The Unity of
William James's Thought

The Unity of William James's Thought

Wesley Cooper

Vanderbilt University Press
Nashville

This book is printed on acid-free paper.
Manufactured in the United States of America

Library of Congress Cataloging in Publication Data

Cooper, Wesley, 1944-
The unity of William James's thought / Wesley Cooper.
    p. cm. — (The Vanderbilt library of American
philosophy). Includes bibliographical references and index.
    ISBN 0-8265-1387-5 (cloth : alk. paper)
    1. James, William, 1842-1910. I. Title. II. Series.
B945.J24 C635 2002
191—dc21   2001005427

The publisher gratefully acknowledges the following original sources
for permission to reprint material based on earlier versions of these
essays: Chapter 3 from "James's Theory of Mental Causation," in
Transactions of the Charles S. Peirce Society, 30:3, 1994. Chapter 4 from
"William James's Theory of Mind," in *Journal of the History of
Philosophy*, 1990. Chapter 5 from "William James's Theory
of the Self," in *The Monist*, October 1992 (© 1992, *The Monist*, Peru,
Illinois 61354). Chapter 6 from "James's God," *American Journal of
Theology & Philosophy*, 16:3, September 1995. Chapter 13 revised from
"Moral Realism, Social Construction, and Communal Ontology," by
Wesley Cooper and Augustine Frimpong-Mansoh, *South African
Journal of Philosophy*, 19:2, 2000.

011603-351602

for kate

Contents

Preface

Gerald Myers's *William James: An Intellectual Biography* was enormously important for me. It edified me and led me to ask the questions that were crucial for developing my own interpretation of James. It became an invaluable companion as I studied James. So my first thanks are to Gerald. After my own interpretation of James had taken shape, I encountered Richard Gale's *The Divided Self of William James*. I recognized it as an inspired and spirited interpretation, one which put my own to a severe test. I found my own view of James taking on increased focus as I traced its relationship to Gale's; his book too became an invaluable companion. So my next thanks are to Richard. My thanks to other philosophers will take the form of references to them in this essay. My final thanks are to my wife, Kate, my essential companion.

Quotations from secondary works are accompanied by a bibliographical reference and page number; references to James's work are indicated by the following abbreviations:

ECR	*Essays, Comments, and Reviews*
EP	*Essays in Psychology*
EPH	*Essays in Philosophy*
ERE	*Essays in Radical Empiricism*
ERM	*Essays in Religion and Morality*
MEN	*Manuscript Essays and Notes*
MT	*The Meaning of Truth*
P	*Pragmatism*
PBC	*Psychology: Briefer Course*
PP	*The Principles of Psychology*
SPP	*Some Problems of Philosophy*
VRE	*The Varieties of Religious Experience*
WB	*The Will to Believe*

The Unity of
William James's Thought

1

Introduction:
James's Philosophical System

James's Beans

Lincoln, Mass., Aug. 5, 1907

Dear Miller—

I got your letter about "Pragmatism," etc., some time ago. I hear that you are booked to review it for the "Hibbert Journal." Lay on, MacDuff! As hard as you can—I want to have the weak places pointed out. I sent you a week ago a "Journal of Philosophy" with a word more about Truth in it, written *at* you mainly; but I hardly dare hope that I have cleared up my position. A letter from Strong, two days ago, written after receiving a proof of that paper, still thinks that I deny the existence of realities outside of the thinker; and [R.B.] Perry, who seems to me to have written far and away the most important critical remarks on Pragmatism (possibly the *only* important ones), accused pragmatists (though he doesn't name *me* of ignoring what ideas are true). I confess that such misunderstandings seem to me hardly credible, and cast a "lurid light" on the mutual understandings of philosophers generally. Apparently it all comes from the *word* Pragmatism—and a most unlucky word it may prove to have been. I am a natural realist. The world *per se* may be likened to a cast of beans on a table. By themselves they spell nothing. An onlooker may group them as he likes. He may simply count them all and map them. He may select groups and name these capriciously, or name them to suit certain extrinsic purposes of his. Whatever he does, so long as he *takes account* of them, his account is neither false nor irrelevant. If neither, why not call it true? It *fits* the beans-minus-him, and *expresses* the *total* fact, of beans-*plus*-him. Truth in this total sense is partially ambiguous, then. If he simply counts or maps, he obeys a subjective interest as much as if he traces figures. Let that stand for pure "intellectual" treatment of beans, while grouping them variously stands for nonintellectual interests. All that Schiller and I contend for is that there is *no* "truth"

[1]

without *some* interest, and that non-intellectual interests play a part as well as intellectual ones. Whereupon we are accused of denying the beans, or denying being in anyway constrained by them! It's too silly! . . .

> —William James, to Dickinson S. Miller
> (Hardwick 1961)

James bequeathed his pragmatism[1] and radical empiricism to the philosophical tradition, displaying over a sprawling range of topics and a long career the
fruitfulness of this pair of innovations. James's beans are the particulars of pure
experience; pragmatism is his account of how the beans should be sorted. This
study is an attempt to unpack the simile and underscore the value of James's
bequest. I will not be arguing that James was a systematic philosopher, since
others have convincingly made the case that the rigors of a technical style of
presentation did not interest him, or were beyond his gift (Gavin 1992). I will
be arguing rather that there is a systematic philosophy in James's writings, however it may have been with the philosopher. As for the beans, I theorize them
in the early chapters but especially in Chapter 8, the heart of my interpretation, which details the doctrine of pure experience with a Ramsey-sentence
analysis that was not available to James. The pragmatic sorting becomes salient
in the later chapters.

The most general thematic idea of this study is that of *construction*, which
encompasses the construction of physical and mental reality from pure experience, and the construction of social and moral reality through pragmatic efforts to give the world a *good* shape. There are the pure-experiential "beans,"
and there is their pragmatic "sorting." Who does the sorting? Not a Cartesian
ego or a transcendental subject, but rather a bean with the capacity to know its
relationship to others, knowledge that comes to take the form of awareness of
an external physical world and an interior stream of consciousness. The mental and physical are *functions* of this epistemic relationship between one bean
and others; this means that physicality and mentality are not brute facts, but
rather constructs. What God is responsible for the patterns—of personhood,
physicality, mentality, society, morality—that emerge among the beans? Not a
transcendent God but an imminent one, and not physically imminent like Zeus
on Olympus nor mentally imminent as though there were a stream of consciousness in every atom, but rather an historical pattern among the beans that
expresses overwhelming if not omnipotent goodness, a pattern that is woven in

part by the free agency of beans like us. Where is this pattern headed? Its *telos* is toward a future consensus among all knowing beans, a universal consensus that the content of morality is a set of absolute moral facts by which to measure the earlier stages of moral progress. This too is a form of construction. The future consensus is not a mere possibility but a construct from earlier historical stages, and it is a construct from the actual acceptance of future morally aware beans.

Enthusiasts for Jamesian pragmatism have generally neglected his metaphysics, specifically his realism about pure experience; his commitment, that is, to a world that is independent of our representations of it. This is a mistake which fosters the accusation that James's pragmatism was epistemically irresponsible, and it aligns him much too closely with murky postmodern irrealism of the 'there-is-nothing-outside-the-text' variety. There is scope for *the will to believe*, which goes beyond the self-fulfilling prophecy in the power of positive thinking. (James was a partisan of the "mind-cure" movement of his day, which dwelt on this power, but his pragmatism has additional philosophical ambitions.) James was aware that this additional scope is tightly constrained, as indicated by the letter quoted above, and my account will emphasize these constraints.

James's radical empiricism attempts to construe experience in such a way that everything philosophy needs for understanding can be found within it. Critical of traditional empiricism for its atomistic division of experience into simple units and its consequent inability to deal *in experience* with the question, How do these units get glued together in everyday experience? James expands empiricism so that it embraces not just objects of reference but relations between them, not just the "substantive parts" of experience but the "transitive parts" as well, not just the perchings but the flights, too; not just the pails and pots in the stream of thought, but the free water as well. "Like a bird's life," experience "seems to be made of an alternation of flights and perchings" (PP, 236). "The traditional psychology," James asserts, "talks like one who should say a river consists of nothing but pailsful, spoonsful, quartpotsful, barrelsful, and other moulded forms of water. Even were the pails and the pots all actually standing in the stream, still between them the free water would continue to flow. It is just this free water of consciousness that psychologists resolutely overlook" (PP, 246).

The upshot for radical empiricism is the view that what is experienced is not a set of units but a conjunctively related whole. James's words, always worth quoting, deserve to be quoted at length at this point:

> The conjunctive relation that has given most trouble to philosophy is *the co-conscious transition*, so to call it, by which one experience passes into another when both belong to the same self. About the facts there is no question. My experiences and your experiences are "with" each other in various external ways, but mine pass into mine, and yours pass into yours in a way in which yours and mine never pass into one another. Within each of our personal histories, subject, object, interest and purpose *are continuous or may be continuous*. Personal histories are processes of change in time, and *the change itself is one of the things immediately experienced*. "Change" in this case means continuous as opposed to discontinuous transition. But continuous transition is one sort of a conjunctive relation; and to be a radical empiricist means to hold fast to this conjunctive relation of all others, for this is the strategic point, the position through which, if a hole be made, all the corruptions of dialectics and all the metaphysical fictions pour into our philosophy. The holding fast to this relation means taking it at its face-value, neither less nor more; and to take it at its face-value means first of all to take it just as we feel it and not to confuse ourselves with abstract talk *about* it, involving words that drive us to invent secondary conceptions in order to neutralize their suggestions and to make our actual experience again seem rationally possible. (ERE, 25)

Radical empiricism is not just "Hume with glue." Its centerpiece is a doctrine of pure experience, which is about the nature of this conjunctive experience and the topology of its flow into mind and body—the stream of thought and the physical world. In Chapter 2 I suggest that pure experience is protomental in nature, having some of the qualities of thought but not all of them, and that the topology of its flow involves separate channeling into the stream of thought and the physical world. This contrasts with a topology in which pure experience flows into a physical world and the mind is a feature of this physical construct, the topology favored by some other turn-of-the-century neutral monists.

The reader will have noted that my references to *The Principles* show James talking about sensation rather than experience. It is a basic interpretive hypothesis for me that the sensations of James's early psychological writing are the pure experiences of his later metaphysical writing. Pure sensations in *The Principles* are objective, exterior, extended, and voluminous. "It is surely subjectivity and interiority which are the notions *latest* acquired by the human mind," James says in the "Sensation" chapter of *The Principles*.

Concepts expressive of our needs and interests are our tools in the constructive work of building the physical world and our subjective, mental course through it (the stream of thought). Experience for us is always conceptualized rather than pure, with the possible exception of the baby assailed by "one great blooming, buzzing confusion" (PP, 462); otherwise pure experience is an abstraction (PP, 653). Truth operates within a realm defined by this conceptual work on experience. James's pragmatic theory of truth requires that the truth should be thought of in terms that always relate to the flow of actual experience:

> Pragmatism, on the other hand, asks its usual question, "Grant an idea or belief to be true," it says, "what concrete difference will its being true make in anyone's actual life? How will the truth be realized? What experiences will be different from those which would obtain if the belief were false? What, in short, is the truth's cash-value in experiential terms?"
>
> The moment pragmatism asks this question, it sees the answer: *True ideas are those that we can assimilate, validate, corroborate and verify. False ideas are those that we cannot.* That is the practical difference it makes to us to have true ideas; that, therefore, is the meaning of truth, for it is all that truth is known as.
>
> This thesis is what I have to defend. The truth of an idea is not a stagnant property inherent in it. Truth *happens* to an idea. It *becomes* true, is *made* true by events. Its verity *is* in fact an event, a process: the process namely of its verifying itself, its veri-*fication*. Its validity is the process of its valid*ation*. (P, 97)

This passage can be interpreted in a variety of ways. I will interpret it in a way that is cautious about subjective implications. Truth can happen to an idea in the future, and an actual consensus about truth in the future might be more true than the truth that happens to ideas along the way, in particular the happenings *now*; such a future consensus might indeed be the "cash value" of absolute truth.

One-sided attention to James's pragmatism also tends to obscure the moral-realist dimension of his thought. Realism in this sense is distinct from realism about pure experience. It signifies commitment to the idea of universal moral truth, despite the diversity in pragmatically guided moral thinking, in history so far. James's realism about morality, like his account of mind and body, is constructivist, but in this case the construction is a future universal consensus about right and wrong. Moral truth is what *will* be believed about morality in such a consensus. The fragile historical contingency of this realism is to be underscored. Moral truth is not counterfactually what would be believed in a hypothetical future consensus. It must be "made flesh," as James put it, in actual agreement.

James's conception of God, an austere empiricist conception of an evolving structure in the world of pure experience, is a reason for optimism about this "religion of humanity," as James called it. The structure is good and purposes getting better; human beings, to the extent that they make themselves good, contribute to the structure, though theirs is not the only contribution, nor necessarily the greatest. It could be said of James's God that it intends the religion of humanity, intending that the world of pure experience should evolve in such a manner that the historical fact of morality-made-flesh is brought about. Furthermore James's conception of God is essential to the bridge I attempt to build in Chapter 2 to panpsychist interpreters of James; it can be granted that every item of pure experience is a mind, when this proposition submits to the austere interpretation that it contributes to a purposive structure in the whole world of pure experience or, in other words, if it is internally related to God. Ultimately I think this teleological interpretation of pure experience is optional, as I indicate in Chapter 8, but there can be no doubt that it belongs in the version of James's system that James himself would want to salute. For those of us a century later who are able to take seriously the possibility of God's existence, James's conception of God is worthy of study.

Another general thematic idea is the Two-Levels View, according to which James's philosophical system has empirical and metaphysical levels, which must be respected in order to appreciate the system's unity and power. Claims that James makes must be categorized by reference to their metaphysical or empirical intent, in order to avoid unnecessary contradiction. The Two-Levels View should be understood as an alternative to the dominant view in contemporary philosophy, naturalism, according to which the full story about reality is told by the natural sciences. The alternative does not deny the naturalistic story, but rather consigns it to reality's empirical level. The metaphysical level is not an incredible Rube Goldberg Machine operating in a world beyond experience, but is rather the pure-experiential content of things conceptualized at the empirical level—persons, streams of consciousness, the physical world, society, morality. The notion of such preconceptual content is surprisingly robust, as Chapter 8 makes out, despite what have seemed decisive objections to some formulations of it, including nineteenth- and early twentieth-century phenomenalist formulations.

There is a theoretical unity to James's writing in psychology, metaphysics, epistemology, philosophy of religion, and ethics. A view of his system as having two levels, empirical and metaphysical, helps to bring this unity into clear relief. The empirical level recognizes a world of physical processes, some of which are correlated with mental processes ("streams of thought" or "streams of consciousness") in a manner that scientific psychology can describe in its laws. The metaphysical level posits a world of pure experience out of which the empirical world is *constructed*, in ways that James documents encyclopedically in *The Principles of Psychology*. The "sensationalism" of *The Principles* is the theory that objective sensation, not yet interiorized in a stream of thought nor congealed in physical objects, is the material of construction.

The dual role of sensation in *The Principles* coheres with the doctrine of pure experience in *Essays in Radical Empiricism*, showing how the empirical leads to the metaphysical; and the doctrine of pure experience grounds the later pragmatism, emphasizing experiential constraints on pragmatically guided concept formation. Moreover, James's philosophical system is not as vulnerable to well-known objections to phenomenalist or sense-data theories as has been assumed during the past half century. It is as plausible as contemporary functionalism about the mind, which is widely regarded to be very plausible indeed. This point, established in Chapter 8, leads the way toward integration of James's pragmatism and radical empiricism, distinguishing it from other views that emphasize the unity of James's thought, such as Rorty (1986) and Bird (1986), which highlight the pragmatism but neglect the radical empiricism: all sorting and no beans, so to speak.

I hope that my readers will return to James's work with the thought that they are entering a philosophical system that just might be true. In order to facilitate that, I have had to criticize several interpretations that take note of only the flux in his thought, or emphasize only one philosophical moment in his intellectual career at the expense of the others. And in the case of Myers (1986), I often take issue with him only because he is our ablest guide to James, and where he is wrong he is almost right. Similarly, I have responded frequently to Gale (1999), because his Divided-Self interpretation of James is by far the most powerful critique that we have.

The first six chapters attempt to establish the Two-Levels View in this forensic way, as the correct account of what James was up to philosophically. Later chapters are more focused on the question of truth. Chapter 8 is pivotal, breathing life into the doctrine of pure experience, thereby reviving the metaphysical/empirical distinction, and anchoring the Two-Levels View's claim to truth. Mind and body are essentially predicative of something that is neither, according to the global functionalism I attribute to James. This "something," according to the Two-Levels View, is the world of pure experience; pure experiences are James's beans. The logical pattern is the same as the familiar functionalist view of the mind, according to which the concept of mind is essentially predicative of something with a certain causal role, the "something" turning out to be the brain, according to the physicalism that usually motivates such accounts. But for James the "something" is pure experience. And just as physicalism speculates that a physical "something" constructs the mental, our mental life ultimately being constructed out of physical events causally interacting with other physical events, analogously the pure-experiential "something" constructs *both* the mental and the physical.

James was not a physicalist, according to the Two-Levels View, although others have interpreted him that way. He rejects any form of reduction of the mental to the physical, but he accepts a broader reduction of both the mental and the physical to pure experience. This broader reduction may be a place where mental-to-physical reductionists and their opponents, advocates of irreducible subjectivity, *qualia*, and the like, can meet. Experience makes us imminently aware of something nonphysical, as the "qualia freaks" have always insisted; but we are not aware of something irreducibly mental, as the physicalists have always insisted. We are aware rather of pure experience.

James's ideas about the mind-body relationship require the hypothesis that thought is a function of the brain. This is his cerebralism. He had another set of ideas, which the ordinary psychophysiologist leaves out of his account, which led him to think the function very special, not a simple causal dependency. In Chapter 3 I attempt to connect the two sets of ideas with the notion of mental events and their physical correlates as *simultaneous nomic equivalents*. This notion does useful work at the level of empirical psychology, while leaving open the possibility of interpreting psychophysical correlation laws in terms of the metaphysics of pure experience. I explore the metaphysical possibilities that James is protecting in Chapter 8.

What I call "James's Shoehorn" is his method, just noted in connection with conjunctive relations, of finding a way to ascribe to experience what less austerely empiricist philosophers would attribute to something nonexperiential, or that other empiricists would attempt either to eliminate or arrive at as a construct out of experience. I find the Shoehorn at work in his views about the purposiveness of the universe (Chapters 2 and 3), freedom of the self (Chapter 5), and God's existence (Chapter 6). Examples in his system abound. Berkeleyan empiricism faced the question, How do we arrive at experience of three-dimensional space on the basis of acquaintance with two-dimensional sense impressions? James simply denied the question's assumption, holding that experience is natively "voluminous." In the chapter "The Perception of Space" in *The Principles*, for instance, he contrasts his position with the Berkeleyans as follows:

> Berkeleyans unanimously assume that no retinal sensation can primitively be of volume; if it be of extension at all (which they are barely disposed to admit), it can be only of two-, not of three-dimensional extension. At the beginning of the present chapter we denied this, and adduced facts to show that all objects of sensation are voluminous in three dimensions (cf. p. 778ff). It is impossible to lie on one's back on a hill, to let the empty abyss of blue fill one's whole visual field, and to sink deeper and deeper into the merely sensational mode of consciousness regarding it, without feeling that an indeterminate, palpitating, circling depth is as indefeasibly one of its attributes as its breadth. (PP, 847)

Another example of the Shoehorn at work: Lockean empiricists faced the question, How do we arrive at experience of duration on the basis of the succession of our ideas? He skewers Locke for intellectualizing duration in a typically substantial footnote:

> Locke, in his dim way, derived the sense of duration from reflection on the succession of our ideas (*Essay*, book II, chap. xiv, 3; chap. xv, 12). Reid justly remarks that if ten successive elements are to make duration, "then one must make duration, otherwise duration must be made up of parts that have no duration, which is impossible. . . . I conclude, therefore, that there must be duration in every single

interval or element of which the whole duration is made up. Nothing indeed is more certain than that every elementary part of duration must have duration, as every elementary part of extension must have extension. Now, it must be observed, that in these elements of duration, or single intervals of successive ideas, there is no succession of ideas, yet we must conceive them to have duration; whence we may conclude with certainty, that *there is a conception of duration, where there is no succession of ideas in the mind*" (*Intellectual Powers*, essay III, chap. v). "Qu'on ne cherce point," says Royer-Collard in the "Fragments" added to Jouffroy's Translation of Reid, "la durée dans la succession; on ne l'y trouvera jamais; la durée a précédé la succession; la notion de la durée a précédé la notion de la succession. Elle en est donc tout-à-fait indépendante, dira-t-on? Oui, elle en est tout-à-fait indépendante." (PP, 574)

Instead of intellectualizing duration, James shoehorns duration into experience, in his well-known notion (borrowed with attribution from E. R. Clay) of "the specious present," writing that "the practically cognized present is no knife-edge, but a saddle-back, with a certain breadth of its own on which we sit perched, and from which we look in two directions into time. The unit of composition of our perception of time is a *duration*, with a bow and a stern, as it were—a rearward- and a forward-looking end" (PP, 574). James's application of the Shoehorn to the self's free will, the purposiveness of the universe, and the existence of God is more complex. Whereas space and time are fully accessible to the empirical sciences, James holds that ascent to the metaphysical level is necessary in order to tell the whole story about these other matters. What enables ascent is a feature of his pragmatism that was evident from the early psychological writings, namely, what I call "James's Tie-Breaker." This is the principle that when there are two comparably credible live options for belief, the one that will serve as a better guide to life should be adopted, especially because of its better moral or aesthetic consequences. (This is a first approximation of the principle; I will attempt to polish it in what follows.) The Tie-Breaker is partly "built-in," a human tendency to prefer the simpler hypothesis, for instance. But James's Tie-Breaker is intended not only as a description of human dispositions but as a principle of rational belief formation. It is to be compared with Ockham's razor ("Do not multiply entities beyond necessity"), understood as a normative methodological principle in science, and indeed the Razor would be a subprinciple within the Tie-Breaker.

Seven Obstacles

Several obstacles to arrival at James's constructivism will be overcome by honoring the two levels of James's system.

Obstacle 1. The physical world poses an obstacle by virtue of the apparent fundamentality of its reality, but this is overcome by viewing the physical as empirically fundamental, while pure experience is metaphysically so. Consider space, for example. Reading Chapter 22 of *The Principles of Psychology,* one would learn much about space perception but might ask oneself: What about space itself? Is it Euclidean? Is it absolute or relative? What exact technical relations hold between space and time (Myers 1986, 114)? The Two-Levels View must be borne in mind. At the empirical level, space will be whatever physicists determine that it is in their quest for a theory of space the predictions of which will survive their tests. At the metaphysical level, however, there is no "space itself" to contrast with space perception, and consequently there is no issue about whether it is Euclidean or not, absolute or relative, and so forth. In this sense psychology is the grand portal to metaphysics, for the sensations it studies contain the basic ingredient of space, voluminousness, which makes possible the experience of a spatiotemporal order that physicists can go on to study. These voluminous sensations are not yet space, not only because the undifferentiated vastness needs to be organized and stabilized through a process of association, discrimination, and selection, but also because some of them are to be classified as belonging to the stream of consciousness rather than to space; sensations of pain are voluminous in just the same generic way that sensations of sight are. The feeling of voluminousness or extensity is a sui generis quale, "an entirely peculiar kind of feeling indescribable except in terms of itself," producing a sense of spatial vastness in three dimensions, not only in the visual sensation when we lie on our back and fill the entire field of vision with the empty blue sky but also in tactile sensations, and in particular those untutored tactile sensations experienced when objects are brought close to the ear (PP, 778).

With the voluminous spatial quale in place, construction of the physical world can proceed without going beyond experience and habit. As James explains in *The Principles,*

I think it obvious—granting the spacial quale to exist in primitive sensations—that discrimination, association, addition, multiplication, and division, blending into generic details, are quite capable of giving us all the space-perceptions we have so far studied, without the aid of any mysterious "mental chemistry" or power of "synthesis" to create elements absent from the original data of feeling. It cannot be too strongly urged in the fact of mystical attempts, however learned, that there is not a landmark, not a length, not a point of the compass in real space which *is* not some *one* of our feelings, either experienced directly as a presentation or ideally suggested by another feeling which has come to serve as its sign. In degrading some sensations to the rank of signs and exalting others to that of realities signified, we smooth our wrinkles of our first chaotic impressions and make a continuous order of what was a rather incoherent multiplicity. But the content of the order remains identical with that of the multiplicity—sensational both, through and through. (PP, 838)

One might characterize the process by which sensation is organized into the experience of space as one in which the knowing subject "creates the illusion of a single continuum of space," but this would contain the false suggestion that there is a difference between subjects' constructive activity and a Real Space to which it corresponds. James does not use the word *illusion*, writing rather that "the primordial largenesses which the sensations yield must be measured and subdivided by consciousness, and added together, before they can form by their synthesis what we know as the Real Space of the objective world" (PP, 787). Whereas an illusion is parasitic on a background of reality, there is no background of Real Space to contrast with the "illusion" that we construct from our sensations. Instead we must ask, "How do we *arrange* these at first chaotically given spaces into the one regular and orderly 'world of Space' which we all know?" (PP, 787).

Sensation has no greater philosophical friend than James. Of course, he demands a lot of this friend. Relations are sensations; for instance, he emphasizes that "*Rightness and leftness, upness and downness, are . . . pure sensations*" (PP, 791). Sensation must contain the categories of space, causality, unity, substantiality, and so forth that are needed to perceive and think about the world:

The first sensation which an infant gets is for him the Universe. And the Universe which he later comes to know is nothing but an amplification and an implication of that first simple germ which, by accretion on one hand and intussusception on the other, has grown so big and complex and articulate that its first state is unrememberable. In his dumb awakening to the consciousness of *something there*, a mere *this* as yet (or something for which even the term *this* would perhaps be too discriminative, and the intellectual acknowledgement of which would be better expressed by the bare interjection "lo!"), the infant encounters an object in which (though it be given in a pure sensation) all the "categories of the understanding" are contained. *It has objectivity, unity, substantiality, causality, in the full sense in which any later object or system of objects has these things.* Here the young knower meets and greets his world; and the miracle of knowledge bursts forth, as Voltaire says, as much in the infant's lowest sensation as in the highest achievement of a Newton's brain. (PP, 658–89)

That sensation should have these powers is why he argues so strenuously against the notion that sensations, in their pure or essential form, are simply subjective effects produced by things external, and the corollary notion that that they seem to inform us of an external world only because we unconsciously "project" them outside of us. On the contrary, "seeming to be in real space" is a native property of sensation, and it is an achievement for the baby to develop a conception of an inner, subjective sensational life. The subject's process of classifying sensation as inner or outer, psychological or physical, takes place because sensation natively has the capacity to produce this bifurcation. On one hand, as I have noted, it has spatiality, objectivity, unity, causality, and substantiality "built in," so it can coalesce into a physical world of substances interacting with each other in a spatial community, without the aid of pre-sensational cognitive machinery. On the other hand, it has the capacity to acquire the characteristics of the stream of thought, and to be a bearer of unchanging conceptions or meanings that relate the ever-changing stream to the physical world and its regularities.

Obstacle 2. Consciousness poses problems, the mind-body problem or "world-knot" being near the top of the list. James identifies five "characters" of thought, as follows:

1. Every thought tends to be part of a personal consciousness.
2. Within each personal consciousness thought is always changing.
3. Within each personal consciousness thought is sensibly continuous.
4. It always appears to deal with objects independent of itself.

5.   It is interested in some parts of these objects to the exclusion of others, and welcomes or rejects—*chooses* from among them, in a word—all the while. (PP, 220)

In Chapter 2 I argue that James conceives of pure experience (or objective sensation) as having some features akin to some of the items on this list, especially 2 and 3, but not enough to justify the label *panpsychist*; the term *neutral monist* is less misleading. (He flirted with panpsychism in *Some Problems of Philosophy* [SPP, 109], but only fleetingly and without conviction.) From a stance that James found natural, the world of pure experience as a whole is purposive, and this suggests a kinship, at least for pure experience taken collectively, with consciousness's character 5. I discuss this stance in Chapter 6.

I will interpret James's cerebralist approach, always looking for dependencies of mental events on brain events, as hypothesizing a form of parallelism between the mental and physical which preserves the causal efficacy of the former, avoiding the threat of a repugnant epiphenomenalism. By examining his discussion in *Principles* of the "mind-dust" theory, I will reject the suggestion that James's psychology overlooks the realm of subconscious mental events that Freudian theory and recent cognitive psychology have explored. I show that the empirical level of James's system, specifically the particulars of his conception of psychology as a natural science, is sufficiently robust to block the threat and dismiss the suggestion as false.

Perception entails sensation for James. This does not mean that sensation is part of a larger perceptual mental state, but rather that one's perceptual state *is* the sensation *plus* the effect on past experience, especially recollections of the object of perception in question. The sensation which is the perception is not internalized, of course. That justifies Hilary Putnam and others who hold that James was perhaps the first to theorize that we directly perceive an external world, rather than being separated from the external world by a veil of interior perceptual ideas. (This veil is *one* of James's targets when he denies that consciousness exists, but it would be wrong to infer that he denies the interiority of the stream of thought, and more wrong still to associate his psychology with behaviorism.) He is not against the notion that perception involves interpretation of sensation. Indeed, he relies on misinterpretation to explain so-called fallacies of the senses such as a pea's seeming double when rolled between crossed fingers. But it is not the sensation which is responsible for misinterpretation, but what comes out of our own heads. If the influence of evolution and culture count as sources of interpretation, then James is fully aware of the influence of these sources of interpretation on perception, and as his pragmatism developed they were emphasized more and more. But interpretation does not, so to speak, go all the way down. He rejected Helmholtz's psychological hypothesis that, because a bright object placed in an even brighter context will appear darker, the same sensation is subjected to faulty interpretation; he prefers the hypothesis that what happens in such cases is that there are changes in the neural system that produce a different sensation.

A metaphysical problem for this view is raised by the question, How do you and I perceive (see, feel, etc.) the *same* pencil? As the Two-Levels View implies, James's psychology can simply assume that we do so, since our bodies are both pointed in the right direction, our visual systems are both functional, and so forth. A residual question is kicked up to the metaphysical level of his system. Given that our pencil-percepts are ultimately sensational, how do we both have the same sensation to trigger our two perceptions? The distinction just noted, between sensation-as-interiorized and sensation-as-objective does important work in dealing with this problem, since the relevant sensation for our two percepts is not interiorized; if it were, the problem would be insoluble. The relevant sensation is rather, by James's hypothesis about sensation in *The Principles* and about pure experience in *Essays in Radical Empiricism*, objective and external to the two subjects, and consequently is not debarred from being something that would ground both subjects' perceptions. How exactly objective-sensation-pure-experience does so is a mystery. There are related mysteries about James's radical empiricism, such as the question of how some items of experience are capable of constructive activity in building selves, streams of thought, and so forth; the question of how a world of pure experience happens to channel into psychological and physical forms; and others as well. These aren't necessarily cause for panic. Every philosophical theory has an agenda of unsolved problems, or else it is sterile, and every theory reaches bedrock where problems are converted into axioms or simply accepted as insoluble mysteries.

Obstacle 3. The nature of the self poses an obstacle, for scholastically informed common sense would view it as *beneath* experience, a transcendent subject, whereas constructivism brings with it the danger that the self dissolves into

motley patterns of experience. The Two-Levels View shows how James's thinking about the self subtly navigates the border zone between the empirical and
metaphysical levels. James's account begins with a sensation or experience that
has a capacity that lifts it beyond itself, into relationships with other experiences, some of which it constructs into a conception of the physical world and
others which it *appropriates* to itself, either (i) because of a peculiar "warmth
and intimacy" that it detects in the other, by virtue of which the other becomes
integrated as a past stage into the history of the stream of thought of which the
appropriating experience (the "passing Thought") is the temporal leading edge;
or (ii) because something external to the stream of thought—one's body, one's
family, one's clothes, or whatever—is apprehended as having "a glow and a
warmth" such that it becomes an ingredient of the self.

Contemporary echoes of James's philosophy are worth looking out for, and
I will draw attention to them now and then. Here is one, from Nozick (1989,
144–45), describing "a process within which the self gets constructed," which
will be useful in summarizing how James avoids a Cartesian or transcendental
subject:

> Let us look more closely at the self's organization and particular functions. . . . Let
> us begin, then, with many bits of consciousness: experiences, thoughts, etc.—iso-
> lated bits. Some of these bits of consciousness are about other bits—for example,
> one bit might be a memory of an earlier conscious event. One of these bits of
> awareness, however, is very special. This bit is an awareness *of* many of the other
> bits of experience and thought, *plus* an awareness of itself, a reflexive self-aware-
> ness. Let us hypothesize that the self *is* or *begins* as that special awareness: aware of
> other contents of consciousness and also reflexively aware of itself *as* being aware
> of these other contents of consciousness and also of itself. This particular piece of
> consciousness, this "self," groups various experiences and bits of consciousness;
> these are the ones it is aware of—including itself. There also may be other bits of
> consciousness it is not aware of; these do not fall within the group. Thus far, all the
> self is entitled to say is "I know of, I am aware of, bits of consciousness, experi-
> ences, thoughts, feelings, etc., including this very self-reflexive bit." Somehow the
> step gets made from being aware of these bits of consciousness to *having* or *pos-
> sessing* them. The self comes to think of these as *belonging* to it. The self is born,
> then, in an act of appropriation and acquisition. How does it do this? And when it
> claims what amounts to ownership over these other bits of consciousness, is that
> claim legitimate?

James writes in Chapter 10, "The Consciousness of Self," that "The Empirical Self of each of us is all that he is tempted to call by the name of *me*. But it is clear that between what a man calls *me* and what he calls *mine* the line is difficult to draw" (PP, 279). This would not be true if James were wedded to a traditional conception of personal identity, according to which it depended on the persistence of Cartesian *res cogitans*, or what James dismissively called a "soul pellet." Were that the case, the difference would be fundamental and simple: the *me* is that which thinks, or the pellet, and everything else about me is *mine*, not me.

The empirical self's appropriation of its various dimensions prevents collapse into a passive Locke-Hume bundle theory, anticipating the Closest-Continuer theory of contemporary theorists such as Nozick and Parfit, which construes personal identity as a function of weighted dimensions. The basic idea about identity is contained in the Closest-Continuer solution to the puzzle about the ship of Theseus; parts are gradually taken from the ship as it sails and stored somewhere as the old parts are replaced by new ones, until the ship comes to port alongside a qualitatively identical ship, assembled from the old parts. Which is identical with the ship that set sail? The solution is that there is no closest continuer, because two dimensions, continuity of shape and continuity of parts, are relevant to the identity of ships, and they are of equal weight. So in this special situation neither of the ships is the ship that set sail. The extra complications introduced by *personal* identity are that there is a variety of dimensions and weights and that these are to a degree determinable by the subject; people are "self-defining" in ways that ships are not.[2]

The close connection between James's theory of the self and the Closest-Continuer theory can be brought out by thinking of his idea of the constituents of the self as a broad pass at the idea of dimensions or vectors that are relevant to personal identity. The constituents he lists are

1. the material self,
2. the social self,
3. the spiritual self, and
4. the pure ego.

The first three do serious work for him, whereas the fourth does not. Under the material self he discusses various subdimensions: "The body is the innermost part of *the material Self* in each of us; and certain parts of the body seem more intimately ours than the rest" (PP, 280). Next, somewhat surprisingly, come "the clothes," after which come immediate family, our home, and property, especially that which is saturated with our labor. The particular weights that James has assigned are less important here than the fact that he assigns them and makes them determinative of the self:

> There are few men who would not feel personally annihilated if a life-long con-struction of their hands or brains—say an entomological collection or an exten-sive work in manuscript—were suddenly swept away. The miser feels similarly towards his gold; and although it is true that a part of our depression at the loss of possessions is due to our feeling that we must now go without certain goods that we expected the possessions to bring in their train, yet in every case there remains, over and above this, a sense of the shrinkage of our personality, a partial conver-sion of ourselves to nothingness, which is a psychological phenomenon by itself. (PP, 281)

Under a man's social self he gathers "the recognition which he gets from his mates," adding that "Properly speaking, *a man has as many social selves as there are individuals who recognize him* and carry an image of him in their mind" (PP, 281–82). This is easily assimilable to the Closest-Continuer theory if these various selves are understood as various vectors of different weight, de-pending on the man's degree of regard for the opinion of the individual who has an opinion about him.

Under the spiritual self James understands "a man's inner or subjective being, his psychic faculties or dispositions, taken concretely," including our ability to argue and discriminate, our moral sensibility and conscience, our indomitable will, and so forth (PP, 283). He is careful to prevent some portion of the stream of thought from being abstracted from the rest and pressed into duty as an ersatz soul pellet, "a sort of innermost centre within the circle, of sanctuary within the citadel," a central nucleus of the self, the central active self:

> But when I forsake such general descriptions and grapple with particulars, com-ing to the closest possible quarters with the facts, *it is difficult for me to detect in the activity any purely spiritual element at all. Whenever my introspective glance*

succeeds in turning round quickly enough to catch one of these manifestations of
spontaneity in the act, all it can ever feel distinctly is some bodily process, for the
most part taking place within the head. . . . [T]he "Self of selves," when carefully
examined, is found to consist mainly of the collection of these peculiar motions in
the head or between the head and throat. (PP, 287–88)

This deflationary account of the 'Self of selves' does not deflate the importance of the stream of thought, or subjectivity, to personal identity. The appropriating activity of the stream's current "section" (the passing Thought), as I
noted above, is centrally important. Furthermore, deflation from the perspective of empirical psychology might be met by reflation from a metaphysical
perspective, should a case be made for the contracausal free agency of the passing Thought. James would have welcomed this, but the Two-Levels View requires him to keep his metaphysical hunches in check when doing psychology.

There may be more for the metaphysician to say about James's theory of
the self, including an account of its contracausal free agency; or its empirically
hidden relationship to other pure-experiential structures, a matter related to
James's religious and mystical views; and so on. But radical empiricism places
strictures on speculative metaphysical possibilities. So the thought that one's
metaphysical essence is to be a Cartesian ego, for instance, either has a pure-
experiential "cash value," or else it is an "overbelief" that might be tolerated
because of its association with a religious credo but not seriously entertained as
philosophical doctrine.

Under the pure ego there is, in James's account, after a long and scathing
discussion of Cartesian and Kantian conceptions, "simply *nothing.*" Specifically, there is nothing to contradict, or serve as objective background to, the
subjective sense of personal identity, which by the agency of the passing
Thought gathers the ingredients of the self together "much as out of a herd of
cattle let loose for the winter on some wide Western prairie the owner picks out
and sorts together, when the time for the round-up comes in the spring, all the
beasts on which he finds his own particular brand" (PP, 317).

James recognizes that the "cattle," such as past stages of my stream of
thought, are "branded" because they are mine, and not mine because they are
branded. So, what makes them mine? We have noted his answer, the appropriating activity of the passing thought. But must there not then be, after all, an

underlying Thinker that unifies the many passing Thoughts that occur through time? James rejects the suggestion:

> For how would it be if the Thought, the present judging Thought, instead of being in any way substantially or transcendentally identical with the former owner of the past self, merely inherited his "title," and thus stood as his legal representative now? It would then, if its birth coincided exactly with the death of another owner, *find* the past self already its own as soon as it found it at all, and the past self would thus never be wild, but always owned, by a title that never lapsed. We can imagine a long succession of herdsmen coming rapidly into possession of the same cattle by transmission of an original title by bequest. May not the "title" of a collective self be passed from one Thought to another in some analogous way? (PP, 321–22)

James successfully develops a theoretical alternative to the Cartesian ego and the transcendental subject. Moreover, the theory's crucial parts, about the passing Thought and the ingredients of the self, are echoed in Nozick's account of the self's construction (from the appropriating activity of bits of consciousness) and the Closest-Continuer Theory of identity through time.

Obstacle 4. God poses an obstacle to James's constructivism, especially when understood as transcendent to experience, having no place *in* "a world of pure experience." The Two-Levels View offers an account of James's God which is consistent with the radical animus of his empiricism, while being tolerant of overbeliefs about the transcendental nature of God, on much the same pattern as just noted with regard to the self. The goodness, knowledge, and power of God are a function of the corresponding qualities to be found in the world of pure experience; for instance, the corresponding qualities to be found in human beings, but also perhaps other beings with far greater portions of these qualities. This function, God, is not static but progressive or not, depending at least in part on what we pure-experiential *beings* do, how we exercise our freedom. God might be understood as a pattern *of* the world of pure experience rather than a being *in* it; not transcendent to it, but not internal to it either. The pattern is noticeable by those who adopt a certain stance toward experience, a religious stance whether or not it involves overbelief. There is nothing inevitable about adopting this stance, however, and those who cleave to a view of the world as simply a physical mechanism will be persuaded, if at all, by ethical considerations such as those that led James away from a mechanistic world-view.

James's God is of a piece with the pluralistic or melioristic universe of which James often speaks; God is its pattern:

> Finally, if the "melioristic" universe were *really* here, it would require the active good will of all of us, in the way of belief as well as of our other activities, to bring it to a prosperous issue. . . .
>
> The melioristic universe is conceived after a *social* analogy, as a pluralism of independent powers. It will succeed just in proportion as more of these work for its success. If none work, it will fail. . . .
>
> "*If we* do *our* best, *and* the other powers do *their* best, the world will be perfected"—this proposition expresses no actual fact, but only the complexion of a fact thought of as eventually possible. As it stands, *no* conclusion can be positively deduced from it. A conclusion would require another premise of fact, which only we can supply. The original proposition *per se* has no pragmatic value whatsoever, apart from its *power to challenge our will to produce the premise of fact required.* Then indeed the perfected world emerges as a logical conclusion. (SPP, 116)

This passage ties James's conception of God to his pragmatism and his ethics. The pragmatic meaning of *God exists* is given by the ways in which it *leads* believers to make the world better. It is pragmatically rational to believe that God exists when that is epistemically justified, where epistemic justification is understood as having a practical element as well as a cognitive one, and the practical element favors belief in God, perhaps because that will help make the world better. Pragmatic half-truth, or truth in context, is just pragmatically rational belief. Pragmatic absolute truth, including objective moral truth, requires premises of fact about a future universal consensus, to which previous generations are related, not counterfactually or passively, but as cocreators, "in the way of belief as well as of our other activities." To "testify against villainy, is practically to help" bring about "the perfected world," including the consensus conditions for absolute truth (SPP, 115). Perhaps believing in God now sets the stage for the absolute truth that God exists.

Obstacle 5. James's pragmatism itself poses an obstacle, since it is easy to construe, notably in the fashion of postmodernist admirers of James, as entirely at odds with philosophy's metaphysical aspiration, in particular with James's radical empiricist metaphysics. I argue rather that James's empiricism and pragmatism work together, within the structure of the Two-Levels View. Chapter 8 especially aims to show that the marriage of pragmatism and pure experience is a live option for belief. The basic argument is that this marriage is just as plausible as functionalism about the mind; since this latter is a virtual orthodoxy in the philosophy of mind and cognitive psychology, the argument is a formidable challenge to those who would decouple pragmatism and radical empiricism, as well as those who assume that physical facts or mental facts, or both, are brute.

Although James's pragmatism had not fully developed when he wrote *The Principles of Psychology*, it is present there embryonically in his emphasis on the aesthetic and practical interests that guide us in conceptualizing things and separating the real from the illusory: "Out of all the visual magnitudes of each known object we have selected one as the REAL one to think of, and degraded all the others to serve as its signs. This 'real' magnitude is determined by aesthetic and practical interests. It is that which we get when the object is at the distance most propitious for exact visual discrimination of its details" (PP, 817). The fundamental principle guiding our pursuit of our interests is a law of economy that disposes us to simplify, unify, and identify as much as we can. This affects the way we formulate concepts, including our concepts of "things": "Whatever sensible data can be attended to together we locate together. Their several parts seem one extent. The place at which each appears is held to be the same with the place at which the other appears. They become, in short, so many properties of *one and the same real thing*" (PP, 821). Several discrete doctrines are often packed together under the rubric of James's pragmatism. I distinguish three: a pragmatic theory of meaning, a pragmatic theory of rational belief, and a pragmatic theory of truth. The pragmatic theory of meaning is straightforwardly an application of James's extensive discussion of meaning or conception in *The Principles*, an application to the clarification of our ideas, especially ideas that get us into problems in philosophy. Meanings allow a thinker (the passing Thought) to rise above her isolation by leading her to a physical world and a stream of consciousness, permitting her to spot regularities and continuities and use this information to her advantage. That is what meanings *function* to do. But they can function badly, as meanings born of superstition tend to do. They can go on holiday, sounding nice but not leading their users fruitfully into experience. (James thought that the meanings used by the Hegelians of his time were on year-round holidays.) I argue in Chapter 9 that *The Principles'* account of meaning is at work in *Pragmatism*.

As mentioned above, I interpret James as having a conception of epistemic justification that includes a practical, pragmatic element as well as a cognitive one, the former being constrained by the latter. Since exaggeration of James's "voluntarism" is a philosophical cottage industry, I theorize these constraints in some detail in Chapter 11.

Obstacle 6. James's commitment to the natural sciences, and to psychology as such, creates an obstacle when construed as being at odds with the personal, the religious, the emotional, and so many other sources of values that are important to James's system. I will be arguing for an integrated philosophical system rather than such fissure. For one thing, James's distinctive mysticism is closely related to the sensationalism that informs his psychology and, in his pragmatic writings, to the emphasis on concepts arising from and leading to experience.

James was self-professedly a "positivist" in his philosophy of science, and in particular his philosophy of psychology, but his positivism was of a nineteenth-century sort, associated with Auguste Comte and John Stuart Mill, as opposed to the twentieth-century sort associated with the Vienna Circle and its "logical positivism." This difference is crucial. For instance, as I will show later, it bedevils interpreters who read Wittgenstein's neutral monism in the *Tractatus* into James's neutral monism in *Essays in Radical Empiricism*. Both versions of positivism are broadly empiricist in outlook, but logical positivism takes its lessons in empiricism from Hume, whereas James introduced fundamental innovations in the empiricist tradition. Logical positivism employed the new logic of Frege, Russell, *et al.* in order to develop a more sophisticated version of Hume's "fork" between matters of fact and relations of ideas—condemning to the flames, as nonsense, any empirical statement that doesn't ultimately decompose into references to atoms such as Hume's simple impressions. Although the empiricist roots of James's philosophy are deep and a conception of verifiability is central to his pragmatic method, Humean atomism and the methodological primacy of logic were alien to him. His positivism about psychology amounted to an insistence that it be pursued as a science, and in particular that it should be an observation-driven and law-seeking enterprise, informed by evolutionary theory. Other nineteenth-century positivists were distrustful of metaphysics (and theology), not for the sophisticated twentieth-century reason that it was meaningless-because-unverifiable, but simply because they thought it false and laden with superstitions. But on this point James's positivism was highly qualified, especially by the Two-Levels View : he was distrustful of metaphysical and theological intrusions into empirical sciences like psychology, but he felt that vigorous pursuit of these sciences, not to mention deep human needs, would lead to legitimate metaphysical inquiry. He was critical from *The Principles of Psychology* till his final work, such as *Some Problems of Philosophy*, of that strain of nineteenth-century positivism which recommended science *as opposed to* philosophy and metaphysics (SPP, 17). The moral I would draw is that readers should beware of interpretations which dismiss James's psychological writings as "positivism," the word's effectiveness as a term of abuse being inversely proportional to the clarity with which it is used and understood. I attempt to draw out the character of James's positivism in Chapter 3, expanding on his thought in *The Will to Believe* that "a thoroughgoing interpretation of the world in terms of mechanical sequence is compatible with its being interpreted teleologically, for the mechanism itself may be designed" (WB, 66).

James's philosophical system is far from perfect as found. As a result, interpreters predictably divide between "the glass is half empty" and "the glass is half full" responses. I have indicated that I belong to the latter group. Richard Gale belongs to the former, and one of his chief reasons for this response has to do with detecting "Poohbahism" in James's theorizing. This diagnosis ties in nicely with the beans-on-the-table theme of James's letter to Miller and supplies the reader with motivation for the chapters to come, so I want to say a preliminary word or two about it, although I won't come fully to grips with Poohbahism until Chapter 8 and beyond.

Gale is alluding to *The Mikado* and specifically the following passage, which illustrates, he says, how James "implicitly prefaces his every remark with a 'qua this official' restriction" (Gale 1999, 190):

> KOKO. Pooh-Bah, it seems that the festivities in connection with my approaching
> marriage must last a week. I should like to do it handsomely, and I want to
> consult you as to the amount I ought to spend upon them.
> POOH-BAH. Certainly. In which of my capacities? As First Lord of the Treasury,

Lord Chamberlain, Attorney-General, Chancellor of the Exchequer, Privy Purse, or Private Secretary?

KOKO. Suppose we say as Private Secretary.

POOH-BAH. Speaking as your Private Secretary, I should say that, as the city will have to pay for it, don't stint yourself, do it well.

KOKO. Exactly—as the city will have to pay for it. That is your advice.

POOH-BAH. As Private Secretary. Of course you will understand that, as Chancellor of the Exchequer, I am bound to see that due economy is observed.

KOKO. Oh! But you said just now "Don't stint yourself, do it well."

POOH-BAH. As Private Secretary.

KOKO. And now you say that due economy must be observed.

POOH-BAH. As Chancellor of the Exchequer.

KOKO. I see. Come over here, where the Chancellor can't hear us *(They cross the stage.)* Now, as my Solicitor, how do you advise me to deal with this difficulty?

POOH-BAH. Oh, as your Solicitor, I should have no hesitation in saying "Chance it."

KOKO. Thank you *(Shaking his hand.)*

POOH-BAH. If it were not that, as Lord Chief Justice, I am bound to see that the law isn't violated.

KOKO. I see. Come over here where the Chief Justice can't hear us *(They cross the stage.)* Now, then, as First Lord of the Treasury?

POOH-BAH. Of course, as First Lord of the Treasury, I could propose a special vote that would cover all expenses, if it were not that, as Leader of the Opposition, it would be my duty to resist it, tooth and nail. Or, as Paymaster General, I could so cook the accounts that, as Lord High Auditor, I should never discover the fraud. But then, as Archbishop of Titipu, it would be my duty to denounce my dishonesty and give myself into my own custody as First Commissioner of Police.

KOKO. That's extremely awkward.

POOH-BAH. I don't say that all these distinguished people couldn't be squared; but it is right to tell you that they wouldn't be sufficiently degraded in their own estimation unless they were insulted with a very considerable bribe. (Gale 1999, 191)

In Gale's view James is a metaphysical Pooh-Bah, his many different selves corresponding to Pooh-Bah's many different officials, the different interest-determined worlds of the Jamesian selves corresponding to the officials' different responsibilities. The moral is that James cannot provide a coherent conception of an integrated self or a reality external to these various interest-sculpted worlds.

In the next chapter I begin to set out a theoretical structure with metaphysical and empirical levels, within which, I think, James's philosophical system can be defended against the charge of Poohbahism. I will ascribe to him a neutral-monist or highly qualified panpsychist metaphysics, a world of pure experience which will ultimately be vindicated in Chapter 6. Facts at the empirical level can be sufficiently inconclusive as to leave open certain options for belief at the metaphysical level, at which, furthermore, ethical reasons for belief become relevant which would be out of place in empirical inquiry. James's belief in free will is such a live option, he thinks, although its status as such is not guaranteed: the future of empirical inquiry could make such a convincing case for determinism that belief in free will would cease to be a live option, just as, right now, believing that I am scuba-diving in the Bahamas is not a live option for me. As for James's many selves, they should be viewed as dimensions of a person's identity, along the lines of the Closest-Continuer theory, rather than being compared to "hats" that one puts on *seriatim*. Thinking of the self in terms of such dimensions preserves the concept of personal identity despite the absence of an unchanging "soul pellet." The moral I want to draw is that James can provide a coherent conception of an integrated self and a reality external to our various interest-sculpted worlds.

Obstacle 7. Society and morality present obstacles, since James's relative silence on these topics is a sign to many that his treatment of them is not motivated by a systematic philosophy. I extend the Two-Levels View to them, in such a way that the empirical level represents the various moral half-truths we discover at different historical stages of moral progress, and the metaphysical level stands for a possible future moral consensus that would vindicate belief in absolute moral truth. I offer an alternative to the standard reading of James as a utilitarian. Rather, he is only a *consequentialist*, whose criterion for evaluating moral progress is that "the best whole" eventuates. But this criterion does not favor our using a principle of utility over other moral principles when we reflect on what to do; rather, we should be guided by a plurality of principles, generally the ones that capture the inherited wisdom of our communities. Moreover, his consequentialist criterion of rightness by no means guarantees that the principles that guide us, or the ones that may one day be accepted in a universal consensus, are themselves consequentialist. For all that the criterion stipulates, a deontological respect for rights or a virtue of strenuousness may be morally fundamental.

These remarks signal the tenor of this study of James. It argues the unity of James's thought, taking seriously his radical empiricist metaphysics and trying to unite it — through the Two-Levels View, constrained pragmatism, global functionalism, and constructivism — with his psychology and philosophy of science on one hand and, on the other, his ideas about religion, truth, and other philosophical matters. James did not choose to do this. It suited his temperament to move on, as my brief sketch of his life indicates. He once wrote to a friend, "I'm sorry you stick so much to my psychological phase, which I care little for, now, and never cared much. This epistemological and metaphysical phase seems to me more original and important" (James 1920, 331–22). This supports the view that he gave up psychology after writing *The Principles* and *The Briefer Course*, but it doesn't imply that there is no underlying theoretical unity to the "phases." My study takes up several central Jamesian doctrines with a view to revealing their unity, but it does not attempt a synoptic description of James's work. Gerald Myers's indispensable *William James: His Life and Thought* has accomplished this task with admirable critical perspective.

I echo Owen Flanagan's sentiment when he wrote recently, "William James is my favorite philosopher," and I understand why he would feel this way despite agreeing with almost no view that James holds. One loves James, not just for allowing his person to shine forth from his philosophy with such refined yet down-to-earth exuberance, but for being a model of a person doing philosophy, as Flanagan says: "[T]here is no hiding the person behind the work, no way of discussing the work without the person, no way to make believe that there is a way to do philosophy that is not personal" (Flanagan 1997, 47). I am less certain than Flanagan that I disagree with James's views, and in what follows I have tried to present some of them in such a way that they are live options for belief. Further, I would identify the person behind the work as James's philosophical-cum-literary persona, a skillfully molded writing style, "voice," and sense of character, and separate this as much as possible from psychological and political speculation.

A Brief Biography

William James was born in 1842 and died in 1910. He was the eldest of five children (among them Henry and Alice) of the one-legged Svendborgian eccentric Henry Sr., independently wealthy thanks to contesting the will of his Irish-American father, William Sr. He grew up in a family environment that has been described as an out-clinic for papa, an environment which may have contributed to his lifelong psychological and psychosomatic difficulties, the subject of much speculation by Freudian biographers. Through his father's connections to the literary and theological circles of America and England, the young James met Ralph Waldo Emerson, Henry David Thoreau, Amos Bronson Alcott, Albert Brisbane, Horace Greeley, William Cullen Bryant, Thomas Carlyle, Alfred Tennyson, and John Stuart Mill. He was described as short, wiry, intense, alert, masculine, and energetic, with striking blue eyes set beneath bushy brows (Myers 1986, 41). He customarily wore a Norfolk jacket, bright shirts, and flowing ties, and he was given to an unusually broad grin. He was a loyal and generous friend, notably to Charles Peirce and John Dewey. To blind and deaf Helen Keller he brought an ostrich feather, telling her, she recalls, "I thought you would like the feather, because it is soft and light and caressing." He opposed American imperialism, advocated better care of the insane, deplored trampling of minority rights, proposed more equitable distribution of wealth, and attempted to protect animals from cruelty.

In 1860, at eighteen, he decided to take up a career as a painter, despite his father's disapproval, which he comments upon in a letter from Bonn on August 24, 1860: "I was very glad to get your preceding letter, although its contents were not exactly what I expected. What I wanted to ask you for at Mrs. Livermore's were the reasons why I should not be an 'artist.' I could not *fully* make out from your talk there what were *exactly* the causes of your disappointment at my late resolve, what your view of the nature of art was, that the idea of my devoting myself to it should be so repugnant to you" (Hardwick 1961, 8). But in 1861 he changed his mind, judging his talent insufficient, and entered the Lawrence Scientific School to study chemistry, shifting later to anatomy and physiology, this time imagining that he was making a choice against "worldly fatness," a life of business, that his mother would have made for him, a matter he discusses in a letter to her from September, 1863:

I feel very much the importance of making soon a final choice of my business in life. I stand now at the place where the road forks. One branch leads to material comfort, the flesh-pots; but it seems a kind of selling of one's soul. The other to mental dignity and independence; combined, however, with physical penury. If I myself were the only one concerned I should not hesitate an instant in my choice. But it seems hard on Mrs. W. J., "that not impossible she," to ask her to share an empty purse and a cold hearth. On one side is *science*, upon the other *business* (the most honorable, honored, and productive business of printing seems most attractive), with *medicine*, which partakes of [the] advantages of both, between them, but which has drawbacks of its own. I confess I hesitate. I fancy there is a fond maternal cowardice which would make you and every other mother contemplate with complacency the worldly fatness of a son, even if obtained by some sacrifice of his "higher nature." But I fear there might be some anguish in looking back from the pinnacle of prosperity (*necessarily* reached, if not by eating dirt, at least by renouncing some divine ambrosia) over the life you might have led in the pure pursuit of truth. It seems one *could* not afford to give that up for any bribe, however great. Still, I am undecided. The medical term opens tomorrow and between this and the end of the term here, I shall have an opportunity of seeing a little into medical business. I shall confer with Wyman about the prospects of a naturalist and finally decide. I want you to become familiar with the notion that I *may* stick to science, however, and drain away at your property for a few years more." (Hardwick 1961, 14)

Physical frailty was a factor in his life even at this early age, preventing him from enlisting in the Civil War in 1861. In 1864 he entered Harvard Medical School and would have graduated in 1869, but he interrupted his studies in 1865–66 to follow Alexander Agassiz on an expedition to Brazil, discovering he was not cut out to be a seafarer, as he recounts in a letter to his parents dated April 21, 1865, from Rio de Janeiro:

Every one is writing home to catch the steamer that leaves Rio on Monday. I do likewise, although so far, I have very little to say to you. You cannot conceive how pleasant it is to feel that tomorrow we shall lie in smooth water at Rio and the horrors of this voyage will be over. O the vile Sea! the damned Deep! No one has a right to write about the "nature of Evil," or to have any opinion about evil, who has not been at sea. The awful slough of despond into which you are there plunged furnishes too profound an experience not to be a fruitful one. I cannot yet say what the fruit is in my case, but I am sure some day of an accession of wisdom from it. My sickness did not take an actively nauseous form after the first night and second morning; but for twelve mortal days I was, body and soul, in a more indescribably hopeless, homeless, and friendless state than I ever want to be in again. We had a head wind and tolerably rough sea all that time. The trade winds, which I thought were gentle zephyrs, are hideous moist gales that whiten all the waves with foam. (Hardwick 1961, 18)

His famous depression descended in 1867, leading him to read Charles Renouvier, to whom he wrote on November 2, 1872:

I must not lose this opportunity of telling you of the admiration and gratitude which have been excited in me by the reading of your *Essais* (except the third, which I have not yet read). Thanks to you I possess for the first time an intelligible and reasonable conception of freedom. I accept it almost entirely. On other points of your philosophy I still have doubts, but I can say that through that philosophy I am beginning to experience a rebirth of the moral life; and I assure you, Monsieur, that this is no small thing!

His experience with depression led him to become interested in psychology, and finally, at a moment of crisis in 1870, it led him to "will to believe" in free will: "I think that yesterday was a crisis in my life. I finished the first part of Renouvier's second *Essais* and see no reason why his definition of free will — 'the sustaining of a thought because I choose to when I might have other thoughts' — need be the definition of an illusion. At any rate, I will assume for the present — until next year — that it is no illusion. My first act of free will shall be to believe in free will" (Myers 1986, 46). From 1872 he taught physiology at Harvard. (At roughly the same time, in 1877–78, his lifelong[3] friend Charles Peirce was publishing his best-known articles on pragmatism, "The Fixation of Belief" and "How To Make Our Ideas Clear," in the *Popular Science Monthly*.) In 1878 he married Alice Gibbens and signed a contract with Holt and Company to write a volume on psychology, promised for 1880 and delivered in 1890 as *The Principles of Psychology*, which was immediately accepted as a basic book in the field and is widely regarded as his masterpiece, a classic contribution to both psychology and philosophy. He tried to elide the philosophical elements of the book in the abridged edition of 1892, dubbed "Jimmy" by his students to distinguish it from "James," the unedited original.

In 1897 *The Will to Believe* was published, dedicated to Peirce. Mountain climbing in the Adirondacks in 1898 strained his heart, but during the subsequent period of "collapse" he produced the Gifford lectures, delivered in Edinburgh in 1901 and published as *The Varieties of Religious Experience* in 1902. Both "Does 'Consciousness' Exist?" and "A World of Pure Experience" were published in 1904. In 1905 he declined at least one hundred invitations to speak, and in 1906 he was on hand for the San Francisco earthquake, as well as giving the Lowell Institute lectures, which became in 1907 the monograph *Pragmatism*. The Hibbert Lectures at Manchester College, Oxford, in 1908 were published as *A Pluralistic Universe* in 1909. Failing to find a proper treatment for his heart disease in Europe, he returned to his place in Chococorua, New Hampshire, accompanied by his brother Henry, dying there at the age of sixty-eight, occasioning his celebrated brother's words, "I sit heavily stricken and in darkness—for from far back in dimmest childhood he had been my ideal Elder Brother. . . . His extinction changes the face of life for me—besides the mere missing of his inexhaustible company and personality, originality, the whole unspeakably vivid and beautiful presence of him" (Myers 1986, 21).

Before his death James remarked that his philosophy was "too much like an arch built only on one side" (Gavin 1992, 8). He made a start at completing the arch in *Some Problems of Philosophy: A Beginning of an Introduction to Philosophy*, incomplete at his death, in which he aimed to overcome what he called his "intellectual higgledy-piggledyism" and finally round out his philosophical system (SPP, xv). But it is hard to see that the book does anything like that. My view is that the system had become sufficiently well developed that "completing the arch" had to become the work of many philosophers. I would like to think that I am making a contribution, along with the contemporary philosophers whose ideas I will be discussing.

John Dewey rated James as perhaps the greatest psychologist of any time: "By common consent he was far and away the greatest of American psychologists—it was a case of James first and no second. Were it not for the unreasoned admiration of men and things German, there would be no question, I think, that he was the greatest psychologist of his time in any country—perhaps of any time" (Myers 1986, 1). The arguable poverty of behaviorism such as Watson's, which purports to advance beyond James by eschewing inner states of mind or brain, and of Freudianism, which postulates in-principle unconscious inner states, and of the computer model of the mind, which seems to overlook consciousness, are all reasons to keep an open mind about James's contribution to psychology. And Alfred North Whitehead ranked him among the greatest philosophers of all time: "In Western literature there are four great thinkers, whose services to civilized thought rest largely upon their achievements in philosophical assemblage; though each of them made important contributions to the structure of philosophical system. These men are Plato, Aristotle, Leibniz, and William James" (Whitehead, *Modes of Thought*, quoted in Myers 1986, 15).

James's solution to the mind-body problem is a form of neutral monism (or a qualified form of panpsychism), which posits a metaphysically primary stuff, pure experience, that is neither mental nor physical, getting constructed into streams of thought and physical objects by the pure-experiential subject, which James sometimes called *Sciousness*, to distinguish it from the consciousness it composes. As James wrote in *Essays in Radical Empiricism*, "There is only one primal stuff of material in the world, a stuff of which everything is composed" (ERE, 4). This doctrine of pure experience, the centerpiece of his radical empiricism, is implicit in the "sensationalism" of *The Principles*, which treats sensation as originally objective, its internalization into the stream of thought being an infant's achievement, as is its "physicalization" into a world of physical objects in space.

I shall argue in the pages to follow that James's pragmatism, however it may be understood by Jamesian neopragmatists on the contemporary scene, is grounded in pure experience, which sets limits on the extent to which pragmatic concept formation can helpfully guide experience. (The physical world can't set such limits, because, by the hypothesis of James's neutral monism, it is the spawn of pragmatic constructive activity.) On this theme of the unity of James's thought, the self is a construct out of pure experience; God is a pattern of good purpose in the world of primal stuff; his celebrated and reviled will-to-believe doctrine explores the extent of our power to construct ourselves and the physical world; and his mysticism is both an attempt to get closer to God, the pattern of pure-experiential good purpose in history, and to acquaint himself, so to speak, with the deepest preconceptual wells of everyday experience.

James's spirit has become part of the background of philosophizing in many circles, as in his notion of the "cash-value" of a philosophical concept, or his disposition to take abstract claims down to brass tacks by examining particular cases. Also in the milieu are his distinctions between hard and soft deter-

minism, between tough-minded and tender-minded philosophical tempera-
ments, and between knowledge-by-acquaintance and knowledge-by-descrip-
tion. And his lack of tolerance for obscurantism in metaphysics might also be
mentioned as one of his legacies to the temper of much contemporary philosophical thought, although a legacy in danger of being lost.

Methodological Considerations

Perhaps it goes without saying at this point that my analysis of James is a very
different enterprise from that of what Nabokov called "the Viennese set," who
have ventured to psychoanalyze the James family, rich as it is with material
drawn from a religious-eccentric father, a sensitive younger brother who would
become an important novelist, an intellectually gifted but handicapped sister,
and so on through the James clan. I am concerned foremost with James's philosophy, which makes claims to truth that should be examined on their own
merits, rather than trivialized by mapping them onto personal idiosyncracies.
His personal crises, except when James-the-philosopher chooses to develop his
theory by reference to them, are irrelevant to me, as a student of his theory.

While the philosophy is not to be dismissed for biographical reasons, neither should it be treated simply as a precious historical artifact. It is something
to build with, its insights developed and its blind spots left behind. It is a theory,
or perhaps a prototheory, true, approximately true, or false.

I have tried to be more restrained in my reconstruction than I find some
postmodern and depth-psychology interpretations to be, for instance. "Rational reconstruction" can mean different things, of course, but I will mean by it
an interpretation of James's philosophical writing in a manner that reveals it as
the best philosophical theory it can be. This goes beyond making it intelligible. I want to show that these ideas are live options for belief, and this sometimes involves going beyond simply making sense of his writings; it involves
pursuing his theory's claim to truth, showing how it might be true. Consequently, I have emphasized themes in common between James and contemporary philosophers, including James's approach toward consciousness and
John Searle's Connection Principle; James's account of the relationship between conceptualization and pure experience, and the Ramsey-sentence
pattern of analysis defended by functionalists such as David Lewis; James's account of the mind-body relationship and Alvin Goldman's notion of simulta-

neous nomic equivalence; James's account of the will to believe and Robert Nozick's decision-value theory of the role of symbolic utility in rational belief; James's empirical self and Nozick's Closest-Continuer theory of personal identity; and so on.

There are many methods of making sense of James, several of which I shall have occasion to examine. A particularly luminous recent example is Richard Gale's *The Divided Self of William James* (1999), in which acute philosophical analysis is guided by depth-psychological speculations that treat James as a "hipster" whose philosophizing is "deeply rooted in the blues," its immediate aim "to keep him sane and nonsuicidal," while the philosophical upshot, according to Gale, is a philosophy that tries to have it all,[4] and as a result lacks the theoretical integrity I will be attempting to establish, expressing instead, in Gale's reading, a tendency that "bordered on philosophical satyrism" (Gale 1999, xi, 20). I find the chiaroscuro effect of Gale's psychologizing too dark for my taste, and its speculations about James's psychological frailties, whatever the truth in them,[5] are less interesting to me than the prospect of the power of James's philosophical system. As for the man, the James I admire is the persona James constructed in his writing: erudite, witty, cosmopolitan, visionary. More to the philosophical point, I find that Gale's interpretive framework, especially what he calls James's Master Syllogism, is deeply flawed; I make the case for this in Chapters 10, 11, and 12.

I do not think that interpretation of James is well served by piling up citations and concluding, for a given issue, that the larger pile wins. James had a long career, wrote for different types of audiences, and is associated with publications that are sometimes highly polished and at other times unfinished or little more than day-journal jottings. Philosophical interpreters should give greater weight to those writings in which they think James is doing his best philosophy. Many have in effect done this by emphasizing *Pragmatism, The Varieties of Religious Experience*, late unfinished work like *Some Problems of Philosophy*, or even *Manuscript Essays and Notes*. We now have a good idea of what insight that emphasis affords. If only to cast a different light on James's legacy, there is reason to emphasize his *Principles of Psychology*, as I do in the pages that follow. But there are other reasons as well. *The Principles* is surely James's magnum opus, the work in which he discusses issues for professional psychologists and philosophers at a level of argumentation and detail that is unrivaled elsewhere in his work. So when a later popular lecture, say, is liable to divergent interpretations, it makes sense to see whether the crucial concept or proposition in the lecture is examined in *The Principles*. There is a significant difference of emphasis between this approach and Gale's methodological prescription that "greater weight should be accorded to the later publications, as they represent his more mature, all-things-considered view" (Gale 1999, 21). This difference will be crucial in Chapter 9, where I invoke *The Principles'* account of meaning to clarify an ambiguity in James's discussion in *Pragmatism*.

My own prescription is not a fool-proof procedure; James might have changed his mind or forgotten what he wrote earlier. But there is a burden of proof on the claim that he did so, simply because, other things being equal, a principle of charity in interpretation requires that one construe another's writings as a rationally unified whole when it is possible to do so. The whole may be larger or smaller, of course. The reader will notice that I have ignored James's lifelong interest in paranormal phenomena, which turned out to be, I believe, a blind alley. This interest was not at odds with the psychological and metaphysical foundations of his system, but rather was one way of exploring it, one which bore no fruit. Should I be wrong, I think it would be possible to expand the theory to encompass these phenomena, but I have made no such effort here.

A principle of charity becomes especially important when the larger pile of words, or what is perceived to be so, leads to the conclusion that the other is an irrationally fragmented Pooh-Bah, guilty of "philosophical satyrism" (Gale 1999, 21). I believe that building one's interpretive house on the foundations of *The Principles*, tracing its sensationalism to the doctrine of pure experience in *Essays in Radical Empiricism*, and interpreting *Pragmatism, The Varieties of Religious Experience, The Will to Believe, Some Problems of Philosophy, Manuscript Essays and Notes*, and the rest by harking back to the psychological and metaphysical foundations is the best way to appreciate James's philosophical genius. It is not enough to make James's writings "the star performer," as Gale advises, but rather one should try to determine when the star is at the top of his form and organize the performances so that the performer is shown at his best. The case for this may rest in part on the continuity of James's thought with strands of contemporary thought, our sense now of what is best, so I will bring several supporting actors from contemporary philosophical theater to the stage on which, in the following pages, James will play the lead role.

2

Consciousness I: The Two-Levels View

It rustles, so to speak. (MEN, 30)

In the next three chapters I begin to remove the first obstacle in the path toward acceptance of James's constructivism, namely, the appearance that the physical and mental are ultimate features of the world, an appearance that must be challenged by a radical-empiricist metaphysics which regards both features as constructs out of pure experience. (The removal is completed in Chapter 8.) Psychology's basic physical and mental facts, as well as psychological science itself, are like a ship afloat in a sea of pure experience, which leaks into it at every joint. In this chapter I show that the naturalistic reading of James ignores this leakage; the phenomenological reading wrongly questions the seaworthiness of the ship, the legitimacy of the empirical level of natural-scientific psychology; the neutral monist reading understates the affinity between pure experience and the mental; and the panpsychist reading overstates it. Chapter 3 takes up the central question for philosophy's old mind-body problem, the problem of the relationship between mind and body, defending James's firm conviction that there must be causal interaction and applying this defense to interpretation of the James-Lange theory of emotion. Chapter 4 makes the case that James's assumption that mental life is conscious is well motivated, by associating his criticism of "mind dust" with trends in contemporary philosophy of mind that are critical of Freudian and cognitive-psychological postulations of subconscious mental states.

Four Interpretations

For James, the study of psychology was the grand portal to metaphysics, leading in particular to pure experience, which, though neither mental nor physical, has certain features of the stream of consciousness; it is *protomental*. I hope to show that the idea of pure experience as protomental and as constitutive of both mind and body, couched within a view of James's system as having empirical and metaphysical levels, reconciles four plausible but apparently conflicting interpretations of James's theory of mind. This extraordinary diversity of scholarly opinion represents just about every interpretive live option, construing James variously as a neutral monist, a naturalistic physicalist, a panpsychist, and a phenomenologist. The key to the reconciliation is to take seriously James's own distinction between scientific and metaphysical levels of inquiry and to assign the four readings different roles within the two-level structure. The price of the reconciliation, that substantial tenets of these readings must be rejected, is offset by the prospect of both interpretive consensus and the emergence of an overarching philosophical system within James's work, a system that remains a candidate for belief. I hope to show that the Two-Levels View, as I shall call it, is securely anchored in James's magnum opus, *The Principles of Psychology*, an anchor which secures a flotilla of metaphysical, epistemological, religious, and ethical ideas associated with James's oeuvre. This view has the hermeneutic virtue of finding more coherence and good sense in James's theorizing than the interpretive alternatives, and at the end of this chapter, and indeed throughout the book, I will suggest that the Two-Levels View's claim to truth cannot be dismissed.

A. J. Ayer presents the definitive reading of James as a neutral monist who dissolved the mind-body problem by giving primacy to a single stuff which is metaphysically more fundamental than mind or body, and neutral with respect to the difference between them; this stuff, which James called pure experience, is the material out of which each of us somehow constructs the private, subjective world of one's mind and the public, objective world of body. Owen J. Flanagan's naturalistic reading of James, by contrast, gives primacy to the body: James ended the hegemony of Cartesian assumptions and initiated the reign, in twentieth-century psychology and philosophy, of the naturalistic assumption that a person is a physical thing with no metaphysically odd, nonphysical properties. Marcus Ford, by contrast with Ayer and Flanagan, gives primacy to the mind, seeing in James a panpsychist who believed that every existent thing has mental attributes. Not only do persons have metaphysically odd properties, contrary to Flanagan's lights, but everything has them. And so there can be no primally neutral stuff that lacks them, as Ayer's James insists.

Finally, there is Bruce Wilshire's James, for whom questions of metaphysical primacy are replaced by subtle descriptions of mental states, anticipating Husserl's case for a phenomenological science of the mind that would be autonomous and not dependent, in particular, on data drawn from the natural sciences.

Wilshire's James is a phenomenologist who emphasizes the importance to psychology of introspection, especially for describing mental life in a vocabulary that does not distort it, whereas Flanagan finds James's reliance on introspection to be the least attractive aspect of his theory of psychology. Wilshire takes for granted that James was a naturalist in the sense that he sought psychophysical correlation laws, but he deplores this commitment as being at odds with James's phenomenological insights. In short, there is a profound lack of consensus among James scholars about how to interpret his theorizing about the mind. I have chosen to discuss these four scholars because they represent, in clear and persuasive fashion, four current and often conflicting interpretive schools. Their statements are extreme, and more moderate ones would be less open to the criticisms I shall raise. The extreme statements are the best foils for the Two-Levels View, and moreover, they expose characteristic interpretive errors of each of the four schools.

I shall argue that the neutral monist reading is fundamentally correct at the metaphysical level of James's theory, but it must concede to the panpsychist account that pure experience is protomental; that is, although more basic than mind or body, pure experience is more akin to mind than to body. I shall argue further that the naturalistic reading is fundamentally correct at the psychological level, by emphasizing James's conception of psychology as a law-seeking science like other natural sciences, and by doing justice to his Darwinian commitments. The strength of the phenomenological view is its emphasizing that Jamesian psychology requires precise phenomenological descriptions of mental states as a preliminary to seeking psychophysical correlations. John Wild is right to insist in *The Radical Empiricism of William James* that "the first task of psychology, as James conceived of it, is to describe these phenomena of mental life exactly as they are lived, so far as this is possible, and then to find out something concerning their relations and the patterns into which they fall" (Wild 1969, 4). Where I disagree with Wild, and where I find a characteristic interpretive error in the phenomenological reading of James, is in the decision to concentrate on James's admittedly extraordinary phenomenological descriptions and to subordinate or dismiss James's conception of psychology as a law-seeking natural science. Wild makes the crucial error when he writes, "Hence we shall concentrate our attention upon [the phenomenological description], and subordinate the rest" (Wild 1969, 4).

James makes plain his dim view of such merely descriptive psychologies in his review of George T. Ladd's *Psychology: Descriptive and Explanatory.* "I find this whole descriptive sort of treatment tedious," James writes, "as few things can be tedious, tedious not as really hard things, like physics and chemistry, are tedious, but tedious as the throwing of feathers hour after hour is tedious" (ERC, 484). Like Ladd before him, Wild thinks that psychology does not inquire into causes in the manner of the natural sciences. Furthermore, he attempts to distance James from such inquiry by attributing to him a distinction between a causal relation and a "leading to" relation: "bodily conditions [of mental life], while necessary, are not sufficient, and, therefore not to be confused with causes," Wild claims on James's behalf, adding that bodily changes only "lead to" mental changes and vice versa (Wild 1969, 3–4). I do not deny that the "leading-to" relationship is important to James. It is clearly at work in this theory of conception or meaning in *Principles,* which informs his notion of pragmatic meaning in *Pragmatism* and elsewhere. But I see no reason to deny that the leading-to relation is a causal one.

Whatever the merits of Wild's exclusive disjunction between the causal and "leading-to" relations, it is a mistake to attribute it to James, and a greater error to use it as the basis for denying that Jamesian psychology is causal inquiry. Commenting on Ladd's view that all attempts to assimilate psychology to other natural sciences are "misleading," James says: "To me this lack of craving for insights into causes is most strange" (ERC, 485). And in *The Principles* James could scarcely be more explicit about the appropriateness of seeking causes in psychology: "As in the night all cats are gray, so in the darkness of metaphysical criticism all causes are obscure. . . . But Psychology is a mere natural science, accepting certain terms uncritically as her data, and stopping short of metaphysical reconstruction. Like physics, she must be naïve; and if she finds that in her very peculiar field of study ideas seem to be causes, she had better continue to talk of them as such" (PP, 83).

None of this gainsays the phenomenological insight that psychology must rely on introspection to identify and describe mental phenomena. The phenomenological reading is also important in illuminating the metaphysical level of James's system, for techniques of phenomenological description may help to get at *just what appears*, the pure experience, which is encrusted by conceptualization and the mind-body dichotomy in adult experience. It is a mistake however, according to the Two-Levels View, to suppose with Gale (1999, 222) that James gave "pride of place to introspection over the way of objective analysis in terms of cause and effect." At which level should this claim be assessed? At the empirical level, as I argue in the next chapter, introspection functions in the discovery and deployment of laws of correspondence between the mental and the cerebral. Psychology must rely on introspection first and foremost and always, James famously wrote, but that is because discovery of mental-physical correlations cannot even begin without introspection's fixing the reference of the mental. It would be different if subconscious mental states played a role in James's psychology, but they do not, as I argue in Chapter 4. Then how should the pride-of-place claim be evaluated at the metaphysical level? Here the problem is that objective analysis of cause and effect has *no* role, rather than a role that is subservient to introspection; indeed, introspection itself has no role here, because introspection is necessarily related to the stream of thought. The stream of thought, like the physical world, is a product of construction with the materials given by pure experience. Introspection then, understood as introspection of the stream of thought, doesn't directly apprehend pure experience (though mystical experience, James thought, might have this power).

Protomental and Essentially Mental

For James there is a legitimate but circumscribed level of theorizing about the relationship between mind and body, and he hoped to erect a science of psychology in this area by discovering psychophysical correlation laws. This science would provide the empirical grounding for speculation at a metaphysical level, where the methodological assumptions made by the various sciences might be questioned. For instance, it can be questioned whether thoughts and physical states really exist in the final, metaphysical analysis.

Many of the questions posed by scientific psychology receive broadly naturalistic answers from James, but he insists on a firm demarcation between the domain of the natural sciences, in which these answers are appropriate, and the domain of metaphysics, where they may or may not be. James draws the basic distinction as follows in the preface to *The Principles*:

I have kept close to the point of view of natural science throughout the book. Every natural science assumes certain data uncritically, and declines to challenge the elements between which its own "laws" obtain, and from which its own deductions are carried on. Psychology, the science of finite individual minds, assumes as its data (1) thoughts and feelings, and (2) a physical world in time and space with which they coexist and which (3) they know. Of course these data themselves are discussible; but the discussion of them (as of other elements) is called metaphysics and falls outside the province of this book. This book, assuming that thoughts and feelings exist and are vehicles of knowledge, thereupon contends that psychology when she has ascertained the empirical correlation of the various sorts of thought or feeling with definite conditions of the brain, can go no farther-can go no farther, that is, as a natural science. If she goes farther she becomes metaphysical. (PP, vi)

The natural sciences do the indispensable empirical spade work for metaphysics, and they may point suggestively away from or toward a metaphysical conclusion; but typically they leave options open with respect to ultimate questions. Among the metaphysical options left open about the nature of mind and body is neutral monism. The genetic psychological accounts in *The Principles*—of the subject's gradual construction of an inner, mental world and an outer, public world, organizing sensations which are originally experienced as belonging to neither category—strongly suggests that scientific psychology points toward a radical empiricist metaphysics of pure experience.

The Two-Levels View requires a distinction between the protomental and the essentially mental. Observing this distinction makes it possible to create a middle way for James between neutral monism and panpsychism, for then it can be said that both the neutral stuff of neutral monism and the psychic stuff of panpsychism are protomental rather than essentially so. The mentality which panpsychism affirms is minimal, amounting to the insistence that pure experience has at least three of the five features that James regarded as characterizing the stream of consciousness, namely, purposiveness, changingness, and continuity. These features are appropriately termed protomental, because they characterize the stream before as well as after the subject's achievement of dividing his or her experience into inner and outer, public and private. So experience that has these protomental features is suited to being organized into physical objects as well as mental states. That is, such experience can function as the neutral primal stuff of neutral monism. Of these three features, two may be regarded as absolute or nonrelational features of pure experience, while the third, purposiveness, must be construed in relation to other pure experience, as detailed in Chapter 7, on James's conception of God. Its purposiveness cannot be a particular person's purposiveness, since that brings in the characters of thought, personal ownership, and privacy, which are to be excluded. Pure experiences are to comprise a world external to human beings and independent of their existence, so it would be unsatisfactory to presuppose human purposes in theorizing them; they are mindlike in their purposiveness, but that feature requires a different story (the story attached to James's conception of God) from the story to be told about human purposiveness.

A narrower conception of the mental, essentially conscious rather than protomental, would describe it as necessarily private, inner, and subjective. Mentality in this sense is what James has in mind when he denies that pure experience is mental; it is also what is different from but correlated with the physical, in the psychophysical correlation laws that psychology is responsible for discovering. At least one of the five characters in the process of thought seems to imply this narrower sense of mentality. When James discusses the first character, that every thought tends to be part of a personal consciousness, he is led into emphasizing privacy: "No thought even comes into direct sight of a thought in another personal consciousness than its own" (PP, 221). I think it is worth mentioning, however, that even in connection with the personal character of thought, James seems to be driving partly at a point which need not imply privacy, viz., that "the elementary psychic fact [is] not thought or this thought or that thought, but my thought, every thought being owned" (PP, 221). Personality in this sense need not imply privacy, as can be seen by noting that a person's money can be the elementary budgetary fact for a science of personal accounting; the "my-ness" of my money does not prevent others from coming within sight of it. My-ness in this sense, carefully distinguished from privacy, can be a protomental feature of pure experience.

It is vital to distinguish the protomentality of pure experience from naïve panpsychism, according to which the world of pure experience would have *all* the features of consciousness. My account is not Gale's, when he writes, "What [James] finds through introspection of what goes on when he endures over time and acts intentionally so as to bring something about is a fusing or melting together of neighboring conscious stages; and he then assumes that there is a similar sort of mushing together between all spatial and temporal neighbors, the result of which is panpsychism, since only in consciousness can such mushing together occur" (Gale 1999, 15). I am recommending a reading according to which it is *false* that such mushing can occur only in consciousness; it can occur also in pure experience, which has protoconscious features but is external to consciousness. Pure experience is public, capable of being apprehended by different consciousnesses. Instead of saying, with Gale (1999, 222), that for James consciousness is the stuff of everything, I recommend saying that consciousness is one of the two basic categories of fact at the empirical level of James's system, whereas, at the metaphysical level, pure experience is basic and is indeed the stuff of everything; but it is not consciousness, though it has *some* of the features of the stream of thought.

Trimming panpsychism to an attenuated form of panpsychism—a theory of the protomentality of pure experience—gains plausibility when it is recalled that James had an austere conception of what is involved in a thought's being "personal." The personal character of thought does not imply that behind the steam of consciousness, and uniting it, there is a deep further fact, like the Cartesian ego. One robust form of panpsychism would hold that everything has such an ego, soul, or substantial mind. But James is certainly not a panpsychist in this sense. For him "the Ego is simply nothing: as ineffectual and windy an abortion as philosophy can show" (PP, 345). He diagnoses its currency as "an outbirth of that sort of philosophizing whose great maxim, according to Dr. Hodgson, is: 'Whatever you are totally ignorant of, assert to be the explanation of everything else'" (PP, 329). James assigns the unity of consciousness to it simply as a brute fact, just as he attributes a personal, "for itself," feature to it as a brute fact. This characteristically Jamesian strategy helps to make his empiricism radical in the way he desires. Rather than positing a subject behind experience, an anterior unifier and owner of experience, James holds that the unity and the sense of being "owned" are given in experience, and that there is no license for inferences to explanatory posits. James resorts to the same shoehorn strategy in his discussion of space, for instance, when he attributes voluminousness, or three-dimensionality, to spatial qualia as a brute fact about the qualia, instead of following Berkeley in attempting to construct it out of originally two-dimensional qualia. Like Ockham's razor, James's Shoehorn permits one to keep ontological commitments minimal. The Razor does so by eliminating unnecessary entities, the Shoehorn by attributing a psychological "sense" of the unnecessary entities to the necessary one. There is no purposive agent that unifies and directs pure experience, according to James's radical empiricism; rather, pure experience, when it becomes a thought that appropriates other experiences to itself, natively contains the sense of being personally owned and purposefully directed by such an agent.

The Two-Levels View's distinction between protomental and essentially mental readily fits James's most explicit statements of his position, such as the following: "My central thesis," he says in "The Place of Affectional Facts in a World of Pure Experience," is that "subjectivity and objectivity are affairs not of what an experience is aboriginally made of, but of its classification. Classification depends on our temporary purposes" (ERE, 71). Purpose and subjectivity are related here in just the way the Two-Levels View relates the protomental to the essentially mental.

James's universe was ultimately teleological, but it was not ultimately private, subjective, and inner, just as it was not ultimately physical, intersubjective, and outer. These intermediate categories get a grip only when the primal stuff has organized itself in the various ways that *The Principles* describes, creating for the first time inner and outer, private and public, subjective and intersubjective. It is fundamental to the Two-Levels View that *The Principles* accounts of the genesis of mind and body—of the stream of thought and of space and its contents—anticipates the radical empiricist metaphysics of the later ERE. The unclassified sensations of early life, in *The Principles*, become the pure experiences of the ERE.

My view of the continuity of *The Principles* and the ERE leads me to question Ignas K. Skrupskelis's assertion that "the concept of pure experience is only weakly embedded in James's published writings; it is found in the *Essays in Radical Empiricism* and nowhere else" (MEN, xxii). This is true of the term "pure experience," but not of the concept. The concept of that which is neither mental nor physical, but which becomes so, is clearly at work in *The Principles*; it is simply termed, somewhat misleadingly, sensation. Skrupskelis may be misled in reading *The Principles* as affirming that "there is a mental stuff and a physical stuff and that in the original experience the two stand fused" (MEN, xxii). If the reference to fusion is taken at face value, then Skrupskelis is saying that the original experience of *The Principles* is both mental and physical, creating a gratuitous mystery about how such experience could be the pure experience of the ERE, which is neither mental nor physical. I see nothing in *The Principles* to recommend the "fusion" reading of original experience. At one point indeed James criticizes a theory according to which an infant's experience is a fusion of many sensations, dismissing the theory as "pure mythology" (PP, 496).

Naturalism

Flanagan's naturalism is found in the essay "Naturalizing the Mind: The Philosophical Psychology of William James." He sees James's work as "the first formulation of the naturalistic position in the philosophy of mind," in which view "mentality has no metaphysically odd properties [but rather] the world [is] comprised of physical objects, their properties, and their relations," and "mental states are functional states and functional properties of the complex commerce we have with the outside world" (Flanagan 1984, 24).

With the idea of a two-level structure in place, it can be said that naturalism is simply not plausible as an account of the metaphysical level of James's thought. Its seeming so can be accounted for only by supposing that the interpreter has conflated the metaphysical and psychological levels of James's theory. Although the conflation leaves open the possibility that naturalism is correct as an account of James's conception of scientific psychology, I shall argue that it is partially mistaken even here. James was a naturalist in psychology to the extent that he wanted psychology to become a law-seeking natural science, but its laws link brain states to mental states, construed as irreducibly different, as far as psychology is concerned, from physical states. So James is committed, contrary to Flanagan's view, to odd properties in Flanagan's sense, both at the metaphysical and scientific levels. The pure experiences of James's radical empiricist metaphysics are nonphysical things, hence "metaphysically odd." And scientific psychology should treat states of consciousness as nonphysical, whatever their ultimate nature, rather than reducing them somehow to the physical.

Flanagan is not clear about what constitutes the sort of "metaphysically odd property" of which naturalism is skeptical. On one hand, he is inclined to think that a property is metaphysically odd if it is not either a physical property or a relational property, e.g., a functional property describing the "complex commerce" between one physical thing (an organism) and another physical thing (the outside world). James's philosophy of pure experience (his "radical empiricism") is a philosophy of odd properties in this sense, for pure experience is not a physical thing, nor a physical or relational property of a physical thing. On the other hand, if by "metaphysically odd property" one understands a property not referred to by scientific psychology—that is, if one reads Flanagan as describing James's psychology rather than his metaphysics, then James is still committed to metaphysically odd properties in Flanagan's sense, because it is central to his view of human psychology that consciousness is a nonphysical causal force which stabilizes the brain's activity. Consequently, scientific psychology must refer to such causes in its psychophysical laws. In claiming this efficacy for consciousness James is not simply noting that there is a functional commerce between an organism and its environment, but rather he is explaining this functional relationship by referring to a nonphysical cause. I note the concurrence of Myers on this point: "James's testimonial words to it [consciousness] lead us irresistibly to view it is not merely as a function but as something with an inherent nature, by which it is a causal agent that produces effects" (Myers 1986, 64).

Like many other commentators, however, Myers is puzzled by James's holding this view while also wanting to deny that consciousness exists. "James wanted to hold that in one way consciousness does not exist, but that in another way it does," Myers writes, "yet he was never able, even to his own satisfaction, to define the two ways clearly enough to show that they are consistent rather than contradictory" (Myers 1986, 64). This last judgment is too pessimistic, and in Chapter 7 I will set out a full solution to the puzzle. For now it will be enough to say that The Two-Levels View solves the apparent puzzle by restricting the proposition that consciousness does not exist to the metaphysical level of James's system and by restricting the proposition that consciousness interacts with the body to the level of scientific psychology. So consciousness does exist as pure experience, but it does not exist as something distinct from pure experience and essentially different from the physical. In logicians' parlance, James quantifies pure experience, not consciousness and bodies, in his metaphysics; in his psychology he quantifies both consciousness and bodies.

This way of solving the puzzle is consistent with the attitude that James expresses in the paper "Does 'Consciousness' Exist?" from ERE. According to that attitude consciousness is not an intrinsic but rather a relational property of a state. So a careful introspective analysis of an electrically induced visual appearance of a blue expanse, for instance, in which that state was abstracted from its relationship to other mental states, would reveal no quality of the state which would intimate that it was an illusory state of consciousness rather than, say, a directly perceived blue wall. Consciousness is not self-intimating. It intimates itself, rather, through such relations as it may have to the experience of, for example, groping unsuccessfully for the seemingly present blue wall. But the visual appearance of a blue expanse, though it does not reveal itself to awareness as being mental or physical, genuinely exists. James was not attempting a behaviorist reduction of such appearances when he denied that consciousness exists, as Naturalist interpreters of James are wont to suppose.

James returns to this neutral aspect of present experience in a remarkable passage from *Manuscript Essays and Notes*, anticipating the intimate connection between the present subject, the relationship between mind and body, and the subject of Chapter 5, the self:

> As I pause in my writing I perceive the rustling of the leaves of a breeze-swept maple hard-by. That rustling has gone on for many minutes, yet I only just now notice it. It probably gave me a "sensation'," but the sensation lapsed immediately, for my Self of subsequent moments ignored & dropped it. What shall we call it? Was it "rustling," or was it "sense of rustling"? Was it a mysterious two headed entity, both in one? What was it? Obviously what we mean by objective "rustling" is just that pure experience; and that pure experience is also what we mean by sense of rustling. If there were no other experience in the world than that, the question whether it were objective or merely conscious, or both in one, would never have arisen. The rustling would be the world, and if anyone asked us then of what kind of stuff the world consisted, we should say of just *that* stuff, or *rustle*, if you need an appellation. . . . We call the rustling physical when we come to connect it with other features of the tree and with the wind; we call it mental when we connect it with our listening and with the stream of our thinking which it interrupts.
>
> Now the immediately present moment in everyone's experience, however complex the content of it may be, has this same absolute character. It rustles, so to speak. The vastest "field of consciousness," when *there*, does not yet figure either as a field of consciousness or as a reality outside. It figures as just *that*. (MEN, 30)

I turn now to arguing for the construal of naturalism as expressing methodological posits of scientific psychology, rather than metaphysical tenets. I do so while acknowledging that the line of demarcation between them is vague, uncertain, and contested:

When, then, we talk of "psychology as a natural science," we must not assume that that means a sort of psychology that stands at last on solid ground. It means just the reverse; it means a psychology particularly fragile, and into which the waters of metaphysical criticism leak at every joint, a psychology all of whose elementary assumptions and data must be reconsidered in wider connections and translated into other terms. It is, in short, a phrase of diffidence, and not of arrogance; and it is indeed strange to hear people talk triumphantly of "the New Psychology," and write "Histories of Psychology," when into the real elements and forces which the word covers not the first glimpse of clear insight exists. (PBC, 400)

I begin with some observations about James's rejection of epiphenomenalism, which will require leaving some implications of naturalism behind.

James's youthful enthusiasm for epiphenomenalism,[1] or what he called "the conscious automaton theory," was firmly curbed by the time of his writing, in *The Principles*, "It is to my mind quite inconceivable that consciousness should have nothing to do with a business which it so faithfully attends." Yet James's insistence on the dependency of the mental on the physical — especially in Chapter 2 of *The Principles*, "The Functions of the Brain" — veers close to that doctrine. His psychology is saved from the "brain-automatists," however, by his hypothesis that the brain's structure is so complex that it has a "hair-trigger organization," which would make of it "a happy-go-lucky, hit-or-miss affair" were it not that consciousness increases the brain's efficiency by "loading its dice," which means "bringing a more or less constant pressure to bear in favor of those of its performances which make for the most permanent interests of the brain's owner; it would mean a constant inhibition of the tendencies to stray aside" (PP, 143). The how of such influence he is content to put aside as a mystery for metaphysics to solve; psychology will simply affirm the appearance that there is such an influence. The upshot is that James is committed in psychology to a methodological dualism of mind and body.

Flanagan fails to appreciate this dualism and its methodological character. The error may be illuminated by comparing it to a related one in Charlene Seigfried's *Chaos and Context: A Study in William James*. Seigfried appreciates the dualism but not its methodological character. "In his landmark work, *The Principles of Psychology*," she says, James "reluctantly allowed the dichotomy [between mind and body] to stand. Later on, with more consistency, he abandoned this dualism. What allows him to abandon consciousness as an equi-primordial entity along with physical things is his liberating hypothesis of pure experience " (Seigfried 1978, 39). The Two-Levels View implies by contrast that James never abandoned the methodological dualism of *The Principles*, as this would have been tantamount in his eyes to despair of putting psychology on a scientific footing. It is true that he came to dwell on metaphysical questions rather than psychological ones, but this is consistent with his accepting a division of labor between psychological and metaphysical levels of inquiry.

To digress for a moment: The interpretive mistake instanced by Siegfried is a common one, and I am inclined to trace it back to the influence of Ralph Barton Perry's *The Thought and Character of William James*. Perry, too, fails to appreciate the methodological character of James's psychological dualism when he contrasts it with Berkeleyan idealism—a metaphysical doctrine, of course—and says" that James "saw with increasing clearness that he could not hold one view as a psychologist and another as a philosopher; and as his rejection of dualism became a more and more dominant motive in his thought, he saw that he would have to correct his psychology" (Perry 1935, 273). Although the Two-Levels View does not purport to be intellectual biography, on the point that Perry raises I suspect it can be defended on biographical grounds as well as the hermeneutical ones I mentioned at the beginning of this study. What James saw clearly as early as *The Principles* is that any natural science, including scientific psychology, will raise and leave unanswered many metaphysical questions. He called psychology "the antechamber to metaphysics,"[2] and as his career developed, James walked through the psychological antechamber and began a metaphysical analysis which reached a high point in the *Essays in Radical Empiricism*, sputtering however to an inconclusive end in the writings collected in *Manuscript Essays and Notes*. His ideas at the metaphysical level, unfortunately, never received the definitive statement that *The Principles* represented at the empirical-psychological level.

To return to Flanagan's naturalism: It views James as offering a metaphysical alternative to Cartesian dualism, an alternative according to which people have no "metaphysically odd," i.e., nonphysical, properties. But it is plain that James's remarks about the influence of consciousness on the brain imply that mentality has metaphysically odd properties in Flanagan's sense: they are nonphysical causal forces which affect the brain. James offers not the least hint that the influence of consciousness on the brain is the influence of a physical force, such as one part of the brain stabilizing the rest. On the contrary, he seems at pains to distinguish it from the various physical processes going on inside the skull.

It is a mistake to draw inferences from *The Principles* about what James regards as metaphysically fundamental, so it would be a mistake to infer a metaphysics of Cartesian dualism from James's insistence in this context on the difference between the brain and consciousness; but equally it would be a mistake to infer from James's commitment to a Darwinian perspective in psychology that he was a metaphysical naturalist in Flanagan's sense.

Flanagan's major piece of evidence for James's "underlying naturalism" is "his unwavering commitment to evolutionary theory," which Flanagan interprets as ruling out a view of mental states as "an extra added attraction conferred by God" (Flanagan 1984, 44). He quotes James as saying, "We ought therefore ourselves sincerely to try every possible mode of conceiving of consciousness so that it may not appear equivalent to the irruption into the universe of a new nature non-existent to then" (Flanagan 1984, 44). But in his partisanship for naturalism Flanagan overlooks the method of avoiding the irruption which James actually chose—namely, his metaphysics of radical empiricism with its doctrine of pure experience. Consciousness is not an irruption into the physical universe of a new nature, because both consciousness and the physical universe are different arrangements of the same nature, namely, pure experience. A metaphysics of naturalism is not entailed by a commitment to evolutionary theory, for this theory can be subsumed under a radical empiricist metaphysics. Given the fundamental natural-scientific assumption of a physical world, Darwinian evolutionary theory is true of that world; but the natural science of psychology also assumes nonphysical thoughts and feelings, which evolutionary theory cannot ignore. Besides, what is a given for science is not a given for metaphysics; James's doctrine of pure experience recognizes neither the physical world nor thoughts and feelings in its ontology.

James does not attempt to deal with the problem of continuity between physical and mental phenomena at the level of scientific psychology; rather, he says, "the ascertainment of a blank unmediated correspondence, term for term, of the succession of states of consciousness with the succession of total brain-processes [is] the simplest psycho-physical formula, and the last word of a psychology which contents itself with verifiable laws, and seeks only to be clear, and to avoid unsafe hypotheses" (PP, 182). As far as psychology is concerned, panpsychism is just as capable as naturalism to meet evolutionary psychology's demand for continuity: if "each atom of the nebula . . . had an aboriginal atom of consciousness linked with it," then it would not be necessary to posit a new nature, mind, as abruptly coming into existence at some stage of evolution" (PP, 149).

Far from his Darwinism's leading to Flanagan's naturalism, James reasons in a Darwinian fashion for the efficacy of consciousness understood as a nonphysical force. After remarking in the 1879 paper "Are We Automata?" that "mental and physical events are, on all hands, admitted to present the strongest contrast in the entire field of being," James goes on to argue that the "presumptive evidence wholly favors the efficacy of Consciousness," as having been "slowly evolved in the animal series" so as to "determine its brain to prosperous courses" (PP, 40–41). James even presents this conclusion as rebutting the objection to Darwinian theory that evolution would have taken longer to give rise to such a complex organism as the human being: "But give to consciousness the power of exerting a constant pressure in the direction of survival, and give to the organism the power of growing to the modes in which consciousness has trained it, and the number of stray shots [i.e., mutations without survival value] is immensely reduced, and the time proportionally shortened for Evolution. It is, in fact, hard to see how without an effective super-intending ideal the evolution of so unstable an organ as the mammalian cerebrum can have proceeded at all" (EP, 54). It is plain that the "training" of the brain is done by a nonphysical force, namely, mental events which "present the strongest contrast" with physical events.

On top of all this it must be remembered that the complex evolutionary process is ultimately understood to be a construction out of pure experience. So for example the pragmatic "cash value" of claims about the history of evolution resides in the experiences that substantiate these claims (anthropologists' experiences of fossil remains, etc.). It is hard to understand how this might be so, and Flanagan's naturalism may seem much more plausible, since it takes for granted, in a way that is congenial to the common sense of most modern people, the independent existence of a physical world, a world which is not "made up" of experience. But the evidence is compelling that physical objects do not constitute a metaphysically fundamental category for James and that his commitment to evolutionary theory does not entail metaphysical naturalism. Moreover, I will conclude by offering some considerations suggesting that James's theory of mind should be viewed as a live, if unlikely, option.

Phenomenology

The phenomenological tradition of Husserl *et al.* has recognized an affinity with William James's philosophy, especially when James is describing the stream of consciousness, in memorable passages like the following one from the chapter "The Stream of Thought" in *The Principles of Psychology:*

> Now what I contend for, and accumulate examples to show, is that "tendencies" are not only descriptions from without, but that they are among the *objects* of the stream, which is thus aware of them from within, and must be described as in very large measure constituted of *feelings of tendency*, often so vague that we are unable to name them at all. It is, in short, the re-instatement of the vague to its proper place in our mental life which I am so anxious to press on the attention. Mr. Galton and Prof. Huxley have, as we shall see in Chapter XVIII, made one step in advance in exploding the ridiculous theory of Hume and Berkeley that we can have no images but of perfectly definite things. Another is made in the overthrow of the equally ridiculous notion that, whilst simple objective qualities are revealed to our knowledge in subjective feelings, relations are not. But these reforms are not half sweeping and radical enough. What must be admitted is that the definite images of traditional psychology form but the very smallest part of our minds as they actually live. The traditional psychology talks like one who should say a river consists of nothing but pailsful, spoonsful, quartpotsful, barrelsful, and other moulded forms of water. Even were the pails and the pots all standing in the stream, still between them the free water would continue to flow. It is just this free water of consciousness that psychologists resolutely overlook. Every definite image in the mind is steeped and dyed in the free water that flows round it. With it goes the sense of its relations, near and remote, the dying echo of whence it came to us, the dawning sense of whither it is to lead. The significance, the value, of the image is all in this halo or penumbra that surrounds and escorts it, — or rather that is fused into one with it and has become bone of its bone and flesh of its flesh; leaving it, it is true, an image of the same *thing* it was before, but making it an image of that thing newly taken and freshly understood. (PP, 246)

Although such typical descriptive power is inseparable from the genius of James's literary muse, phenomenologists have seen in it an anticipation of the autonomous science of mental life to which they lay claim. However, James never asserted autonomy for his descriptions; they were always integrated with his "cerebralist" assumptions. This has led some phenomenologist readers of

James to detect a fundamental contradiction in James's philosophy of mind. Particularly notable is Wilshire's phenomenology as found in "Protophenom-enology in the Psychology of William James." The Phenomenological reading aims to establish James's connection with the phenomenological movement, but also to show that his Protophenomenology is at odds with his natural-scien-tific program in *The Principles of Psychology*. I want to exclude the latter claim from the Two-Levels View.

Wilshire reads James's *Psychology: Briefer Course* as "decisively reversing his natural-scientific program" in *The Principles*. Wilshire correctly interprets James as stepping directly toward his metaphysics of pure experience, espe-cially with the claim in the *Briefer Course* that a phenomenon which presents itself immediately to mind is in some way identical to both the mental state and the mental state's object. But then Wilshire goes on, incorrectly, to assert that "everything in the preceding two volumes of *The Principles of Psychology* gets turned around by this move" toward radical empiricism (Wilshire 1969, 26–27). In particular, Wilshire affirms, "James's belated philosophical reversal upends his whole natural-scientific program for psychology" (Wilshire 1969, 27). I note that James M. Edie, in *William James and Phenomenology*, enthusi-astically endorses Wilshire's reading of James, and specifically his thesis that James's phenomenological insights are at odds with his natural-scientific pro-gram for psychology, in such a way that *The Principles* comes to seem seriously flawed.

Rather than accede to this violent image of *The Principles* being turned around and reversed, the Two-Levels View emphasizes the continuity between that book's sensationalist accounts of perception and the philosophy of radical empiricism that James developed later. In *The Principles*, however, there is only the seed of radical empiricism, because the sensational analyses are officially psychological rather than metaphysical. So the psychologist is still supposed to recognize a physical world, but he analyzes his subject's perception of it as ultimately a sensational affair. This is an awkward position, in which the psy-chologist qua psychologist is related unproblematically to the physical world, whereas her human subject is related to it only in a mediated way, *via* his sen-sations. For instance, the psychologist is related to physical space, but for his subjects "space means but the aggregate of all our possible sensations" (PP, 682). So it is not surprising that the psychologist's privileged access to a physi-cal world is finally eliminated in favor of a metaphysics of radical empiricism.

Everyone's perceptual transactions now take place, from a metaphysical point of view, in the medium of pure experience . The pure experiences of the *Essays in Radical Empiricism* are what the sensations of *The Principles* become when sensations are no longer being classified as mental or physical. This classification is still legitimate; it is salient for ordinary life and fundamental for scientific psychology. But for metaphysical purposes it is superficial. At this level phenomenology legitimately presupposes the classification of pure experience as mental or physical, confining itself to description of the mental states which are to be correlated by law with brain states.

Wilshire holds that scientific naturalism is only an embarrassment to James. He is much impressed by James's saying in the *Briefer Course*—Wilshire calls it a confession—that he did not know what a mental state is. "His embarrassment is complete," according to Wilshire's diagnosis, "for it is absurd to seek correlations between mental states and brain states without first knowing what could possibly count as a mental state" (Wilshire 1968, 27). But the overstatement here is highly misleading. For one thing, the so-called confession in the *Briefer Course* is only a variation of a theme in *The Principles*, that "the boundary-line of the mental is certainly vague," and that psychology should tolerate this vagueness rather than get caught up in metaphysical speculation (PP, 19). More importantly, metaphysical insights into the nature of mental states are not necessary for the scientific project of predicting and controlling behavior by discovery of psychophysical correlation laws. James was an instrumentalist about scientific theory. As the Two-Levels View's division of labor between scientific and metaphysical levels would lead one to expect, prediction and control are essential to the scientific enterprise, in James's view, not disclosure of the ultimate nature of reality. "All natural sciences aim at practical prediction and control," James says, "and in none of them is this more the case than in psychology today" (EP, 272). "The kind of psychology which could cure a case of melancholy, or charm a chronic insane delusion away," James says in the spirit of instrumentalism, "ought certainly to be preferred to the most seraphic insight into the nature of the soul" (EP, 277). Psychologists are able to identify and individuate mental states, and correlate them with cerebral states, and perhaps cure a case of melancholy, without need for metaphysical insight into the nature of mental states.

I believe that the following passage from "A Plea for Psychology as a 'Natural Science,'" which was published in the same year as *The Briefer Course*, counts decisively against the implications of upheaval which Wilshire extracts from James's remark in the latter work:

> Whatever conclusions an ultimate criticism may come to about mental states, they form a practically admitted sort of object whose habits of coexistence and succession and relations with organic conditions form an entirely definite subject of research. Cannot philosophers and biologists both become "psychologists" on this common basis? Cannot both forego ulterior inquiries, and agree that, provisionally at least, the mental state shall be the ultimate datum so far as "psychology" cares to go? (EP, 274)

This remark strongly suggests that there was continuity rather than conflict in the transition from *The Principles* to *The Briefer Course*. James's alleged confession in the latter is only a repetition of his insistence in the former that psychology can be pursued scientifically without addressing metaphysical issues, or "ultimate criticism." Wilshire's view seems more plausible than it is, should one fail to distinguish between science and ideologies that can surround science. Science facilitates measurement, prediction, and control; a scientific ideology, *scientism* if you will, or *the mechanical philosophy* in terms James used, asserts that there is nothing in the world except those things that can be measured, predicted, and controlled in scientific fashion, all else being illusion; such scientism is mechanistic and materialistic. James was deeply committed to science, not at all to scientism. Gale's divided-self interpretation of James is misdirected to the extent that it overlooks this distinction, James the scientist tugging in one direction and James the person tugging in another. "James accepts without question the bifurcationist upshot of science," Gale writes (1999, 220), quoting James (PP, 1230) as holding that "the essence of things for science" is their atomic microstructure rather than the way they appear to us, explaining that James means by this that, in James's words, "Sensible phenomena are pure delusions for the mechanical philosophy based on modern science" (PP, 1258). But the mechanical philosophy based on modern science is one thing, and modern science itself is another. Only the former denies *dulcissima mundi nomina*, all the things and qualities men love. Overlooking this, Gale continues: "This scientific image of the world challenges our deepest humanistic longings and aspirations. Some of the most eloquent and poignant passages in James attest to the sense of alienation and forlornness wrought by this bifurcation. Science holds that "all the things and qualities men love, *dulcissima mundi nomina*, are but illusions of our fancy attached to accidental clouds of dust which will be dissipated by the eternal cosmic weather as carelessly as they were formed" (Gale 1999, 208, quoting PP, 1260).

However, this is the view that James introduces a few lines previous as "the modern mechanico-physical philosophy" which, with its mathematical world-formula, "butchered at a blow" the sentimental facts and relations; and it is the view that, in a few lines consequent, he dismisses as "utterly absurd": "The popular notion that 'Science' is forced on the mind *ab extra*, and that our interests have nothing to do with its construction, is utterly absurd" (PP, 1260). It is not science that is absurd, *nota bene*, but a popular notion about it. Gale goes on to quote James as writing, in *Essays in Psychical Research*, that our personal and romantic view of life is incompatible with the mechanistic and materialistic world view of science, but here too he overlooks the distinction between science and scientism, between science and popular or philosophical notions about it:

> Science has come to be identified with a certain fixed general belief, the belief that the deeper order of Nature is mechanical exclusively, and that non-mechanical categories are irrational ways of conceiving and explaining even such a thing as human life. Now this mechanical rationalism, as one may call it, makes, if it becomes one's only way of thinking, a violent breach with the ways of thinking that have until our own time played the greatest part in human history. Religious thinking, ethical thinking, poetical thinking, teleological, emotional, sentimental thinking, what one might call the personal view of life to distinguish it from the impersonal and mechanical, and the romantic view of life to distinguish it from the rationalistic view, have been and even still are, outside of well-drilled scientific circles, the dominant forms of thought. But for mechanical rationalism, personality is an insubstantial illusion; the chronic belief of mankind that events may happen for the sake of their personal significance is an abomination; and the notions of our grandfathers about oracles and omens, divinations and apparitions, miraculous changes of heart and wonders waked by inspired persons, answer to prayer and providential leadings, are a fabric absolutely baseless, a mass of sheer *un*truth. (Gale 1999, 221)

Surely one of James's intellectual gifts to posterity is his demonstration of how to be a scientist without thinking exclusively in scientific categories, without converting science into the scientism of mechanical rationalism. Far from showing that James accepts without question the bifurcationist upshot of science, this passage shows us how to reject the bifurcationist upshot of scientism.

With the distinction between science and an optional mechanical philosophy that some (not James) would impose on it, I return to Wilshire: the suspicion that Wilshire has attempted to extract too much from the remark in *The Briefer Course* is confirmed by an unconvincing attempt to put James on the horns of a dilemma. Because James must "specify what he means by mental states in order to look for correlations," Wilshire reasons, and because the specification of this meaning will lead him eventually to his doctrine of pure experience, he claims that James is "forced to conclude that such a metaphysics must be logically prior to his natural-scientific psychology, and that his psychology cannot stand by itself as an autonomous endeavor" (Wilshire 1968, 27). But surely it can stand by itself, to the extent that it can pick out the mental and physical events that it hopes to correlate. If what one means by a mental state can be specified to this extent, thereby enabling prediction and control, this is meaning enough, and autonomy enough, for James's instrumentalist conception of scientific psychology. Cerebralist correlation laws don't promise the independence from natural science that phenomenologists seek, but they are fully compatible with acknowledging that they must be reconsidered in the broader context of the metaphysics of radical empiricism, as the quotation at the top of this chapter emphasizes.

The natural-scientific program of *The Principles* is not reversed or upended by the later development of James's philosophy of pure experience . Rather, James first adopted the psychologist's viewpoint and accepted the mental state as a fundamental datum. Then he took up the metaphysician's perspective and made "ulterior inquiries" which revealed that pure experience, and not mental or physical states, is metaphysically fundamental.

At the scientific level the Phenomenological reading rightly asserts the indispensability of introspection for acquiring knowledge about the mental. "Introspective observation," James says, "is what we have to rely on first and foremost and always" (PP, 185). The Two-Levels View appropriates this role for introspection on the grounds that it must be relied upon to confirm or falsify claims of psychophysical correlation. Scientists must ask people whether they are in the appropriate psychological state when the alleged physical correlate occurs, and the subjects answer by introspecting. However, Flanagan's skepti-

cism about introspection may be justified to the degree that contemporary cognitive psychology is credited with discovering levels of mentality which are not
open to introspection. On the other hand, Searle (1992) has recently mounted
a serious critique of the idea of unconscious mind, which tends to vindicate
James's assimilation of mind and intentionality to consciousness. (See Chapter
4 for a discussion of this topic.)

Phenomenology has a more distinctive role to play at the metaphysical
level, where it offers descriptions of the homogeneous material which neutral
monism identifies—the primal stuff of pure experience. A phenomenological
description in this sense is one which is free of implications about whether
what is being described is to be classified as mental or physical. It employs
techniques for describing "all that the thought thinks, exactly as the thought
thinks it" (PP, 266)—techniques memorably deployed in the chapter "The
Stream of Thought" of *The Principles*. Accordingly it will describe pure experience so as to reveal its protomental features and its neutrality with respect to
the categories of mind and body. Its task is to make articulate the reference to
pure experience that James makes in the following passage: "If you ask what
any one bit of pure experience is made of, the answer is always the same: 'It is
made of that, of just what appears, of space, of intensity, of flatness, brownness,
heaviness, or what not' " (ERE, 14–15). Phenomenology describes "just what
appears," in a vocabulary which is purified of mentalistic or physicalistic implications. This task is not easy because a normal adult's regimentation of her
experience puts her at a distance from pure experience. James puts the point
this way in "The Thing and Its Relations": "Only newborn babes, or men in
semi-coma from sleep, drugs, illnesses, or blows, may be assumed to have an
experience pure in the literal sense of a that which is not yet a definite what,
tho' ready to be all sorts of whats" (ERE 46). So it is not a conclusive objection
to James's radical empiricism to observe that physical objects do not seem to be
constructs out of pure experience. A *fortiori*, it is not an objection to the Two-
Levels View that physical objects do not seem to be purposive or teleological
in the attenuated sense that it attributes to pure experience. This attenuation
does not presuppose individual consciousness, but rather has to do with the
teleology of the universe as a whole—James's God, as I argue in Chapter 6.
The fundamental question is whether the appearance that the physical world
presents can be explained fully by referring only to pure experience and how it

comes to be classified in the transition from the experience of a newborn babe to a mature adult. Chapter 8 argues that this question can be answered affirmatively.

I conclude this section by commenting on Skrupskelis's view that James equivocates between two conceptions of pure experience . One of them, he says, is the conception of a "stuff that accepts all predicates except those that would characterize it as subjective or objective" (MEN, xxii). The other "appears to accept no predicates at all, and thereby becomes something much like the immediacy of many idealists" (MEN, xxii). My own view is that Skrupskelis's second notion of pure experience is only a special case of the first; there is no need to attribute an equivocation to James. The special case occurs in the circumstances such as those that James mentions in the passage just quoted, of "experience pure in the literal sense of a that which is not yet a definite what, tho' ready to be all sorts of whats." This is simply the idea of a pre-conceptual "given" in experience, an idea I will attempt to analyze and defend in Chapter 5.

Panpsychism

Ford's panpsychism is set out in *William James's Philosophy*. Ford holds that James's "metaphysical position is a panpsychic type of metaphysical realism," according to which the pure experiences that constitute reality are "intrinsically psychical" (Ford 1982, 7). By this Ford means that pure experiences "are or have been experiences for themselves," where the phrase "for themselves" serves to indicate the purposive character of the primal stuff (Ford 1982, 84). Panpsychism construes James's world as teleological at bottom.

Ford is tempted to defend panpsychism by assigning it validity relative to this or that phase of James' career. He concedes that James espoused neutral monism in the *Essays in Radical Empiricism* of 1904–5, but he views this as an aberration. "The evidence suggests that James was a panpsychist," he says, "who, for a brief period of time, was interested in phenomenism [i.e., neutral monism] and not, as most believe, a phenomenist who, for a brief period of time, was a panpsychist" (Ford 1982, 77). The main problem for this approach is that James's later panpsychism becomes of merely biographical interest if it cannot be integrated with the texts in which he dealt extensively with the nature of mind, viz., *The Principles* and ERE, and the Two-Levels View claims that this can be done only by construing panpsychism in such an attenuated fashion that it becomes compatible with the Neutral Monist reading of James's metaphysics.

In *William James: His Life and Thought* Myers writes, in the spirit of panpsychism, "It can be argued that the later notion of pure experience presupposes that of consciousness, and that pure experiences, far from being neutral occurrences, are described in terms of conscious sensations" (Myers 1986, 63). He notes that "the concept of consciousness was doomed to an ambiguous status in [James's] philosophy," so that "the project of his later metaphysics—to analyze consciousness in terms of a neutral notion of pure experience—thus remains a hazy one" (Myers 1986, 63). Where I differ from Myers is in taking this ambiguity as a starting point for developing a rational reconstruction of James's theory of mind. Where he sees a haze-inducing ambiguity, I see the essential ingredients of the Two-Levels View. The features that James associated with consciousness can be gathered into two groups, such that one group of features characterizes pure experience and the other group characterizes consciousness as it is studied by psychology. But if the Two-Levels View is correct, pure experiences are conscious sensations only in the sense that they are purposive or teleological, and not in the fuller sense assumed by psychology, in which consciousness is distinguished from the physical by virtue of being not only purposive but also private rather than public, subjective rather than objective, inner rather than outer, etc.

The textual evidence cited by Ford suggests that James's favorable references to panpsychism in his later writings were prompted by his reflecting on the purposive and perhaps "self-owning" properties of things. There is, for instance, his cryptic remark from his syllabus for Philosophy 1a at Harvard, "Our only intelligible notion of an object in itself is that it should be an object for itself, and this lands us in panpsychism and a belief that our physical perceptions are effects on us of 'psychical' realities. . . . That something exists when we as individuals are not thinking of it, is an inexpugnable conviction of common sense. The various stages of idealist reflection are only as many successive attempts to define what the something is that thus exists. The upshot tends pretty strongly towards something like panpsychism" (Ford 1982, 84). Ford concludes that "the neutral events of his phenomenism [i.e., neutral monism] gave way to self-experiencing actualities" (Ford 1982, 77). This conclusion is not forced, however, for there is another interpretation which makes it possible to affirm the unity rather than the fragmentation of James's thought, and to this I now turn.

One gets the sense from James's pro-panpsychist passages that it dawned on him that, as he said on February 11, 1909, in the "Miller-Bode" notebooks, "the constitution of reality which I am making for is of the psychic type" (Ford 1982, 84). This could be explained in Ford's way by supposing that he finally left behind the broadly neutral-monist view of *The Principles* and *Essays in Radical Empiricism*, or by supposing that James became aware for the first time of an implication of that view.

If the former option is to be avoided, then the problem to be addressed is this: it seems unlikely at first that panpsychism could be an implication of neutral monism, rather than a contradiction of it. The Two-Levels View solves this problem by identifying an attenuated form of panpsychism as implicit in James's characterization of the stream of thought in *The Principles* as being ever-changing, sensibly continuous, and purposive. I have called these the protomental features of thought.

They are closely related to, but distinct from, the "five characters in thought" that James sets out in Chapter 9 of *The Principles*. They are, first, that "every thought tends to be part of a personal consciousness"; second, "within each personal consciousness thought is always changing"; third, "within each personal consciousness thought is sensibly continuous"; and fourth, thought "is interested in some parts of those objects to the exclusion of others, and welcomes or rejects-chooses from among them, in a word-all the while" (PP, 220).[3] It is the first and fourth of these features, the personal and the purposive, which figure prominently in the evidence cited by Ford. The Two-Levels View accepts the purposive character of pure experience, but it rejects the implication that pure experience is private to the owner, subjective and interior. If "being owned" has these implications, pure experience is not owned; if it is construed as tantamount to "purposive," then pure experience is owned, in an attenuated sense given by James's notion of the purposiveness of the universe as a whole.

Assuming now that pure experience for James has the protomental features of continuity, changingness, and (collectively) purposiveness, panpsychism succeeds in forcing a concession from neutral monism, as follows. Although pure experience is neutral with respect to the difference between mind and body, nevertheless it has some features which are characteristic of the mental. More specifically, these protomental features may be understood as characterizing the physical world as well as the essentially mental, since both are constructed out of the purposive material of pure experience. This is the same as saying that the universe is fundamentally purposive, according to James, thus confirming one of panpsychism's insights. But this is not the same as saying that the world is populated by egos, souls, or substantial minds; and it is not to say that there is no legitimate distinction between the privacy and subjectivity of consciousness, on the one hand, and the publicity and objectivity of external, physical objects, on the other hand.

James observes in *The Principles* that an infant's original experience cannot be classified in terms of the mental/physical dichotomy. "The baby, assailed by eyes, ears, nose, skin and entrails at once, feels it all as one great blooming, buzzing confusion," James writes in a famous passage (JPP, 462), and elsewhere he clearly states that the baby's experience is not subjective or mental in the manner of the stream of thought, for "so far as it is from being true that our first way of feeling things is the feeling of them as subjective or mental, the exact opposite seems rather to be the truth. Our earliest, most instinctive, least developed kind of consciousness is the objective kind; and only as reflection becomes developed do we become aware of an inner world at all. . . . [S]ubjective consciousness, aware of itself as subjective, does not at first exist" (PP, 679). So this least developed form of consciousness becomes the stream of thought: it is protomental. At the same time it becomes the external world. This must be understood in order to grasp characteristic Jamesian epigrams like "Space *means* but the aggregate of all our possible sensations." As well as being protomental, therefore, original experience is protophysical. It has features like purposiveness which prefigure the stream of thought, and features like objectivity which prefigure the external world.

James did not carefully distinguish between the protomental features of thought and its essentially mental ones. The error to which panpsychism is liable is to follow James too closely in his failure to separate the two notions of mentality. The result is that one takes James's remarks about panpsychism as an abrupt about-face—as they would be if they had committed him to a world made up of substantial egos, or if they committed him to the essentially private and subjective character of all experience. But they do no so commit him.

Panpsychism's mistake is to impose derived properties of the mental, such as privacy, onto pure experience. The grain of truth in panpsychism is this: that which is private, viz., the mental, has features such as purposiveness which are lacking in the physical, and these features characterize pure experience.

Neutral Monism

Ayer propounds neutral monism in *The Origins of Pragmatism*, where he continues James's project of "cashing" statements about the physical in the coin of pure experience, hoping "to give James most of what he wanted" by making out a general case that our conception of the physical world can be exhibited as a theory with respect to our experiences" (Ayer 1968, 292–93).

I note in passing that Ayer does not often use the phrase "neutral monism," which derives from Russell's discussion of James. It is slightly misleading, since James's monism is a highly pluralistic one, as the following passage from "Does 'Consciousness' Exist?" suggests:

> First of all, this will be asked: "If experience has not 'conscious' existence, if it be not partly made of 'consciousness,' of what then is it made of 'consciousness,' of what then is it made? Matter we know, and thought we know, and conscious content we know, but neutral and simple 'pure experience' is something we know not at all. Say what it consists of—for it must consist of something—or be willing to give it up!"
>
> To this challenge the reply is easy. Although for fluency's sake I myself spoke early in this article of a stuff of pure experience, I have now to say that there is no general stuff of which experience at large is made. There are as many stuffs as there are 'natures' in the things experienced. (ERE 14)

The Two-Levels View accepts the Neutral Monist reading that the mental and the physical, in James's theory, differ in no intrinsic property but only in respect of the arrangement and context into which pure experience enters. It sees this view as implicit in James's "sensationalist" analyses of the origins of experience in *The Principles*. These purport to show that and how our sensations develop into perceptions—for instance, our perception of space, physical objects, etc. It also emphasizes the view advanced in *Essays in Radical Empiricism*, which James summarizes as follows: "[T]houghts and things are absolutely homogeneous as to their material, and . . . their opposition is only one of relation and function. There is no thought—stuff different from thing— . . .

but the same identical piece of 'pure experience' (which was the name I gave to the *materia prima* of everything) can stand alternately for a 'fact of consciousness' or for a physical reality, according as it is taken in one context or another" (ERE, 69). Remarks like these certainly justify neutral monism in its denial that the physical is metaphysically fundamental for James, and consequently naturalism is wrong on this score. Less clear is whether neutral monism is justified in denying that the mental is metaphysically fundamental, given the strengths of the panpsychist reading of James. My position is that James put two notions of mentality to theoretical work, the mental as purpose and the mental as private, and that neutral monism is justified in denying the fundamentality of the mental in the latter sense.

But neutral monism is liable to the mistake of failing to separate the two notions of mentality. Ayer rightly presents James's theory of mind as a dissolution of the mind-body problem as it was explored within the Cartesian framework of metaphysical dualism, in favor of the primacy of pure experience, out of which each of us somehow constructs the private, subjective world of one's mind and the public, objective world of body. But Ayer is led, in his haste to deny that pure experience is essentially mental, to the opposite conclusion from the one that can correctly be extracted from the panpsychist reading. Ayer denies that there is something protomental about pure experience. But there *is* something protomental about pure experience, as it dawned on James to affirm.

The Case for Panpsychism

Having argued my case that the Two-Levels View is the truth about James's theory of mind, I turn to considering the prospects for developing its panpsychism. Perhaps suggestively, it resembles an attenuated form of panpsychism proposed by Thomas Nagel as a solution to several intractable problems about explaining mind-body interaction when naturalist or physicalist assumptions are taken for granted. He distinguishes two forms of panpsychism. The first of these posits that physical objects are fundamental but that each physical object, such as an atom or molecule, has protomental properties, and when these objects are arranged in the appropriate way, as they are in the human nervous system, consciousness is the result. The second form of panpsychism affirms that a "common source" of mental and physical properties is fundamental; having neither mental nor physical properties itself, this common source explains the occurrence of things, such as human organisms, that have both physical and mental properties. Nagel's second form of panpsychism is easily interpreted as a variant of James's radical empiricism, Nagel's *common source* being James's *pure experience*. As it happens, Nagel is primarily concerned to defend the first form of panpsychism in his essay, apparently because he does not want to stray too far from the naturalistic assumption that we are physical organisms. He observes that one is led to the first form by supposing that protomental properties are discoverable by explanatory inference from mental phenomena, whereas one is led to the "common source" form of panpsychism by supposing that protomental properties are discoverable only by explanatory inference from both mental and physical phenomena. And he suggests that this supposition is somewhat less implausible than that there are two quite distinct sets of basic properties, the set arrived at by the explanatory path of physics and the set arrived at by theorizing about mental phenomena. In "What Is It like to Be a Bat?" he terms this theorizing about the mental "objective phenomenology."

Although Nagel concludes that this twin-track path toward discovery of protomental properties implies that they are not mental, the panpsychist conclusion of his argument would survive in a modified form, he says: "There would be properties of matter that were not physical from which the mental properties of organic systems were derived. This could still be called panpsychism" (Nagel 1979, 185).

The remark about the relative plausibility of panpsychism in this sense suggests that Nagel would hope to show that it was explanatorily more basic than the first form, and this suggestion is confirmed in the later *The View from Nowhere*, where Nagel envisions a "psychological Maxwell" discovering someday a general theory of mind as different from contemporary physical theories as Maxwell's account of electricity and magnetism was different from the mechanical concepts of matter in motion that characterized the earlier Newtonian science. Then a "psychological Einstein" would follow the psychological Maxwell "with a theory that the mental and the physical are really the same," just as Einstein followed Maxwell in uniting radically different physical phenomena (Nagel 1986, Chapter 3, Section 6). I read this as implying that the psychological Maxwell discovers a theoretically powerful objective phenomenology, to use the terminology of "What Is It like to Be a Bat?," whereas the psychological Einstein discovers the "common source" of the mental and physical, as Nagel puts it in "Panpsychism."

Now James's radical empiricism has at least the general form of Nagel's position, and of both the Maxwellian and Einsteinian moments in the imagined vindication of panpsychism. It offers a theory of mind which, like Nagel's, is very different from the physicalist and dualist accounts which dominate discussion of the mind-body problem. It is "Maxwellian" in the importance it assigns to phenomenologically revealing descriptions of pure experience, and it is "Einsteinian" in holding that the mental and the physical are really the same, in virtue of being made of the same primal stuff. Nagel's vision may one day be borne out by a theory with the general form of James's view.

More recently David Chalmers, influenced by Nagel, has gestured sympathetically toward such a view, particularly when he distinguishes proto-phenomenal properties from phenomenal ones: "There is of course the threat of panpsychism. I am not sure that this is such a bad prospect—if phenomenal properties are fundamental, it is natural to suppose that they might be wide-spread. . . . An alternative is that the relevant properties are protophenomenal properties. In this case the mere instantiation of such a property does not entail experience, but instantiation of numerous such properties could do so jointly" (Chalmers 1996, 154). Though it is hard to see how objective phenomenology might converge with physics on pure experience as their common source, it is equally hard to see how reduction of the mental to the physical is possible. So it is perhaps not excessively speculative to leave open the possibility that "common source" panpsychism might be, in broad outline, true. However, I am inclined, for reasons that will emerge later in this book, to think that this *scientific* form of primal stuff would not be a vindication of James's doctrine of pure experience. It would run counter to what the Two-Levels View would indicate: radical empiricism is a metaphysical view, and as such it should not be confirmed by a scientific theory, even a "common source" panpsychist one. In a sense the scientific possibility misconstrues pure experience and makes the problem of vindicating it seem more difficult than it is. After all, each of us is directly aware of pure experience in James's view, and indeed of nothing else, whether mental or physical, these latter being conceptual constructs out of it. We do not need to wait for a theory to know about it; we know it too well to think we have to wait. James's empiricism invites a kind of mysticism about the imminent-in-experience, traces of which I will have occasion to note in discussing his purposive conception of the universe, his cause-theory of the self, and his conception of God.

In summary, then, it has been proposed here that James's theory of mind has a two-level structure. At the level of scientific psychology there is a methodological dualism of the mental and the physical. Psychology seeks causes and laws like other natural sciences, with which it is closely connected. Biological science and Darwinian theory in particular are fundamental to the outlook of scientific psychology. The Naturalistic reading misses the methodological dualism but is correct in emphasizing James's natural-scientific and Darwinian commitments. At the metaphysical level there is a monism of pure experience which is protomental and protophysical without being either mental or physical. In this respect the Neutral Monist reading is correct. But as protomental, pure experience has the characteristically mental feature of purposiveness, and to this extent therefore there is truth in the panpsychist reading. As for the Phenomenological reading, it is correct to emphasize the importance of introspection at the psychological level, and correct, too, to suppose that one must look elsewhere, to what I have called the metaphysical level, to determine what ultimately exists.

Empirical and Metaphysical Reality

James poses the following question in *The Principles:*

> Suppose a new-born mind, entirely blank and waiting for experience to begin. Suppose that it begins in the form of a visual impression (whether faint or vivid is immaterial) of a lighted candle against a dark background, and nothing else, so that whilst this image lasts it constitutes the entire universe known to the mind in question. Suppose, moreover (to simplify the hypothesis), that the candle is only imaginary, and that no "original" of it is recognized by us psychologists outside. Will this hallucinatory candle be believed in, will it have a real existence for the mind? (PP, 917)

James answers his question affirmatively, but putting the answer in correct context is a delicate matter.

It is not enough to say, though it is true, that there is a basic difference between "real existence for the mind" and "real existence." For one thing, he adds the important qualification, "But when the candle appears at the same time with other objects, it must run the gauntlet of their rivalry, and then it becomes a question of which of the various candidates for attention shall compel belief. As a rule we believe as much as we can" (PP, 928). He also acknowledges the difference when he observes, "A dream-candle has existence, true enough, but not the same existence (existence for itself, namely, or *extra mentem meam*) which the candles of waking perception have" (PP, 920).

But the candles of waking perception, for James, are a "sub-world" among many sub-worlds, including the world of the newborn mind in the thought-experiment: "My world is but one in a million alike embedded, alike real to those who may abstract them. How different must be the worlds in the consciousness of ant, cuttle-fish, or crab!" (PP, 277). He distinguishes in particular the world of sense, the world of science, the world of ideal relations such as mathematics, the world of "idols of the tribe," supernatural worlds, worlds of individual opinion, and worlds of sheer madness and vagary.

He recommends that "the complete philosopher" should seek "not only to assign to every given object of his thought its right place in one or other of these sub-worlds, but he also seeks to determine the relation of each sub-world to the others in the total world which *is*" (PP, 921). At this point, it is tempting to draw irrealist conclusions, perhaps with Protagorean subjectivist content, as suggested when James writes, "Each thinker, however, has dominant habits of attention; and these practically elect from among the various worlds some one to be for him the world of ultimate realities" (PP, 923). But one must remind oneself of the biological and cultural ties that lead human thinkers to inhabit the same world.

And if I am correct in what follows, in arguing that his pragmatism goes hand in hand with his realism about pure experience, one should bear in mind that all of these sub-worlds are different conceptualizations of *sensation*, in the *nonsubjective* sense of the term that' is basic to *The Principles* and anticipatory of the doctrine of pure experience in *Essays in Radical Empiricism*. Pragmatism operates within parameters set by a world of pure experience, a real world external to our pragmatically shaped conceptualizations of it.

James's system implies a doctrine of external realism, according to which there is a world, namely a world of pure experience, which is external to our representations (conceptualizations, ideas, etc.) of it. Moreover, there is a crucial distinction between *an item of pure experience*, on one hand, and *my experience of that item*, on the other hand. James isn't always tidy about this distinction, but it is crucial, and he realizes that it's crucial to his conception of a public world that several people can apprehend. How do you and I see the same pen? The pure experience is "taken" twice over, once by you and once by me. In *The Principles* James is very careful to distinguish between the point of view of the psychologist and the point of view of the subject whom the psychologist is studying, cautioning that the psychologist must detach from his own point of view and study the subject's *au fond*. But psychology is the grand portal to metaphysics, and when the psychologist matures into metaphysical speculation, as James did, this methodological stance is overridden by his radical empiricist metaphysics, which asserts the metaphysical fundamentality of the sensations that James had taken for granted in *The Principles* as the stuff out of which the physical world and the stream of consciousness were built.

James's psychologistic view of metaphysics contrasts instructively with Peirce's. In the following passage Peirce expresses a preference for a logical rather than a psychological portal to metaphysics:

> In one view, metaphysics is a branch of Psychology while in another psychology is but applied metaphysics. This suggests two modes of treating metaphysics, one starts by drawing the conceptions from the system of psychology and reasoning to their logical relations and meaning; the other draws the conceptions from no system but from the thoughts as they present themselves in their logical form — examining them logically — and finally puts them in their right place in the mind. The latter is the only proper course, since it is only after understanding these truths that we can find their logical relations. It may be called the Logical in opposition to the Psychological Treatment of Metaphysics. (Peirce 1982, 63)

By contrast with Peirce, James regards psychology as the grand portal to metaphysics, and the notion of the methodological priority of logical form has no appeal to him.

In the Two-Levels View, James is a realist at the metaphysical level, drawing on his radical empiricism and especially his doctrine of pure experience. At the empirical level he is a pragmatist, broadly speaking, holding that our conceptualizations, and consequently our conceptions of what' is real, are reflections of our interests. But this latter is not an invitation to Protagorean sub-jectivism. *Our interests* are our interests as biologically and culturally situated subjects. Our evolved human nature and our cultural inheritance set param-eters for pragmatic determination of belief, yielding what may be called *empiri-cal reality*, and at the metaphysical level pure experience sets broader param-eters yet, yielding *metaphysical reality*.

Psychologically speaking, *any* experience can constitute "reality." That is well established in *The Principles*, as noted above in the example of the candle. Also well established is the notion that what passes among "us" as "the real world" is a complex function of a race's biological inheritance, a society's cul-tural inheritance, and personal disposition. Given James's "pure experience/conceptualization" dichotomy, any *answer* to the question What is reality? will necessarily fail to capture metaphysical reality, since the answer is conceptual, while metaphysical reality is preconceptual and pure-experiential. At best, the answer would most fully reflect all of our fundamental interests and needs. Metaphysical reality underdetermines any such answer:

> It is conceivable that several rival theories should equally well include the actual order of our sensations in their scheme, much as the one-fluid and two-fluid theo-ries of electricity formulated all the common electrical phenomena equally well. The sciences are full of these alternatives. Which theory is then to be believed? *That theory will be most generally believed which, besides offering us objects able to account satisfactorily for our sensible experience, also offers those which are most interesting, those which appeal most urgently to our aesthetic, emotional, and active needs.* (PP, 940)

The perfect theory of empirical reality, he thinks, has so far evaded us:

> It is undeniably true that materialistic, or so-called "scientific" conceptions of the universe have so far gratified the purely intellectual interests more than the mere sentimental conceptions have. But, on the other hand, as already remarked, they leave the emotional and active interests cold. *The perfect object of belief would be a God or "Soul of the World," represented both optimistically and moralistically (if such a combination could be), and withal so definitely conceived as to show us why our phenomenal experiences should be sent to us by Him in just the very way in which they come.* (PP, 945)

James's marriage of realism and pragmatism provides a credible alternative to scientific realism, which holds that a scientific conception of the universe cuts reality at the joints, and postmodern irrealism, which holds that there is no reality to take into account, only a multiplicity of narratives expressive of this or that interest or need. On Richard Rorty's reading of James on these matters, James subscribes to the view that there is no point to debates between realism and antirealism, "for such debates presuppose the empty and misleading idea of beliefs 'being made true'" (Rorty 1986, 335). Rorty acknowledges that his reading, like mine, is highly selective, prescinding from the moments in which James allegedly fell into error (Rorty 1986, 334). But I don't think his realism about pure experience is an error, so I won't ignore it. Aside from James's insistence on his realism in several places (see the letter to Miller at the beginning of Chapter 1, for instance), Rorty's view has to gloss over James's emphatic endorsement of absolute truth in *Pragmatism*. Moreover, in addition to the coercions of the sensible and abstract orders that James speaks of there are conditions of the world that "make false" the belief that $2 + 2 = 5$ or that I can jump over the moon. Although the role of experience in making-true is more complex, and though he does not want to think of the world of pure experience as articulated in such a way that a sentence is a logical map of this articulation (a "copy"), James's account of truth does not reduce to merely the deconstruction of the copy theory, as Rorty holds.

One of my central aims in this study is to establish that the marriage of pragmatism and radical empiricism does indeed afford a live option to current physicalist and deconstructionist orthodoxies.

Conclusion

I have taken a synthetic approach toward the doctrine of pure experience in this chapter, putting it together from James's texts and prominent interpretations of them. Although pure experience cannot be defined in terms that presuppose individual human psychology, I arrived at its defining features by reference to the five characters of thought listed in Chapter 1 that James lays out in *The Principles*. Pure experience, "just what appears," shares features 2 (changingness) and 3 (continuity) with thought, and a nonpersonal notion of purposiveness, broadly corresponding to the other three characters but abstracted from their presumption of privacy and subjectivity, may be attributed to it if one accepts James's teleological conception of the universe. If not, the analytic approach to the doctrine of pure experience in Chapter 7 will show that a nonpurposive, "mechanical" conception of pure experience is also possible. The changingness of thought is an essential feature of the experience from which it comes. Although he did not explicitly discuss the doctrine of pure experience in the incomplete *Some Problems of Philosophy*, there is a passage in it that nicely captures this feature:

> Nevertheless, *within experience*, phenomena come and go. There are novelties; there are losses. The world seems, on the concrete and proximate level at least, really to grow. So the question recurs: How do our finite experiences come into being from moment to moment? By inertia? By perpetual creation? Do the new ones come at the *call* of the old ones? Why don't they all go out like a candle? (SPP, 29)

As for the sensibly continuous character of pure experience, this is a fundamental line of demarcation between James's conception of empiricism and the atomism about experience of the empiricist tradition from Hume to the "mind-dust" theorists of James's day. Again with the qualification that James in the passage to follow is not explicitly discussing the doctrine of pure experience, what he says in *Some Problems of Philosophy* about percepts is a feature of pure experience generally, not restricted to the percept/concept structure of the stream of thought:

> The great difference between percepts and concepts is that percepts are continuous and concepts are discrete. . . . Each concept means just what it singly means, and nothing else; and if the conceiver doesn't know whether he means this or means that, it shows that his concept is imperfectly formed. The perceptual flux as such, on the contrary, *means* nothing, and is but what it immediately is; and no matter how small a tract of it be taken, it is always a much-at-once, and contains innumerable aspects and characters which conception can pick out and isolate, and thereafter always intend. It shows duration, intensity, complexity or simplicity, interestingness, excitingness, pleasantness or their opposites. Data from all our senses enter into it, merged in a general extensiveness of which each occupies a big or little share. Yet all these parts leave its unity unbroken. Its boundaries are no more distinct than are those of the field of vision. Boundaries are things that intervene; but here nothing intervenes save parts of the perceptual flux itself, and these

are overflowed by what they separate, so that whatever we distinguish and isolate conceptually is found perceptually to telescope and copenetrate and diffuse into its neighbors. The cuts we make are purely ideal. If my reader can succeed in abstracting from all conceptual interpretation and lapse back into his immediate sensible life at this very moment, he will find it to be what someone has called a big blooming buzzing confusion, as free from contradiction in its "much-at-onceness" as it is all alive and evidently there. (SPP, 32)

A fascinating and problematic aspect of James's solution to the mind-body problem is that the mediating medium, pure experience, is an external reality we directly apprehend. As such, it is diametrically opposed to the recently bruited view, mysterianism or transcendental naturalism, that the relating medium lies forever beyond our ken. Mysterianism however can promise profound (if unknowable!) depth to the mind-body connection, whereas solutions of James's sort—"phenomenological solutions," broadly speaking—have been effectively lambasted as incapable of explanatory depth. A theory that works exclusively with the phenomenologically given, the objection goes, doesn't have much to work with, especially as compared to the impressively deep explanations that the natural sciences provide for the physical world. Mysterians can acknowledge this depth while insisting that the mind-body problem is so hard that there must be a level of natural-scientific description and explanation that is "cognitively closed" to minds like ours. The phenomenological tradition, on the other hand, is accused of constitutional incapacity to acknowledge this depth, much less to compete with it in explanatory power, since it purports to be autonomous from the natural sciences. Its account of the mind-body relationship, drawing exclusively on a mentalistic vocabulary, is bound to be *too light*. I view this objection as devastating to the phenomenological tradition and to James's theory of mind on Wiltshire's protophenomenological reading of it. But James's theory of mind is *cerebralistic*, even if that is perverse from Wiltshire's point of view. So it may be that James's combination of phenomenology and cerebralism isn't devastated by the *too-light* objection. That is what I will explore in the next two chapters.

3

Consciousness II: Mental Causation

Introduction

If James's psychology is to serve as portal to a serious metaphysics, it needs clarification and defense. The relevant material, mainly in *The Principles*, is both rich and difficult, to the despair of some commentators. I aim to bring the reader into the heart of this material and to return with a reconstruction of it which will be a live option for belief. It is essential above all to rescue James's belief in mental causation from the widely accepted view that his cerebralism leads him inescapably to an epiphenomenalism which was repugnant to him.

James's treatment of the causal relationship between mind and body in *The Principles of Psychology* should be understood as an expression of a coherent theory of mental causation. There is a need to correct the impression, widespread among readers of *The Principles* and understandably so, that James's theory of mind-body interaction is deeply incoherent. Among the results of the interpretation to be proposed here is that the James-Lange theory of emotion, as James always insisted, has been misunderstood by critics who object to its treatment of emotions as mere by-products of behavior. The point of the theory is not to deny that emotions are causes, but rather to tie such mental causation tightly to physical conditions. This "tying-tightly" is to be construed in terms of the idea that mental events and their physical correlates are simultaneous nomic equivalents, as Alvin Goldman calls them (Goldman 1970, 157–69). After interpreting James's view of the relationship between mind and body by reference to this analysis, I apply it to emotion, responding to Robert M. Gordon's critique of the James-Lange theory.

Typical of the widespread dismissal of James's theory of mental causation is Thomas Leahey's A *History of Psychology*, which views James as involved in a "contradictory view of consciousness [which] proved absolutely fatal to American mentalistic psychology" (Leahey 1980, 266). Leahey finds James guilty of both arguing for the causal efficacy of consciousness and making it impossible. "On one hand James tells us that consciousness directs thought and action," Leahey writes, "while on the other hand he pictures consciousness as only parallel to the bodily nervous processes that are thought and action" (Leahey 1980, 266). I hope to show that such dismissal of James's legacy poses a false dilemma. There is an alternative that combines parallelism with causal efficacy, and this makes good sense of James's theory of mental causation.

Passages can be cited in *The Principles* which support almost every kind of theory of the mind-body relationship, including materialism, Cartesian dualism, epiphenomenalism, and parallelism. The problem of rendering these passages coherent is partly solved by adopting a two-level interpretation of James's system: as having, first, a scientific level at which the difference between mind and body is taken for granted in the quest for psychological, cerebral, and psychophysical laws; and second, a metaphysical level at which mind and body are understood as constructs each of us builds out of the material provided by pure experience, which is neither mental nor physical. I have explored this interpretation elsewhere, explaining how apparently inconsistent claims about the mind can be shown coherent by assigning them to different levels of James's system. But there are important residual doubts about the coherence of James's theory of mind at the level of scientific psychology. I want to assuage these doubts.

The sense that there is a contradiction between James's affirmation that consciousness is causally efficacious, on one hand, and his "cerebralism" or "mechanism" on the other hand, is not confined to psychologists. It pervades the philosophical study by Bruce Wilshire, *William James and Phenomenology: A Study of "The Principles of Psychology."* Wilshire is so impressed by the contradiction that he writes, "We will also observe how the attempt to impute causal properties to mental states dies away after the physiological preliminaries of *The Principles*," adding, "It is surely significant, I believe, that there is only one other place in *The Principles* (as far as I can determine) in which James speaks of consciousness as having causal characteristics" (Wilshire 1968, 29, 39). This is stunningly false on the face of it, since James is continually using causal idioms to describe conscious mental states. One need only turn to the famous "Now how do we ever get up?" passage in the chapter "Will" of *The Principles*. Lying in bed unable to get up, "We suddenly find that we have got up. A fortunate lapse of consciousness occurs; we forget both the warmth and the cold; we fall into some revery connected with the day's life, in the course of which the idea flashes across us, 'Hollo! I must lie here no longer'—an idea which at that lucky instant awakens no contradictory or paralyzing suggestions, and consequently produces immediately its appropriate motor effects" (PP, 1132–33). This is only one of countless examples in which such contents of consciousness as ideas (and sensations, perceptions, willings, and so forth) produce effects. It may be that Wilshire is talking about the word "consciousness," but it would be a triviality even if true that the word doesn't appear after the first six chapters (assuming that's what Wilshire means by "the physiological preliminaries"). Whether this is true or not, what possible difference could it make when James's discussion of specific conscious states is chock full of attributions of causal powers to them?

My general recommendation is that, first, it is fundamental to James's theory of mind that there is a certain kind of parallelism between bodily processes and the stream of consciousness; I shall call this special parallelism the "Correspondence Thesis." And second, the Correspondence Thesis must be interpreted as asserting a relationship of simultaneous nomic equivalence between the corresponding mental and physical processes in order to consort happily with James's conviction that consciousness is causally efficacious. ("It is to my mind quite inconceivable that consciousness should have nothing to do with a business to which it so faithfully attends" [PP, 140].)

The Correspondence Thesis is silent about the causes and effects of the physical and mental events that are in correspondence, but it does not imply epiphenomenalism and is wholly compatible with James's view that mental events are "motor in their consequences."

Simultaneous Nomic Equivalents

The model that helps to make the best sense of James's theorizing about the mind-body relationship is, I submit, the idea that mental events and physical events can stand to each other as simultaneous nomic equivalents (SNEs), a relationship I define as follows: A bodily process of type BP and a stage of the stream of consciousness of type SC are simultaneous nomic equivalents if and only if it is a scientific law (or follows from a scientific law) that BP-type processes occur at time *t* if and only if SC-type processes occur at time *t*.

The general idea here is that events which are simultaneous nomic equivalents are mutually dependent. SC can't occur without BP, but similarly BP can't occur without SC. This mutual dependence is in the nature of things: it is a scientific law. By contrast, the epiphenomenal relationship between the operations of a locomotive's engine and its steam whistle, to use Thomas Huxley's example, involves the dependence of the whistling on the engine's operations, but not conversely: the engine would still run if the whistle were removed. This is not to deny that there could be engineered or artifactual codependence between the two, so that any attempt to remove the whistle would prevent the engine from working, but this codependence would not be in the nature of things. It doesn't follow from scientific law that a locomotive engine works if and only if a steam whistle whistles. What follows rather, from cunning engineering, is that this locomotive's engine can't operate without this whistle's whistling. (This conclusion wouldn't follow if BP had some property that suited it to be the cause of E, and if SC lacked this property. But what would that property be? One important candidate in the history of reflection on causation, recommending itself to a rationalist temperament, is BP's being related to E by a "mechanism" that renders the causal link intelligible. So one could say that BP is a cause of E, but SC is not, because BP but not SC is related to E by a mechanism that renders their causal connection intelligible. But James, the radical empiricist, rejects this demand for a mechanism.)

I propose to interpret the Correspondence Thesis in James's work in light of the SNE model. James's frequent brain/thought analogies clearly rely on the Correspondence Thesis for the power that he evidently sees in them. I have in mind such remarks as "Physiologically considered, we must suppose that a purpose means the persistent activity of certain rather definite brain-processes throughout the whole course of thought" (PP, 549). Or again, in a fine rhetorical question: "But as the brain-tension shifts from one relative state of equilibrium to another, like the gyrations of a kaleidoscope, now rapid and now slow, is it likely that its faithful psychic concomitant is heavier-footed than itself, and that it cannot match each one of the organ's irradiations by a shifting inward iridescence of its own?" (PP, 229). James clearly expects predictively projectable relationships between the "faithful concomitants," by virtue of which a salient structure in one of them would be reason to expect an isomorphic structure in the other. The SNE interpretation of James's theory of mind brings this out, explicating his idea that mental principles and brain laws are codeterminants of behavior. Viewing the corresponding processes as SNEs makes sense of the efficacy that James attributed to consciousness: If BP causes some event E, and if SC is the SNE of BP, then SC causes E, too. For let it be supposed, in the spirit of James's "cerebralism," that a brain event BP causes action E. In James's view this is to say that there is a law which justifies the inference that if BP then SC. Now introduce the premise that mental event SC and cerebral event BP are SNEs. But then it follows from scientific law both that if BP occurs then SC occurs, and that if SC occurs then BP occurs. But then, by transitivity, it follows that if SC occurs then action E occurs. That is to say, there is the same justification for describing SC as the cause of E as there is to describe BP as the cause of E. So mental causation is vindicated.

The SNE account puts the Correspondence Thesis at the foundation of James's system. Part of what it means to do this is to deny the demand for a "mechanism" that would render intelligible the causal connection between mental causes and their physical effects or correlates. James rejects this Lockean demand; in his philosophy of science, at least, he follows Hume rather than Locke. In accordance with his instrumentalist conception of science, James announces in the Preface of *The Principles* that "I have therefore treated our passing thoughts as integers, and regarded the mere laws of their coexistence with brain-states as the ultimate laws for our science" (PP, 6). The problem in the Cartesian tradition of explicating the "mechanism" of interaction between mind and body is not his problem:

> However inadequate our ideas of causal efficacy may be, we are less wide of the mark when we say that our ideas and feelings have it, than the Automatists are when they say they haven't it. As in the nights all cats are gray, so in the darkness of metaphysical criticism all causes are obscure. But one has no right to pull the pall over the psychic half of the subject only, as the automatists do, and to say that that causation is unintelligible, whilst in the same breath one dogmatizes about material causation as if Hume, Kant, and Lotze had never been born. (PP, 140)

With these ideas James can be seen as all but explicitly setting out the nomic equivalents account of the causal efficacy of consciousness. The closer one looks at James's treatment of the issues, the more the SNE account helps to explain the potential and the problems for his vision of a scientific psychology.

A token of the attractiveness of the SNE solution is Andrew Bailey's heroic attempt to save James from epiphenomenalism by reading him as a chaos theorist: "[H]ad William James had the terminology at the turn of the century, he would have described the brain as a chaotic system, and consciousness (including perceptual consciousness) as closely analogous to a strange attractor for that system" (Bailey 1998b, 25). Although Bailey's careful reading sheds considerable light on James's theory of consciousness,[1] the attempt gets into difficulty immediately because chaos theory implies determinism, as Bailey acknowledges: chaos theory is the qualitative study of unstable aperiodic behavior in deterministic nonlinear systems. This is a large problem, from James's perspective, since a brain describable by chaos theory would be unfit for free will. The SNE account, on the other hand, though it insists on laws of correspondence of the form "if this now then that now," does not *require* deterministic laws, of the form "if this now then that later." Although the SNE account is compatible with a general picture of the body as a reflex mechanism, the complexity of the brain is interesting to James in part because it may be an exception to it. And as Bailey acknowledges, consciousness as a chaos-theoretical principle of organization of the brain is inconsistent with the possibility of immortality ("if the system [the brain] did not exist, then neither would the attractor [consciousness]" [Bailey 1998b, 38]), with which James held his own view to be at least consistent. Finally, there is no imminent experiential reality to consciousness on Bailey's interpretation:

> An attractor is merely a topological object in phase space, and has no more reality than this; by contrast, visual sensations of redness, experiences of intense pain, the taste of a lemon, and the smell of rotten eggs have a *much* more forceful claim to ontological existence (even given all of James' positivism). Indeed, how *could* an attractor—a mathematical object—be a phenomenal flux as James describes it, and as we experience it?" (Bailey 1998b, 39).

An excellent and unanswerable question. Bailey is driven to ask it only because the chaos interpretation seems to him the only way of giving James his premise about the causal efficacy of the mental *and* his premise about the denial that consciousness is an entity ("it is difficult to see how James could solve these problems of internal inconsistency *without* endorsing a view of this sort" [Bailey 1998b, 39]). But the SNE account solves these problems. Of course, the SNE model assumes that mental events, states, and processes are genuine events, states, and processes. Bailey was prevented from exploring the SNE reading because he interpreted James's denial that consciousness is an entity as tantamount to denying that there are actual events or processes in the stream of consciousness, and consequently he inferred that, for James, there could be no nonphysical causal events or processes. The correct view, I submit, is that when James denied that consciousness was an entity or a stuff, he was attacking rationalist psychology in general, as well as, in particular, the view that there is a substantial soul and that mental events and processes are *self-intimatingly* mental, revealing themselves in introspection to be mental by virtue of some intrinsic, nonrelational marker. That this notion of self-intimating mentality was James's target is evident from the following passage from "Does 'Conscious- ness' Exist?" quoted by Bailey himself, my emphasis added: "I believe that con- sciousness (as it is commonly presented, either as an entity, or as pure activity, but in any case as being fluid, unextended, diaphanous, devoid of content of its own but *directly self-knowing-spiritual*, in short), I believe, I say, that this sort of consciousness is pure fancy" (Bailey 1998b, 31). James's point in this passage is to pave the way for a reduction of consciousness to pure experience, as well as to tweak the Cartesians' noses; it is *not* to deny that there are mental events, states, and processes (any more than a contemporary functionalist about the mind would deny this).

James could not tolerate the allegedly self-intimating nature of conscious- ness because he anticipated the reduction of the stream of consciousness—of mental processes, events, and states—to pure experience, which, by definition, lacks marking as essentially mental even if, as argued in the previous chapter, it has mindlike qualities. Readings like Bailey's must be avoided by cleaving to the Two-Levels View. At the empirical level, there are nonphysical causal events and processes, but at the metaphysical level both physical and mental causes are episodes in the world of pure experience.

When James wrote that "thoughts in the concrete are made of the same stuff as things are," he meant they are made of the same pure-experiential stuff, not that they are made of physical stuff. Curiously, Bailey insists, rightly, that James would reject mind-brain identity theories, ending his essay by writing, "Unfortunately, however, to abrogate Assumption (b) would be simultaneously to reject large parts of William James' stimulating and filigreed account of the mind" (Bailey 1998b, 31). Assumption (b) is the identity theory. So, since thoughts are not identical with brain processes for James, Bailey should have inferred that they are identical with, or at least in some sense reducible to, pure experience. Only his curious reading of "Does 'Consciousness' Exist?" equating mental events with self-intimatingly spiritual events, prevented him from doing so.

Epiphenomenalism

James's most explicit discussion of the causal relationship between mind and body occurs in Chapter 5 of *The Principles*, "The Automaton-Theory," where he rejects the radical conception of the reflex arc put forward by the physiologists of his day, according to which, "just as the spinal cord is a machine with few reflexes, so the hemispheres are a machine with many," such that, "even where we know consciousness to be there, the still more complicated neural action which we believe to be its inseparable companion is alone and of itself the real agent of whatever intelligent deeds may appear" (PP, 133). Although James rejects the epiphenomenalist conclusion that consciousness lacks causal efficacy, he sympathizes with the physiologists' principle *No psychosis without neurosis*, which serves as a premise toward that conclusion. A large part of the coherence problem is understanding how James could accept what I am calling the Correspondence Thesis, no psychosis without neurosis, without being driven to the conscious-automaton theory:

> Suppose we restrict our view to facts of one and the same plane, and let that be the bodily plane: cannot all the outward phenomena of intelligence still be exhaustively described? Those mental images, those "considerations," whereof we spoke,—presumably they do not arise without neural processes arising simultaneously with them, and presumably each consideration corresponds to a process *sui generis*, and unlike all the rest. In other words, however numerous and delicately differentiated the train of ideas may be, the train of brain-events that runs alongside of it must in both respects be exactly its match, and we must postulate a neural machinery that offers a living counterpart for every shading, however fine, of the history of its owner's mind. Whatever degree of complication the latter may reach, the complication of the machinery must be quite as extreme, otherwise we should have to admit that there may be mental events to which no brain-events correspond. But such an admission as this the physiologist is reluctant to make. It would violate all his beliefs. "No psychosis without neurosis," is one form which the principle of continuity takes in his mind. (PP, 133)

What can be puzzling about the discussion of the conscious-automaton theory in Chapter 5 of *The Principles* is that, after making such a strong case for it, James rather abruptly describes it as "utterly irrational." But this judgment is not puzzling if, as the SNE account implies, one distinguishes sharply between the Correspondence Thesis and the epiphenomenalist interpretation of that thesis, according to which the mental correlate has no causal efficacy. Once the Correspondence Thesis is clearly distinguished from epiphenomenalism, James can keep the former, the plausible aspect, and rail against the latter, the implausible aspect, as he does with gusto. So it is not necessary to interpret James as guilty of "Poohbahism," as Richard Gale does, viewing him as wearing many hats with no way to reconcile them with each other. "Qua the tough-minded scientist," Gale writes, "James affirms determinism and that there is no psychosis without neurosis, but qua the tender-minded moral agent, he rejects both and instead accepts the reality of undetermined acts of spiritual causation" (Gale 1999, 191).

As noted earlier, the idea that mental and physical events are simultaneous nomic equivalents is an elaboration of James's "Humean" reason for saving the appearance that mental events are causes, namely, that the causal connection between a brain event and a bodily event is ultimately just as mysterious as the causal connection between a mental event and a bodily event. So if a physical and a mental event are both related to a bodily action by "constant conjunction," and to each other by "constant correlation," then there is equal justification for each being understood as the cause of the action. But the scruples of the physiologist seem to lead James to add a proviso about the mechanism of mental causation, which might appear incongruent with his Humean defense of it. He writes, "The feelings can produce nothing absolutely new, they can only reinforce and inhibit reflex currents which already exist, and the original organization of these by physiological forces must always be the ground-work of the psychological scheme" (PP, 141).

The brain for James is basically a reflex organ, and a human being a reflex organism. The difference between the older parts of the brain and the hemispheres is a difference in the degree of complexity of the reflex arcs that occur in them, the plasticity of the hemispheres making for a greater number and complexity of these arcs. If thought influences behavior, it does so not by initiating efferent activity of any sort, but only that sort that might issue from the inhibition or reinforcement of reflex arcs that have already traversed their afferent beginnings. This reinforcing and inhibiting role disciplines the complex and unstable brain with real purpose. Consciousness is a fighter for ends, he writes. Whereas the brain's "hair-trigger organization makes of it a happy-go-lucky, hit-or-miss affair consciousness brings a more or less constant pressure to bear in favor of those of its performances which make for the most permanent interests of the brain's owner" (PP, 143). My interest in these passages is not James's dubious doctrine of the happy-go-lucky brain, but rather its congruence with the Correspondence Thesis, as I have called it, and the nomic equivalents account. If mental causation were an entirely anomalous occurrence, a Cartesian bolt from the blue, psychology would have no reason to expect systematic correspondence, and no reason *a fortiori* to expect the correspondence of simultaneous nomic equivalence. These Jamesian commitments presuppose a stable cerebral background in order that mental causation should be possible. If there isn't sufficient stability, there isn't sufficient regularity to ensure that my choosing to perform some action will bring it about, since on the nomic equivalents hypothesis the choice effects action in virtue of a nomic regularity between its occurrence and a particular type of brain event. Against this stable background the nomic equivalents account may offer an interpretation of James's happy-go-lucky brain: At the micro level of fine adjustments to cerebral reflex arcs, where consciousness "fights for ends," the changes in the brain are to some degree indeterministic, which means for James unpredictable, apart from the influence of consciousness as exerted through psychophysical correlation laws. Indeterminism in this context implies that no causal law would be sufficient to predict that the choice or its physical nomic equivalent would occur. But that doesn't make the choice utterly anomalous, for law still requires that it be escorted by its physical correlate.

Materialism

Did James envisage a psychology that relies only on cerebral laws? Gerald Myers suggests this possibility. He writes:

> James's speculations about the physiological correlations of states of consciousness give the impression that he did not cite actual or hypothetical facts about the brain or nervous system merely to locate the physiological causes of conscious states; rather, he often viewed physiological processes as models for understand-

ing states of consciousness. In discussing the stream of thought, he sought to explain how intention connects with linguistic meaning: "Nothing is easier than to symbolize all these facts in terms of brain-action." If we consider a state of consciousness in terms of a conceptual framework taken from biology, James suggested, we may get a superior picture of its nature. The biological perspective is sometimes urged as a corrective to a view that he thought is mistaken; for example, he argued that identical sensations, as theorized by Locke, cannot recur because every sensation corresponds to some brain-state, and brain-states are continually changing. He invoked the biological perspective for rounding out a description of conscious experiences, filling in details perhaps inaccessible to introspection. Although the experiences associated with purposeful thinking may not disclose anything persistent to introspection, James argued: "Physiologically considered, we must suppose that a purpose means the persistent activity of certain rather definite brain-processes throughout the whole course of thought." Speculation about the details of those brain processes is often tantamount in James's writings to speculation about what is happening within associated experiences. (Myers 1986, 191)

I read Myers as claiming that the point of James's analogies between brain events and experiences was to reduce the latter to the former: to affirm that the stream of thought is just a series of brain events. This interpretation goes hand-in-hand with the idea that James adopted a methodological dualism in *The Principles* for forensic reasons rather than as a matter of principle. Knowing that he would alienate many readers if he espoused a materialist theory, he adopted the device of positing a dualism between brain processes and thoughts, officially recommending that psychology seek "correlations" when in fact he anticipated identities. Laws of the form "Mental event M occurs if and only if physical event P occurs" would be less shocking than identifications of the mental with the physical and consequent reliance on brain facts and cerebral laws alone.

This reading has the virtue that it shows how James could conform to the Correspondence Thesis while avoiding epiphenomenalism: he could reduce psychoses to neuroses! But Myers's valid point that James used brain processes as models for understanding the stream of thought doesn't license a reduction. There is every reason, on the contrary, to accept at face value James's repeated methodological claims of the following sort:

The consciousness, which is itself an integral thing not made of parts, "corresponds" to the entire activity of the brain, whatever that may be, at the moment. This is the way of expressing the relation of mind and brain from which I shall not depart during the remainder of the book, because it expresses the bare phenomenal fact with no hypothesis, and is exposed to no such logical objections as we have found to cling to the theory of ideas in combination. (PP, 177)

The fact that there is a systematic correspondence between consciousness and brain activity is reason enough to use the latter as a model of the former. But correspondence is not identity. Besides, we know that James's reductive ambitions lay not in the direction of materialism, but in that of pure experience: consciousness and brain activity will both be reduced to pure experience in his metaphysics of radical empiricism. Myers admits that his materialist reading of James's brain/thought analogies "certainly conflicts with the *esse est sentiri* [to be is to be felt] doctrine of states of consciousness, but both views, contradictory as they are, seem present in *The Principles*" (Myers 1986, 191). There is certainly a conflict in Myers's reading. It would follow from the identity that, since brain activity is composite in that it involves the activity of a myriad of microstructural parts, a thought must be composite in just the same way. But James devotes a Chapter 6, "The Mind-Stuff Theory," to deriding "the theory of ideas in combination," which holds that thought has a composite structure. The tension should be eliminated by retracting the identity interpretation of James's brain/mind analogies. There should be some other way that James can conform to the Correspondence Thesis, without endorsing the atomism and epiphenomenalism he denies so strenuously. The SNE account provides it.

The psychophysical correlation laws of James's psychology point, not toward materialistic reduction, but on the contrary toward a conception of the universe as purposive, as suggested at the outset of *The Principles* in this remark:

Just so we form our decision upon the deepest of all philosophic problems: Is the Kosmos an expression of intelligence rational in its inward nature, or a brute external fact pure and simple? If we find ourselves, in contemplating it, unable to banish the impression that it is a realm of final purposes, that it exists for the sake of something, we place intelligence at the heart of it and have a religion. If, on the contrary, in surveying its irremediable flux, we can think of the present only as so much mere mechanical sprouting from the past, occurring with no reference to the future, we are atheists and materialists. (PP, 21)

It is clear that James had an impression of the universe which "gave him a religion," and the nomic equivalents account imputes to him a conception of the mind-body relationship which coheres with such an impression. The correspondence between the mental and the physical need be no mere mechanical sprouting out of the soil of matter: that route leads towards the conscious-automaton theory. It could rather be a matter of design, an expression of purpose, that the stream of consciousness and brain processes harmonize as they do. It is significant that James quotes approvingly D. P. Bowne's presentation of a dilemma between pre-established harmony on one hand and idealistic phenomenalism on the other. Bowne writes that whatever we know of the outer world is revealed only in and through nervous changes in the brain, and consequently in order to explain this knowledge "it is necessary for us either to admit a pre-established harmony between the laws of nature of thought and the laws and nature of things, or else to allow that the objects of perception, the universe as it appears, are purely phenomenal, being but the way in which the mind reacts against the ground of its sensations" (PP, 216). Commenting, James opts for pre-established harmony, while intimating an "ulterior monistic philosophy." He says, "The dualism of Object and Subject and their pre-established harmony are what the psychologist as such might assume, whatever ulterior monistic philosophy he may, as an individual who has the right also to be a metaphysician, have in reserve" (PP, 216). The harmony could be interpreted materialistically, but materialism is not the only monism that an individual might hold in reserve. James's monism of pure experience is another. The defining feature of pure experience is not mentality or physicality. In a sense there is no defining feature, for pure experience is *just what appears*. But in Chapter 2 I *typified* pure experience as protomental, having the features of continuity and changingness that James attributed to the stream of consciousness, and also a feature of purposiveness, not the purposiveness implicit in James's characterization of the three other "characters'" of the stream (personal possession, object-directedness, selectiveness), but an analog of them that has to do with participation in a larger purposive structure. The impression of which James spoke, that the cosmos is a realm of purpose, grew into a metaphysics, and a conception of psychology as concerned with psychophysical correlation laws was a major part of the scaffolding for this construction.

Anomalism

The SNE interpretation may be brought into more definite relief by contrasting it with another interpretation of the causal efficacy of consciousness, namely, that thought is causally efficacious to the extent that the Correspondence Thesis is restricted, failing to obtain on those occasions when thought makes its force felt in the physical world: when consciousness fights for ends, on this reckoning, it is a psychosis without a neurosis. Textual evidence for this alternative can be found early on in *The Principles*, even as James is describing the functions of the brain. Apologizing for mixing talk about ideas and feelings with his description of the functioning of the brain, James expresses the hope

> that the reader will take no umbrage at my so mixing the physical and mental, and talking of reflex acts and hemispheres and reminiscences in the same breath, as if they were homogeneous quantities and factors of one causal chain. I have done so deliberately; for although I admit that from the radically physical point of view it is easy to conceive of the chain of events amongst the cells and fibres as complete in itself, and that whilst so conceiving it one need make no mention of "ideas," I yet suspect that point of view of being an unreal abstraction. Reflexes in centres may take place even where the accompanying feelings or ideas guide them. (PP, 36)

How must the chain of physical causation be "completed" in order to avoid "unreal abstraction"? In what sense do the mental and the physical "mix"? Granting James his hypothesis about the happy-go-lucky brain, it follows that the chain can't be completed by brain events, since the brain will be too unstable to fight for ends in the way that thought can. So it is natural to suppose that thought, independent from any physical state of the sort implied by the Correspondence Thesis, makes the difference. Call such thoughts free-floaters. This view entails that, when a mental event "completes" a physical causal chain, it does so by supplementing physical causal factors which are not by themselves sufficient to bring about the effect in question. The mental and the physical mix, according to the free-floater view, in the sense that mental events are intervening variables between physical events. By contrast, the nomic equivalents account interprets James's notion of mixing the mental and the physical as implying that they are codeterminants of behavioral effects. The intervening variables view runs counter to the Correspondence Thesis and James's mind/brain analogies, implying causal gaps in brain processes which are filled by mental events alone. But the codeterminants view provides underpinning for the Correspondence Thesis and the mind/brain analogies, helping to justify the theoretical importance James attached to them. There may be causal gaps, as James's indeterminism led him to believe, but when they are filled by free choices they are also filled by the simultaneous physical nomic equivalents of the choices. The SNE account implies that mental causes complete physical causes by being related to them in explanatorily powerful correlation laws. The unreal abstraction of confining one's attention to purely cerebral laws is the mistake of ignoring the predictive power of the broader nomic web, which includes psychophysical correlation laws and psychophysical causal laws.

The issue between the nomic equivalents and free-floater views comes into focus again when James discusses attention: "It goes back to the automaton-theory. If feeling is an inert accompaniment, then of course the brain-cell can be played upon only by other brain-cells, and the attention which we give at any time to any subject . . . is the fatally predetermined effect of exclusively material laws. If, on the other hand, the feeling which coexists with the brain-cells' activity reacts dynamically upon that activity, furthering or checking it, then the attention is in part, at least, a cause" (PP, 424). Feeling's "reacting dynamically" upon brain activity admittedly can be read in the light of the free-floater interpretation, and I do not exclude the possibility that James had this in mind on occasion. My aim is not to provide a philosophical snapshot of what was going through James's mind when he was writing a certain passage of *The Principles*, but to bring a theoretical apparatus to bear on that work which interprets it as an organic unity, a coherent theory with a plurality of sub-theories as constituents, knitted together by the nomic equivalents interpretation of what I call his Correspondence Thesis, his brain-mind analogies, and his talk about the mixing of the mental and the physical. Adopting the free-floater view, on the other hand, leads to a reading of *The Principles* as a hodgepodge of theoretical tensions and outright inconsistencies, as in Leahey's appraisal.

Remarks like James's confessional footnote in "The Automaton-Theory" require the reader to choose between the intervening variables and codeterminants accounts:

> The present writer recalls how in 1869, when still a medical student, he began to write an essay showing how almost everyone who speculated about brain-processes illicitly interpolated into his account of them links derived from the entirely heterogeneous universe of Feeling. Spencer, Hodgson (in his Time and Space), Maudsley, Lockhart Clarke, Bain, Dr. Carpenter, and other authors were cited as having been guilty of the confusion. The writing was soon stopped because he perceived that the view which he was upholding against these authors was a pure conception, with no proofs to be adduced of its reality. Later it seemed to him that whatever proofs existed really told in favor of their view. (PP, 134)

James can be read here as saying that he came to believe that mental processes are "interpolated" between brain processes, floating freely between them. Or he can be read as saying that he came to see the need for an account of brain processes which mentions the mental processes that correspond to them, and which codetermine the effects that the brain processes cause. Mental processes don't literally interpolate between physical processes; that is, they aren't free-floating intervening variables. Rather, there must be interpolations into one's account of brain processes, discussions which will identify their mental correlates and codeterminers, and describe laws of the coexistence of the two kinds of events.

Enough has been said about the nomic equivalents interpretation of James's psychological project to see that he doesn't need free-floaters in order to avoid epiphenomenalism, materialism, and determinism. And dynamic reactivity can be given a nomic equivalents interpretation, as indicated earlier: there is some indeterminacy in the reflex arcs of the cerebral hemispheres, such that thought can further or check brain currents which would otherwise discharge in activity that would not suit the subject's purposes. But thought's reacting dynamically with the brain in this way is consistent with its having physical nomic equivalents. "Mental event M if and only if P" doesn't imply "It is determined by causal law that M" or "It is determined by causal law that P." So the nomic equivalents account *permits* a "cause theory" of attention, as opposed to an "effect theory" which construes attention as the result of antecedent brain events. By contrast, the free-floater view *demands* a cause theory.

Such a demand, as opposed to permission, seems to me quite at odds with the spirit of James's conception of psychology. James had moral reasons to hope and expect that the cause theory is true, but his considered opinion was that scientific psychology will at most leave the option open.

Discussing the question of whether our sense of free will is an illusion, James writes:

> As we grant to the advocate of the mechanical theory that it may be one [i.e., an illusion], so he must grant to us that it may not. And the result is two conceptions of possibility face to face with no facts definitely enough known to stand as arbiter between them. . . . Under these circumstances, one can leave the question open whilst waiting for light, or one can do what most speculative minds do, that is, look to one's general philosophy to incline the beam. The believers in mechanism do so without hesitation, and they ought not to refuse a similar privilege to the believers in a spiritual force. I count myself among the latter, but as my reasons are ethical they are hardly suited for introduction into a psychological work. (PP, 429)

I submit, then, that although James may have been tempted by the free-floater view, and although there are passages in *The Principles* that suggest it, the overall tenor of his theory of the mind-body relationship is better captured by the nomic equivalents account. To put some focus onto this conclusion, I will apply the SNE analysis to my favorite passage in James's entire ouevre, from the chapter "The Will" in *The Principles*.

> We know what it is to get out of bed on a freezing morning in a room without a fire, and how the very vital principle within us protests against the ordeal. Probably most persons have lain on certain mornings for an hour at a time unable to brace themselves to the resolve. We think how late we shall be, how the duties of the day will suffer; we say, "I *must* get up, this is ignominious," etc.; but still the arm couch feels too delicious, the cold outside too cruel, and resolution faints away and postpones itself again and again just as it seemed on the verge of bursting the resistance and passing over into the decisive act. Now how do we *ever* get up under such circumstances? If I may generalize from my own experience, we more often than not get up without any struggle or decision at all. We suddenly find that we *have* got up. A fortunate lapse of consciousness occurs; we forget both the warmth and the cold; we fall into some revery connected with the day's life, in

the course of which the idea flashes across us, "Hollo! I must lie here no longer" — an idea which at that lucky instant awakens no contradictory or paralyzing suggestions, and consequently produces immediately its appropriate motor effects. It was our acute consciousness of both the warmth and the cold during the period of struggle, which paralyzed our activity then and kept our idea of rising in the condition of *wish* and not of *will*. The moment these inhibitory ideas ceased, the original idea exerted its effects. (PP, 1133)

This passage, which James presents as containing "in miniature form the data for an entire psychology of volition," lends itself to the effect theory: ideomotor conditions finally arrange themselves in such a way that they are causally sufficient for getting up. I want to emphasize, though, that the SNE interpretation's *permission* for the cause theory is enough to accommodate Jamesian ideas about free will, suggested in the following passage from the chapter "Association" in *The Principles*:

The effects of *interested attention and volition* remain. These activities seem to hold fast to certain elements and, by emphasizing them and dwelling on them, to make their associates the only ones which are evoked. *This* is the point at which an anti-mechanical psychology must, if anywhere, make its stand in dealing with association. Everything else is pretty certainly due to cerebral laws. My own opinion on the question of active attention and spiritual spontaneity is expressed elsewhere. But even though there be a mental spontaneity, it can certainly not create ideas or summon them *ex abrupto*. Its power is limited to *selecting* amongst those which the associative machinery has already introduced or tends to introduce. If it can emphasize, reinforce, or protract for a second either one of these, it can do all that the most eager advocate of free will need demand; for it then decides the direction of the next associations by making them hinge upon the emphasized term; and determining in this wise the course of the man's thinking, it also determines his acts. (PP, 559)

So, assume that the idea flashes across us, "Hollo! I must lie here no longer" and assume further that the idea, *as conditioned by antecedent cerebral events*, would not have been sufficient to make us rise. What did the trick rather is our emphasizing, reinforcing, or protracting that thought for a second. This is "all that the most eager advocate of free will need demand," James writes, and the SNE interpretation permits it, stipulating only that the emphasizing, reinforcing or protracting has a simultaneous nomic equivalent in simultaneous brain events. It does *not* require that cerebral laws linking earlier to later events should determine the emphasizing, etc. It is consistent with that possibility but also with the possibility that the emphasizing and its physical correlate are free of such determination. The forbidden "free-floaters" are emphasizings, etc., that don't have SNEs in the brain. But the SNE interpretation has already given the free will advocates everything they need demand; free-floaters aren't needed.

Emotions

In conclusion, I want to suggest an application of the foregoing analysis to the vexed question of how to interpret the James-Lange theory of the emotions. I offer an alternative to the view, expressed recently by Robert M. Gordon, that "for James a state such as fear, sorrow, or anger becomes a mere epiphenomenon, an inconsequential by-product of physiological excitation" (Gordon 1987, 88). Gordon correctly deems this view "preposterous" (Gordon 1987, 89). But it is misleading and uncharitable to attribute it to James. James's distinguished intellectual biographer, Gerald Myers, correctly writes that James's "theory of emotion was never intended, despite some misleading language, to deny the common-sense conviction that fear causes running and sadness causes crying" (Myers 1986, 226).

James's theory is an alternative to "our natural way of thinking" about emotions, according to which "the mental perception of some fact excites the mental affection called the emotion, and . . . this latter state of mind gives rise to the bodily expression" (PP, 1065). What James objects to in this picture is not the idea that an emotion might be a cause of bodily movement, but rather the idea that an emotion's role might be understood in abstraction from its physical correlates and causes. Myers helpfully identifies the bone of contention between James and common sense in the following passage:

> To understand the theory, we must appreciate not only what it asserts but also what it denies—the existence of "bodiless" emotions. Consider the emotion of fright caused by perceiving an approaching emu. According to common sense and traditional psychology, James said, the perception of the emu causes a pure, primary feeling of fright—pure in that it is purely mental and independent of

physiological events, primary in that it is the initial or direct effect of the perception. Any associated physical changes, such as running, sweating, heightened blood-pressure, palpitations, or trembling, are called the expressions or effects of the bodiless emotion of fright. Our common sense presumes that fright, considered as an exclusively mental or non-bodily state of consciousness whose nature is given to introspection, was immediately brought into existence by the perception of the emu and then gave rise to the bodily effects of expressions. All emotions are likewise ghostly intermediaries between our perception and our bodily reactions. The James-Lange theory denied this presumption of common sense and traditional psychology, objecting vigorously to the idea that an emotion is a ghostly intermediary. (Myers 1986, 220–21)

Instead of perception of the emu giving rise to a ghostly intermediary or "free-floater," bodily change follows directly upon perception of the exciting fact, "and our feeling of the same changes as they occur IS the emotion" (PP, 1065). Illustrating the point in provocatively memorable prose, he writes that his view is that "we feel sorry because we cry, angry because we strike, afraid because we tremble, and not that we cry, strike, or tremble, because we are sorry, angry, or fearful, as the case may be" (PP, 1066). This manner of speaking got him into trouble with his critics, who noted that there can be trembling without fear, crying without sorrow, striking without anger, and so on. When James returned to the topic in the 1894 essay "The Physical Basis of Emotion" he conceded this much, apologizing for the "slap-dash brevity" of such formulations as "we are frightened because we run." But he insisted that his critics were missing the point of the James-Lange theory. Discussing such cases as the laughter which is a mirthless response to being tickled, or vomiting without a trace of disgust, James writes that "The facts must be admitted; but in none of these cases where an organic change gives rise to a mere local bodily perception is the reproduction of an emotional diffusive wave complete. Visceral factors, hard to localize, are left out; and these seem to be the most essential ones of all. I have said that where they also from any inward cause are added, we have the emotion; and that then the subject is seized with objectless or pathological dread, grief, or rage, as the case may be" (EP, 305).

So the wave of diffusion from the exciting perception has two temporal stages, an essential "visceral" stage and a subsequent behavioral stage which may or may not occur. If you introduce the visceral stage into the process of someone's laughing because of being tickled, you have the case of objectless mirth, someone who is mirthful but not about anything. And if the laughter is inhibited, you have the case of mirth's essential visceral component occurring without its typical behavioral component.

Now these facts that James is trying to assemble in response to his critics are well organized by the SNE account. Mirth's essential visceral component and mirthful feelings that would occur even in the absence of outward behavior are related as SNEs. Let this latter be termed mirth's essential psychological component. Then James's objection to the commonsense view of emotion can be stated in the proposition that mirth's essential psychological component does not occur before the visceral response to an exciting perception but is rather a simultaneous nomic equivalent of that response. But equally, the essential part of an emotion does not occur after the inner processes initiated by the exciting perception. This is what interpreters don't get right when they say, with Flugel in *A Hundred Years of Psychology*, that James's "notorious" theory "reversed the usual assumptions about cause and effect" (Flugel 1964, 130).

It is not as though an emotion is a mere psychological by-product of outward behavior, as Flugel supposes, for the essential psychological component of the emotion will be related to the behavioral component as cause to effect, by virtue of its simultaneous nomic equivalence with the visceral cause. And by virtue of the same relationship the essential psychological component will not be epiphenomenally related to its visceral correlate. Emotions as felt can be "fighters for ends," as James's rejection of the automaton theory requires, and not the Huxleian steam whistle that merely accompanies the work of a locomotive engine.

The SNE interpretation of James's psychology is fully compatible with his materialist orientation (his "cerebralism"): the mind is dependent on the brain. But this dependency doesn't entail epiphenomenalism, because the brain is symmetrically dependent on the mind, by virtue of the simultaneous nomic equivalence of brain processes and stages of the stream of consciousness. This reading reveals deep coherence in James's theory of mental causation, whereas the conventional alternatives find the opposite. In the light of the SNE interpretation James is not caught up in a contradictory view of consciousness. Nor can the James-Lange theory of emotion be dismissed as preposterous. Furthermore, laws of simultaneous nomic equivalence serve as a bridge from scientific psychology to James's broader view of a purposive universe, so the continuity of his scientific and metaphysical theorizing is underpinned. In addition to these general considerations in favor of the SNE reading, there is considerable specific textual evidence for it, especially in James's many remarks having to do with the dependency of the mental on the physical ("cerebralism") and *no psychosis without neurosis*. The conclusion that this reading should be adopted becomes especially strong when a principle of charity in interpretation is invoked, since truth and plausibility replace falsehood and confusion.

The SNE interpretation solves the problem posed at the end of the last chapter, that mental phenomena and pure experience are *too light*, lacking the explanatory depth of the physical sciences. The current proposal is that laws of simultaneous nomic equivalence show how mental phenomena could do the heavy lifting, namely, via their nomic equivalence with physical phenomena. It is not that there is one principle or substance, the physical, which is deeper than the mental. As James remarked, "[I]nstead of being *a principle*, the 'oneness' affirmed may not merely be a name like 'substance,' descriptive of the fact that certain *specific and verifiable connexions* are found among the parts of the experiential flux. This brings us back to our pragmatic rule: Suppose there is a oneness in things, what may it be known-as? What differences to you and me will it make?" (SPP, 66). Oneness may be understood as simultaneous nomic equivalence. The difference it makes to you and me is that it allows our minds to be causally efficacious rather than epiphenomenal.

How does James's theory of mind relate to Donald Davidson's well-known view that psychological laws are impossible because the vocabulary of the mental is *heteronomic*, in contrast with the vocabulary of the physical, which is *homonomic*. This means that the physical vocabulary is capable of being made indefinitely more precise (for instance, by innovation in measurement, mathematics, physical theory, and so forth), whereas the mental vocabulary, because it is used to characterize rational agents, is not; it must be governed by considerations of rationality, rather than the ideal of greater and greater precision. Does this count against James's positivism? In order to do so it would have to be shown, first, that James's conception of a cerebral law was, *inter alia*, the conception of a law that meets Davidson's standards. And second, even if psychological laws were impossible because mental vocabulary is heteronomic, it would have to be shown that psychophysical correlation laws of the SNE sort are impossible for the same reason. As for the first, James's instrumentalist, prediction-oriented conception of science would favor cerebral laws measured by a standard of predictive power in given contexts rather than capacity to be made ever more precise. As for the second, SNE relationships could obtain at a sufficiently coarse level of "granularity," pain being correlated with certain brain events (for example), even though the correlated brain events could be more finely granulated, by virtue of the homonomic character of the physical, whereas there would be no corresponding "pain dust" to correlate with the more finely individuated brain events. So Davidson's view is not a direct threat to James's conception of psychology, though clearly a fuller analysis is called for.

Conclusion

The SNE interpretation of James's theory of mind rescues it from epiphenom-enalism. It provides a unifying and fruitful account of his writings about the relationship between mind and body. His theory has by no means been super-ceded by behaviorism, Freudianism, or the computer model of the mind. On the contrary, the general goal of a psychology with sufficient predictive power, gained from psychophysical correlation laws, to ameliorate the human condi-tion is still a live option for belief. In the next chapter I will pursue this idea further.

4

Consciousness III: Mind Dust

Sciousness

Here I continue to interpret James on consciousness, in accordance with the Two-Levels View, in such fashion that it contributes to a plausible form of his radical empiricism.

"Sciousness" is the term James uses when he wants to emphasize the distance between his position and those broadly Cartesian views which view the mind as an irreducible entity, fit to be studied independently. Sciousness will crop up again in the next chapter, where it will be studied as the passing Thought, which, by its appropriations, constructs the self. Here I examine Sciousness's role in pointing the way toward ontological decomposition of the mental and the physical into pure experience.

When James denies that "consciousness" exists, he means consciousness in the Cartesian sense. When he speaks less guardedly about consciousness, presupposing that it exists, he has in mind the stream of thought separated from the myths of rationalistic psychology. The term "sciousness" anticipates the reduction of both consciousness and the physical world to pure experience, as well as reminding the reader of his "environmentalism" about the mind, his view that mental facts cannot be properly studied apart from the physical environment that shapes them. His commitment to consciousness-as-sciousness is very different from denying the existence of consciousness as contemporary behaviorism and "eliminative materialism" have done. Eliminative materialism implies that consciousness is so myth-ridden that there is no core conception of it which might be an object of scientific study. But sciousness by contrast is just such a core conception:

> *States of consciousness themselves are not verifiable facts.* But "worse remains behind." Neither common-sense, nor psychology so far as it has yet been written, has

ever doubted that the states of consciousness which that science studies are immediate data of experience. "Things" have been doubted, but thoughts and feelings
have never been doubted. The outer world, but never the inner world, has been
denied. Everyone assumes that we have direct introspective acquaintance with
our thinking activity as such, with our consciousness as something inward and
contrasted with the outer objects which it knows. Yet I must confess that for my
part I cannot feel sure of this conclusion. Whenever I try to become sensible of
my thinking activity as such, what I catch is some bodily fact, an impression coming from my brow, or head, or throat, or nose. It seems as if consciousness as an
inner activity were rather a *postulate* than a sensibly given fact, the postulate,
namely, of a *knower* as correlative to all this known; and as if "*sciou*sness" might be
a better word by which to describe it. But "sciousness postulated as an hypothesis"
is practically a very different thing from "states of consciousness apprehended with
infallible certainly by an inner sense." For one thing, it throws the question of *who
the knower really is* wide open again. (PBC, 400)

Eliminative materialism rejects the possibility of reducing the mind to the brain
because the concept of mind is too ill-behaved to participate in a theoretically
valid reduction. James on the other hand expects a reduction of mind, not a
reduction of mind to brain, but rather a reduction of mind and brain to pure
experience, a global reduction which is fully compatible with an empirical
science of psychology which emphasizes the dependence of the mind on the
brain and the environmental shaping of mind. Behaviorism denies that the
mind is a distinct existence from behavior. In its logical form, it assumes that
all talk about the mind can be translated, or reconceptualized, in terms of behavior and dispositions to behave. In its methodological form, it assumes that
scientific psychology should proceed without referring to intervening variables
between afferent stimuli and efferent behavioral responses.

    For James on the contrary sciousness is a distinct existence from behavior,
but it is not self-intimatingly mental. It is mental by virtue of participating in a
stream of thought, that is, by virtue of its relationship to other sciousness; the
circularity in this account will be removed in Chapter 8, when sciousness will
be characterized as what folk-psychological sentences are *about*. If sciousness
were self-intimatingly mental, there would be a nonrelational "sign" of the
mentality of each conscious state, such that its mentality could be read off
from this sign. Sciousness is not *intrinsically* mental, but is rather fit for pure-

experiential reduction. The most straightforward conceptualization of such reduction would *identify* a mental event with its pure-experiential equivalent,
but this is not a live option because any attempt to formulate the identity would
impose a concept on the subconceptual. It turns out that an indirect reduction, via a form of functionalism, best accommodates James's ideas about the
mind, basically because functionalism puts mental states and the self in a
predicative position. They are analyzed as properties of a subject. What sets
James's functionalism apart from its contemporary kin is that James's is not
presumed to be a halfway house to identifying the subject as something physical and conceptualizable as such. For James, the functional analysis is as much
conceptualization of the subject as one can get. The subject "shows" itself in
experience; that is, pure experience is imminent in ordinary experience.

Mind Dust

James's italicized insistence in *The Principles* that *"introspective observation is
what we have to rely on first and foremost and always"* (PP, 185) immediately
follows a ferocious attack on "the mind-dust theory." To understand this attack
is to understand his skepticism about the unconscious, and it brings up a further reason that some continue to have for agreeing with Leahey's assessment,
noted at the beginning of the previous chapter, that James's influence "proved
absolutely fatal to American mentalistic psychology." Is it a good reason?

James's thoughts on mind dust were prompted by contemporaries such as
the German physiologist A. Fick, "who had convinced themselves of the existence of a vast amount of sub-conscious mental life" (PP, 153). Fick had made
experiments in which a subject's skin was stimulated by warmth and by touch
through a hole in a card, the surrounding parts being protected by the card,
finding that mistakes were frequently made by the subject (mistaking radiant
heat for touch, for instance) and concluding that the number of sensations
from the elementary nerve tips affected was too small to sum itself distinctly
into either a feeling of heat or a feeling of touch. Fick then theorized that
ordinary feelings of heat arise "when the intensities of the units of feeling are
evenly gradated, so that between two elements a and b no other unit can spa-
tially intervene whose intensity is not also *between* that of a and b. A feeling of
contact perhaps arises when this condition is not fulfilled. Both kinds of feel-

ing, however, are composed of the same units" (PP, 153). These units are what James derisively called mind dust or mind stuff, and he argued against it, in part, as follows:

> But it is obviously far clearer to interpret such a gradation of intensities as a brain-fact than as a mind-fact. If in the brain a tract were first excited in one of the ways suggested by Prof. Fick, and then again in the other, it might very well happen, for aught we can say to the contrary, that the psychic accompaniment in the one case would be heat, and in the other pain. The pain and the heat would, however, not be composed of psychic units, but would each be the direct result of one total brain-process. So long as this latter interpretation remains open, Fick cannot be held to have proved psychic summation. (PP, 154)

This is a powerful argument, echoed in contemporary theory by philosophers such as John Searle and scientists such as Gerald Edelman, who share James's belief that one should look to biology rather than the unconscious mind, whether in Freud's sense or that of contemporary cognitive psychology, in order to understand the conscious mind. Far from retarding the progress of psychology, James's cerebralism may have been the road that psychology should have taken, instead of the long detours of behaviorism, Freudian psychology, and mind-as-program cognitive psychology.

The Connection Principle

John Searle has recently defended what he calls the Connection Principle, according to which the notion of an unconscious mental state implies accessibility to consciousness. We have no notion of the unconscious, Searle holds, except as that which is potentially conscious. This potential is just a disposition of a neurophysiology to generate conscious states. For instance, the Connection Principle countenances "shallow unconscious" states such as believing something while asleep, since these are patently cases in which the whole force of talking about the belief is given by some such dispositional statement as, "If he were awakened and asked, he would acknowledge that he believes such and such, etc." The Connection Principle also doesn't question repressed mental states, since they are at least in principle conscious states, and it allows "as if" attributions of mentality to the brain that are not to be taken literally, such as saying that the medulla wants to keep us alive, so it keeps us breathing even while we are asleep (Searle 1992, 172). But the principle does not countenance "deep unconscious" mental, intentional phenomena that are not only unconscious but are in principle inaccessible to consciousness. Searle is attacking the effort to separate consciousness from intentionality, just as James attacked Fick's effort to separate consciousness from sensation; Searle's skepticism about "cognitively impenetrable mental modules" involved in "unconscious mental processing of information" has the same motivation as James's skepticism about mind dust.

Searle's main argument for the Connection Principle has to do with the *aspectual shape* of mental states, such that they mean what they are about in a particular way, leaving open the possibility that two mental states could be about the same thing but be different mental states because of their different aspectual shapes. (The aspectual shape of mental states parallels the intentionality of sentences that describe "propositional attitudes" such as desires and beliefs.) If I want an apple and it happens to be poisoned, my mental state is different from wanting a poisoned fruit, different with regard to its aspectual shape. Then Searle's general claim is that microstructural states of the brain do not have aspectual shape, so they could not do the work that deeply unconscious mental states are supposed to do, contrary to the materialism of both Freud and most cognitive psychologists. Searle's aspectual-shape argument is closely related to James's *esse est sentiri* doctrine, since, only as I am aware of my mental states, or potentially (dispositionally) aware of them, do they have aspectual shape; so brain states or deep-Freudian mental states couldn't qualify as mental states, since by hypothesis the subject is not aware of them.

The Connection Principle is important as a defense of James's contribution to psychology, supporting his view that consciousness is essential to mind and validating his skepticism about the unconscious. Although no final conclusions can be drawn, no one can simply assume now that James held psychology back with such skepticism; on the contrary, adherents of the unconscious may be the parties guilty of setting psychology on false trails, and his legacy may be done a disservice by attempts to reinterpret his theory of habits and reflexes, for example, as tantamount to his recognizing the reality of the unconscious. On the contrary, James's theory of habit is better interpreted as presaging ideas such as Searle's "Background," the fundamentally neurophysiological grounding for mental life.

One important difference between Searle's view of consciousness and that of James concerns the latter's commitment to an ontology of pure experience. For Searle the appearance of mental states is their reality, so there can be no question of hiving off how they appear in order to get at their underlying essence. This "hiving" technique is typical of scientific reduction, for example the reduction of colors to wave lengths, where the distinction between observer and observed is taken for granted, and the way something appears to human beings is put to one side in order to get at its objective nature. Searle's view is that the observer/observed distinction is inapplicable to consciousness, so physicalistic reductions (or any others) are nonstarters; the observer/observed model suits things to which there is "third-person access," but it is not suited to "first-person access." But James anticipates a reduction of consciousness to pure experience (in a manner that I describe in detail in Chapter 7), and this motivates him to think of introspection as a kind of observation.

The Taylor–Wozniak Interpretation

Eugene Taylor and Robert Wozniak take the view in *Pure Experience: The Response to William James* that James, far from being skeptical of the unconscious, rejected the positivism of his earlier psychological work for an embrace, especially in *The Varieties of Religious Experience*, of the unconscious that prefigured the work of the depth psychologists and psychoanalysts of the Freudian and contemporary periods:

> By 1904, psychologists had come to believe (and still believe) that James had abandoned psychology following the publication of his *The Principles of Psychology* in 1890. In *The Principles*, James had emphasized a view of psychology as an empirical science that approached its subject matter, states of consciousness, from a positivistic point of view. The major thrust of *The Principles* was James's positivistic emphasis on a cognitively oriented experimental psychology whose subject matter was consciousness conceived as a field within which we become aware of objects that are in focus at the centre.
>
> But *The Principles* also contained another centre of gravity, one that emphasized the fact that there is also a margin, a penumbra or halo that surrounds all our thoughts, warming our bare cognitions and making them our own. This is the domain of the emotions, largely hidden from view, the reservoir of our habits and reflexes, and also the source of our intuitions. Here James hinted at nothing less

than what has since been called the reality of the unconscious. (Taylor and Wozniak 1996, xxii–xxiii)

Taylor and Wozniak confuse James's doctrine of the fringe with recognition of the reality of the unconscious. That doctrine (PP, 446–47) recognizes the important fact that consciousness has a center and a periphery, a focus and a penumbra. This has nothing to do with alleged mental states that are "hidden from view" in the unconscious. The fringe is precisely the fringe of a subjective state, and as such it is something of which one is, if only minimally, aware; unlike its neural counterparts, the essence of a mental state is its being an object of awareness; *esse est sentiri*, as James sometimes said. ("[I]f a certain existing fact is that of a thousand feelings, it cannot at the same time be that of *one* feeling; for the essence of a feeling is to be felt, and as a psychic existent *feels*, so it must *be*" [PP, 165].) For instance, "The sense of our meaning is an entirely peculiar element of the thought," James wrote, which "pertains to the 'fringe' of the subjective state, and is a 'feeling of tendency,' whose neural counterpart is undoubtedly a lot of dawning and dying processes too faint and complex to be traced" (PP, 446). Clearly the fringe in James's reckoning is not hidden from view in the unconscious. And if it were, he and we might well ask, where is it? It is distinct from its "neural counterpart," if it has anything to do with James's doctrine, yet it lacks subjectivity, consciousness; a mental state "with the lights out," so to speak, just the sort of *faux* mind fact that mind dust or mind stuff represented for James and that offends against the Connection Principle. James should be taken at his word when he insists that the reservoir of habits and reflexes, including those that subserve the fringe of consciousness, is filled with brain facts, not mind facts. Shallow unconscious mental states, for example in sleep, are simply tendencies of the brain to give rise to conscious episodes: "Tendencies exist, but they are facts for the outside psychologist rather than for the subject of the observation. The tendency is thus a *psychical* zero; only its *results* are felt" (PP, 246).

Searle's distinction between shallow and deep unconsciousness is crucial at this point, for Taylor and Wozniak cite James's study of the "subconscious" in *The Varieties of Religious Experience* as evidence for their view (which accords with that of Wilshire and Edie, scouted in Chapter 2) that James left behind the basic tenets of *The Principles* by the time of coming to write *The Varieties*. But the subconsciousness of *The Varieties* is shallow, not deep; it does not violate the Connection Principle and consequently does not subvert the doctrines of *The Principles*, specifically James's position on the subconscious.

The "mind-cure" techniques that address the subconscious, such as techniques of relaxation and letting go, do affect the subject's habits and reflexes, and do indeed give rise to healthier mental states; or, at any rate, there is no reason to deny such results here. But the subconscious in this sense is just a neurophysiological disposition of the subject's body to give rise to healthier mental states in response to relaxation techniques and the like. It does not amount to an embrace of subconscious mind facts, contrary to the arguments of *The Principles* against mind dust. (If this were the case, why wouldn't James have said so? He can hardly have forgotten, or have supposed that others had forgotten, the whole of Chapter 6, "The Mind Stuff Theory," from *The Principles*.)

Consider the matter at a slightly greater level of detail, starting with the Taylor-Wozniak position:

> James also launched a six year study in the psychology of religion that culminated in *The Varieties of Religious Experience*. There he developed the theme that the subconscious was the doorway to the awakening of ultimately transforming experiences, the highest of which was the mystical. Mystical consciousness, he suggested, was a state of deep and profound awareness. Once experienced, it led to dramatically changed lives and might, in all probability, be the very source of discursive intellect.
>
> Rather than abandoning psychology in the decade after *The Principles*, in other words, James was actually pioneering the psychology of the abnormal, psychotherapeutics, parapsychology, and the psychology of religion. In doing so, however, James left reductionism and positivism far behind, delving deeply into a domain where most laboratory psychologists have never been able to follow. When James pointed to the reality of a dynamic sphere of experience beyond the bounds of everyday waking material reality, American psychology faltered, leaving exploration of this sphere to generations of depth psychologists and psychoanalysts to follow. (Taylor and Wozniak 1996, xxiv)

I am not disputing the therapeutic benefits that these others, and James himself, speak of. The issue is whether they should be associated with a philosophy of mind that posits deep unconscious mental states. It is parallel to whether behavioral modification techniques should be associated with a behaviorist philosophy of mind that denies the existence of mind. In both cases the techniques and therapies are separable from the corresponding ontologies, and can be used or not used on the basis of estimations of their probable consequences, apart from whether the theories of mind that were historically associated with them are true or not.

Any person has thousands of belief of which he or she is shallowly unconscious. For instance, the reader's belief that the Earth is not flat was no doubt unconscious in this way until my words "brought it to the surface." There are presumably brain facts that explain why people have such beliefs, and there is little or no temptation to suppose that their "subconsciousness" is anything more than the subject's being liable to become aware of them under certain sorts of conditions, like the condition of my drawing your attention to your believing that the Earth is not flat. That is, there is little or no temptation to suppose that there exists "inside" of the subject, *in addition to* facts about his or her neurophysiology and liability to be made aware under certain conditions, a further deep unconscious mental fact, "the unconscious belief that the Earth is not flat."

My claim is that James's references to the subconscious (he preferred this "vaguer term" to "the unconscious") are of this innocuous sort, not anticipating the reality of the unconscious as Freud and other depth psychologists and psychoanalysts construed it, but rather as liabilities to awareness that are perfectly consistent with the thoroughgoing cerebralism of *The Principles*. Even his most enthusiastic references to the subconscious in *The Varieties*, such as the following one in reference to religious mysticism, cite examples that fall within the compass of the shallow unconscious:

> When, in addition to these phenomena of inspiration, we take religious mysticism into the account, when we recall the striking and sudden unifications of a discordant self which we saw in conversion, and when we review the extravagant obsessions of tenderness, purity, and self-severity met with in saintliness, we cannot, I think, avoid the conclusion that in religion we have a department of human nature with unusually close relations to the transmarginal or subliminal region. If the word "subliminal" is offensive to any of you, as smelling too much of psychical research or other aberrations, call it by any other name you please, to distinguish it from the level of full sunlit consciousness. Call this latter the A-region or personality, if you care to, and call the other the B-region. The B-region, then, is obviously the larger part of each of us, for it is the abode of everything that is latent and the

> reservoir of everything that passes unrecorded or unobserved. It contains, for ex-
> ample, such things as all our momentarily inactive memories, and it harbors the
> springs of all our obscurely motivated passions, impulses, likes, dislikes, and preju-
> dices. Our intuitions, hypotheses, fancies, superstitions, persuasions, convictions,
> and in general all our non-rational operations, come from it. (VRE, 381)

This abode of the latent and reservoir of the unrecorded is the brain. The interpreter of *The Varieties* should bear in mind that the basic project of that book is
to show that the cerebralism of *The Principles* does not undermine religious
belief. James points this out repeatedly in the opening chapter of *The Varieties*,
"Religion and Neurology," as in the following passage:

> Let us ourselves look at the matter in the largest possible way. Modern psychology,
> finding definite psycho-physical connections to hold good, assumes as a conve-
> nient hypothesis that the dependence of mental states upon bodily conditions must
> be thorough-going and complete. If we adopt the assumption, then of course what
> medical materialism insists on must be true in a general way, if not in every detail:
> Saint Paul certainly had once an epileptoid, if not an epileptic seizure; George
> Fox was an hereditary degenerate; Carlyle was undoubtedly auto-intoxicated by
> some organ or other, no matter which,—and the rest. But now, I ask you, how can
> such an existential account of facts of mental history decide in one way or another
> upon their spiritual significance? According to the general postulate of psychology
> just referred to, there is not a single one of our states of mind, high or low, healthy
> or morbid, that has not some organic process as its condition. Scientific theories
> are organically conditioned just as much as religious emotions are; and if we only
> knew the facts intimately enough, we should doubtless see "the liver" determining
> the dicta of the sturdy atheist as decisively as it does those of the Methodist under
> conviction anxious about his soul. (VRE, 20)

In short, and mind-cure therapies aside, there isn't much of a case for reading
the deep unconscious into James or denying his fidelity to the cerebralist outlook of *The Principles*.

Esse Est Sentiri

I have argued that James's skepticism about mind dust is justified, and so too
his adherence to the idea that consciousness is essential to the mental. But

Gerald Myers has pointed out that James had a change of heart on the compounding of consciousness and thereby on the *esse est sentiri* doctrine about states of consciousness. I am going to offer an interpretation which minimizes this change of heart, partly because I do not accept Myers's reason for making much of it. He seems to be supposing that unless mental states compound themselves in just the way that, say, chemicals and other physical things compound, James must be committed to a "Cartesian" conception of mental states, despite his having become "increasingly doubtful about a philosophical opposition of consciousness to everything physical" (Myers 1986, 61). But there is no such dilemma. In Searle's view, for instance, mental states have a subjective "first-person ontology," such that the person who has the mental state in question has access to it which no one else has. In contrast, chemicals and brain particles have an objective "third-person ontology," being equally accessible in principle to any observer. Still, as system features of the whole brain, mental states are physical states, albeit physical states with a first-person ontology.

So James isn't facing a dilemma between endorsing Cartesianism, on one hand, or giving up *esse est sentiri* and his opposition to mind dust, on the other hand. He could reply that they are simply "different" from other physical states in these respects. Since the difference between the mental and the physical is the most fundamental tenet of his methodologically dualist psychology, without which his project of seeking psychophysical correlation laws does not even make sense, this reply would help do the crucial work of establishing what that difference is.

Myers thinks that James must have viewed consciousness as an entity in *The Principles* because of the questions he raised about whether it was composed of parts or not. Even though he broke with the tradition that consciousness must be composed of parts, the very idea that "it" is not composed of parts shows that he viewed consciousness as an entity. But in my reading of "Does 'Consciousness' Exist?" where he denies that consciousness is an entity, I take him to be asking whether there is anything about consciousness that stands in the way of a radical empiricist reduction of consciousness to pure experience. This is not best understood as an issue about whether consciousness has parts; after all, James's world of pure experience has a plurality of "parts."

Besides rejecting Myers's reason for emphasizing the change of heart, I want to suggest that the footnote about lemonade that is at issue here should be viewed as a somewhat unfortunately fashioned defense of his position on compounding, rather than being vital to it. Here is how the footnote from *The Prin-ciples* reads, in part:

> I find in my students an almost invincible tendency to think that we can immedi-ately perceive that feelings do combine. "What!" they say, "is not the taste of lem-onade composed of that of lemon *plus* that of sugar?" This is taking the combin-ing of objects for that of feelings. The physical lemonade contains both the lemon and the sugar, but its taste does not contain their tastes; for if there are any two things which are certainly *not* present in the taste of lemonade, those are the lemon-sour on the one hand and the sugar-sweet on the other. These tastes are absent utterly. (PP, 160)

And here is the change of heart:

> In a glass of lemonade we can taste both the lemon and sugar at once. In a major chord our ear can single out the c, e, g, and c′, if it has once become acquainted with these notes apart. And so on through the whole field of our experience, whether conceptual or sensible. . . . The sour and sweet in lemonade are extremely unlike the sour and sweet of lemon juice and sugar, taken singly, yet like enough for us to "recognize" these "objects" in the compound taste. (EPH, 71–72, 87 fn)

What James should have said here is that we can learn how to *partition* our experiences, instead of suggesting that what we learn to partition was already there in the less-sophisticated experiences. (His reluctance about this sugges-tion is evident in his use of scare-quotes around "recognize" and "objects.") The "objects" that the lemonade connoisseur discriminates are high-level achievements, not building blocks of even the most naive lemonade-tasting. A musical person's ear has been educated to articulate the experience of a sym-phony, bringing into existence "objects" that were not there during earlier, less-nuanced listenings. Consequently, these "objects" are quite different from mind dust such as the unfelt sensations that figure in Fick's speculations, which are allegedly there whether they are experienced or not; and consequently James's later acknowledgement of sophisticated articulation of experience doesn't sub-vert his earlier critique of the mind dust theory.

Myers points out that James's uncompromising stance on the unconscious in Chapter 6 of *The Principles*, "The Mind-Dust Theory," gets modified later on in the book. But as Myers himself notes, the modification differs sharply from the Freudian concept of the unconscious. He distinguishes two ways in which James thought mental or subjective states can occur unconsciously. First, we can be unconscious of experiences when we fail to attend to them. "Our insensibility to habitual noises, etc., whilst awake, proves that we can neglect to attend to that which we nevertheless feel," Myers quotes James as writing later in *The Principles*. But this is only shallow unconsciousness; it is just the doctrine of the fringe. In fact Myers interprets such episodes in a manner that is fully consistent with the Connection Principle: "Being felt insures that it [the mental event] is a mental or psychic event and not merely a physiological occurrence not yet translated to the psychological level. However, we may insist that if something is felt then it must, if only minimally, register in consciousness. James agreed. But for all practical purposes, it is ignored by one's conscious attention to such an extent that it is virtually unconscious" (Myers 1986, 59). On this account, I take it, one's believing-while-sleeping that the Earth is not flat has not yet "translated to the psychological level." It is a physiological process of a particular kind, namely, the kind that is liable to such a translation, as in coming to be aware that one disbelieves the Earth is flat.

Myers's second way concerns the abnormal psychology of hysterical blindness, for example, in which "the patient sees at an unconscious level what he cannot see consciously" (Myers 1986, 59). James writes of such cases: "Binet has found the hand of his patients unconsciously writing down words which their eyes were vainly endeavoring to 'see,' i.e., to bring to the upper consciousness. Their submerged consciousness was of course of seeing them, or the hand could not have written as it did. Colors are similarly perceived by the subconscious self, which the hysterically color-blind eyes cannot bring to the normal consciousness" (PP, 206). Such cases are notoriously difficult to describe, and it is not clear to me that talking about "the unconscious level" is the best way to do so. But the important point at present is this: the so-called unconscious level, for James, is in fact the locus of *a secondary self*, and this secondary self *is conscious* of what the primary self fails to see: "These selves are for the most part very stupid and contracted, and are cut off at ordinary times from communication with the regular and normal self of the individual; but still they form conscious unities, have continuous memories, speak, write, invent distinct names for themselves, or adopt names that are suggested; and, in short, are entirely worthy of that title of secondary personalities which is now commonly given them" (PP, 221). So the account of hysterical blindness is a friendly amendment to the earlier dismissal of the unconscious in connection with mind dust and to the *esse est sentiri* principle, as Myers acknowledges in his summary of James's considered position: "Although something may be experienced unconsciously by the primary personality, it must be consciously experienced by someone, a secondary personality in the same body. Cases of multiple personalities or splittings of consciousness associated with a single human body do in fact occur, but nothing that is experienced can fail to be noticed by at least one consciousness. No mental state can occur that is not in some consciousness; nothing can be experienced at an unconscious level that does not register in the consciousness of someone else" (Myers 1986, 60). This is very different from the Freudian unconscious, in which mental states perdure without consciousness, and very different from the "cognitively impenetrable mental modules," such as the module for semantic interpretation of auditory information, of which cognitive psychologists sometimes speak, which modules bear intentional content ("mean" things) although the subject has no consciousness of their doing so. A *fortiori* the James-Searle view stands opposed to Colin McGinn's mysterianism or transcendental naturalism, according to which the essence of consciousness is cognitively closed to the human mind, period.

Conclusion

There is every reason to suppose that a broadly Jamesian psychology is a live option for scientific research, a program which accepts the empirically irreducible reality of conscious mental life and studies its relationship to biology, a program that Searle calls for with his "biological naturalism" and that Edelman is realizing with his "neural Darwinism." As for Leahey's assessment of James's influence, as being absolutely fatal to mentalistic psychology, it is valid only if mentalistic psychology is understood as a psychology of the unconscious, and as I have at least suggested here, the demise of such psychology might be a good thing. If mentalistic psychology is understood as psychology that accepts the reality of mental life and understands it as essentially conscious, then such a psychology has no better friend than James.

5

The Self:
Its Freedom and Unity

Self, God, and Mysticism

The self, God, and mystical experience are all challenges to James's radical empiricism. In the next few chapters I make the case that the self and God may be analyzed as constructs out of pure experience and that the mystical can be understood in pure-experiential terms as well. However, we will observe that James's Two-Levels View is tolerant of "overbeliefs" about these matters, at least up to a point, the point namely where these beliefs become philosophically sophisticated and insist that they refer to something that has more than the referent's experiential "cash value." In the next chapter I make my case for a pure-experiential account of the self, drawing a distinction between an empirical self and a metaphysical self, and theorizing the latter in pure-experiential terms while keeping open the possibility of free will in James's sense, the sense that I interpreted in Chapter 3 as consistent with the requirement that mental events should have cerebral correspondents as simultaneous nomic equivalents. As for James's God, I interpret it as a pattern we can find in experience, when we adopt a certain stance toward it. And as for mystical experience, its philosophical cash value is twofold. It is a particularly intense way in which one may adopt the just-mentioned stance, and also it is a stripping-away of the conceptualization that usually attends experience.

Myers's Mystery

James's constructivism about the universe is threatened by the self and by God, both of them often taken to be transcendent to a world of pure experience, the self because it is thought to be an unchanging thing that has experiences, God because it is beyond the world of experience; the self is underneath experience, so to speak, and God above it. Here I want to explore James's thinking about the self with a view to demonstrating its harmony with a world of pure experience. When this is done, I turn to God. In both treatments there is a constructivist element; both are patterns of pure experience. The passing Thought constructs the self through appropriating other experiences to it, without the need for a metaphysically ulterior witness to this transaction, such as a transcendental ego:

> In contradistinction to this conception [of an ulterior witness], I believe that we describe the facts much better by saying that experiences in their totality are reported *to one another*. The present experience is the only witness we need to suppose of the past one, the future experience the only witness we need to suppose of the present one. If we look at our experiences with the simple aim of describing their succession, we see that they form a stream which in important respects possesses the quality of continuity. . . . An experience is not intrinsically conscious; but another experience beyond it is conscious of it, in the sense of growing out of it and keeping retrospective hold of it. (MEN, 29)

As I will discuss in the next chapter, God too has no need for anything ulterior to experience: God is a discernible pattern of purpose, of good if not omnipotent purpose, in the history of the world. The Two-Levels View is crucial for understanding both topics. The self and God can take on many dimensions at the empirical level. This is attested to by the variety of things that people make constitutive of their personal identity, and by the variety of the world's religions. But the metaphysical cash value of these variegated empirical selves is tendered in the coin of pure experience.

I focus my discussion by offering a solution to a mystery about William James's theory of the self. Among the many students of James who have been mystified is Gerald Myers, who expresses surprise in *William James: His Life and Thought* that, given the religious and mystical overtones of his later metaphysics, James did not abandon the apparent bodily self of the earlier *The Principles of Psychology* for a "non-bodily, spiritual, and mysterious referent for the first-person pronoun" (Myers 1986, 352). Such a shift would reflect the difference between the naturalistic account of the self in *The Principles* and the confession in *The Varieties of Religious Experience* that "If one should make a division of all thinkers into naturalists and supernaturalists, I should undoubtedly have to go, along with most philosophers, into the supernaturalist branch" (PP, 392).

How could James the supernaturalist endorse the earlier James's view that the innermost self, the self of selves celebrated both by religious tradition and common sense, consists of "peculiar motions in the head or between the head and throat"? Instead of declaring a sharp break with the cephalic self of *The Principles*, James adhered, as Myers observes, "to his claims that the body is at the center of any experience of self, that nothing non-bodily shows itself definitely to introspection, and that nothing about using *I* makes a mystery of the self" (Myers 1986, 352).

The same problem can be raised by emphasizing passages in *The Principles* where James seems to veer toward supernaturalism about the self rather than reduction to the body, calling it a spiritual force, passages that Richard Gale reads as committing James to an "immaterial, nonnatural self, which is not a denizen of the natural spatio-temporal order that science describes and explains, but instead a transcendental being or force from James's 'fourth dimension' that brings about effects in this order" (Gale 1999, 76).

The interpretive problem is particularly deep in that James avowed the coherence of *The Principles'* treatment of the self with the later metaphysical treatment, such as the material in *Essays in Radical Empiricism*. Arguing in "Does 'Consciousness' Exist?" from the *Essays* that a metaphysics of pure experience should replace the dichotomy between consciousness and the body, James adduces in support his earlier discussion of the self, "In my Psychology I have tried to show that we need no knower other than the 'passing thought.'"

On the other hand, Myers notes, "if telepathy, clairvoyance, and precognition actually occur," as James was disposed to think, "our everyday equation of the self with bodily experience will surely require some revision" (Myers 1986, 352). Then, too, James's religious convictions as expressed in *The Varieties of Religious Experience* would also seem to call for revision of the earlier equation. James wrote there, for instance, that "the visible world is part of a more spiritual universe from which it draws its chief significance" and that "union or harmonious relation with that higher universe is our true end" (VRE, 382). "Yet instead of suggesting how his psychological concept of the self might have shifted during the progression from *The Principles* to the metaphysics of pure experience," Myers comments with a note of puzzlement, "James wrote in his later period that this concept was a natural ally if not the original herald of that metaphysics" (Myers 1986, 352).

How can the bodily self of *The Principles* be the natural ally and original herald of the nonbodily self of *The Essays* and *The Varieties* and other later writings? The question is important not only because it is posed by the author of James's definitive intellectual biography but also because the answer to it helps to locate James more clearly in the history of philosophizing about the self and personal identity and suggests a deep coherence between James's writings in the earlier and later periods. In addition, the answer to Myers's question will reveal James's connections to contemporary theorizing about these matters. It may even be hoped that James's position is the correct way to keep metaphysical possibilities alive while pursuing naturalistic study of the self.

The Two-Levels Analysis of the Self

The problem, then, is to show how the self of *The Principles* could be the natural ally and original herald of the self in the later writings. The key to solving the mystery is a two-levels analysis of James's theorizing about the mind. The Two-Levels View, as introduced in the previous chapter, distinguishes scientific and metaphysical levels of James's system, minimizing contradiction and maximizing plausibility within it by showing how apparently conflicting claims can cohere by limiting their scope to one or the other of the two levels. Interpretations of James that emphasize his naturalistic and Darwinian commitments are scientifically but not metaphysically true, for instance; James was no metaphysical materialist, yet his biology was Darwinian and his psychology a law-seeking one consciously modeled after the natural sciences. Contrarily, the traditional neutral-monist reading of James, that mind and body are different classifications of the same underlying stuff, is metaphysically but not scientifically true; science should accept the appearance that there is no greater difference in the world than that between mind and body, getting on with the task of discovering predictively useful psychophysical correlation laws and setting the stage for a metaphysical critique of the dualism it assumes. And generally, one should resolve apparent contradictions in James's system by apportioning the conflicting propositions to different levels. With reference to the topic at hand, the alleged "equation" of the self with bodily experiences in *The Principles* falls just short of an equation, in such a way that there is theoretical room for claims about the self's metaphysical dimension. Waiving radical empiricist strictures, this dimension might introduce a transexperiential entity of some sort; when those strictures are imposed, it should be assumed that the self is a construct out of pure experience, although the construct might have a "shape" that is surprising to the human being who is its vehicle. The Jamesian Two-levels theorist will be tolerant of *overbeliefs* about the self, and he will also be tolerant about overbeliefs concerning God, as I will note in the next chapter, as long as the overbeliefs are understood at the empirical level as revelatory of the natural history of thinking about personhood, rather than being construed at the metaphysical level, where they will be trumped by a radical empiricist construction of self and God.

The Self in *The Principles*

The Two-Levels View does not rescue *The Principles'* treatment of the self in the manner of a *deus ex machina*, but rather it is a natural systematization of the outlook of *The Principles*, in particular Chapter 10, "The Consciousness of Self." That chapter includes a sharp attack on the traditional conception of personal identity as requiring an unchanging entity, as well as an alternative account of the sense of self which posits nothing but the continuously changing contents of the stream of thought. James begins there by defining the self as the sum total of all that a person can call his or hers, and divides the self into the material self (e.g., body, clothes), the social self (recognition from others), the spiritual self ("the most enduring and intimate part of the self" [PP, 283]), and the pure ego. This latter turns out to be an illusion of the common man, elevated into a philosophy by theories such as Descartes' and Kant's. James attempts to debunk the illusion by showing that the body is the real object behind notions of a pure ego. Speaking of the emotions of self-satisfaction and self-abasement, for example, he notes: "Each has its own peculiar physiognomical expression. In self-satisfaction the extensor muscles are innervated, the eye is strong and glorious, the gait rolling and elastic, the nostril dilated, and a peculiar smile plays upon the lips" (PP, 307). As for self-seeking and self-preservation, "that self for which I feel such hot regard" is not some abstract numerical principle of identity but primarily the body: "The most palpable selfishness of a man is his bodily selfishness; and his most palpable self is the body to which that selfishness relates. Now I say that he identifies himself with this body because he loves it, and that he does not love it because he finds it to be identified with himself" (PP, 319–20). The sense of personal identity does not require an "absolute Unity in which all differences are overwhelmed" (PP, 335) but is rather "grounded either on the resemblance in a fundamental respect, or on the continuity before the mind, of the phenomena compared" (PP, 334).

James expresses his agreement with the associationist school of Hume and others, who "all describe the Self as an aggregate of which each part, as to its being, is a separate fact" (PP, 336); an empirical and verifiable self as austere as that, he is saying, is all that the data require psychology to recognize. James adds, however, that "in leaving the matter here, and saying that this sum of passing things is all," Hume has "neglected certain more subtle aspects of the Unity of Consciousness" (PP, 336). He offers an account of how these separate facts are "rounded up" by the present judging Thought, relying on a colorful simile to a herd of cattle upon which a herdsman puts his brand: "The passing Thought then seems to be the Thinker," and anything that accompanies the act of thinking, which some might suppose to be a manifestation of a non-physical principle of personal identity, turns out to be, in James's introspective analysis, central adjustments in the head (PP, 341).

James next steps up his attack on the pure ego, rejecting "the substantialist view of the soul" as having no explanatory value, for theorists who rely on it "do not deduce any of the properties of the mental life from otherwise known properties of the soul. They simply find various characters ready-made in the mental life, and these they clap into the Soul, saying, 'Lo! behold the source from whence they flow!'"(PP, 347). Explanatory simplicity favors elimination of the soul, at least elimination from the body of scientific theory: "But when . . . we take the two formulations, first of a brain to whose processes pulses of thought simply correspond, and second, of one to whose processes pulses of thought in a Soul correspond, and compare them together, we see that at bottom the second formulation is only a more roundabout way than the first, of expressing the same bald fact. That bald fact is that when the brain acts, a thought occurs" (PP, 327). And as for the transcendentalist or Kantian notion of the ego, James's severe judgment is that it "is only Substantialism grown shame-faced [and] a 'cheap and nasty' edition of the [Cartesian] soul" (PP, 365). Condemning Kant for failing to stop with the present Thought as the ultimate fact for psychology, James likens the Kantian mind to an "elaborate internal machine-shop" and finds "something almost shocking in the notion of so chaste a function [as thought] carrying this Kantian hurly-burly in her womb" (PP, 363).

Scientific and Metaphysical Levels

The application of the Two-Levels View to the Jamesian self should confirm the former by showing how a coherent and plausible theory of the self emerges when James's remarks are seen in the light of the contrast between the scientific and specifically psychological level, on one hand, and the metaphysical level of analysis on the other. This may have the welcome consequence of permitting interpreters of James to be less reliant on the suggestion that James's writing is pervaded by inconsistencies. Ernest R. Hilgard's commentary in *Psychology In America: A Historical Survey* provides a case in point: "The admirers of James do not take seriously the faults that are found in his system, for there is always so much that is wise and congenial, and his inconsistencies can be tolerated for the value of the rest. It is not surprising, however, that his detailed theories have survived very well, even though he has won a permanent place not only in psychology's past, but in its present. His *The Principles* still remains psychology's great book" (Hilgard 1987, 63).

While taking heed of Hilgard's caution to admirers of James, I find less inconsistency than he in James's remarks about the self, and more coherent theory that has survived very well. I will conclude by drawing some comparisons which suggest that James's theory is alive and well in the form of Robert Nozick's theorizing in this area, including his Closest-Continuer theory of personal identity and the theory of the self's self-synthesis.

What exactly are the faults in James's system that concern Hilgard? He has in mind alleged inconsistencies such as this: "In an early chapter [of *The Principles*] he was not quite sure that he should reject the concept of the soul ("The fact is that one cannot afford to despise any of these traditional objects of belief"). He did reject it, in relation to cognition, however, by introducing the strange doctrine that the only thinker that is required is the passing Thought" (Hilgard 1987, 61). Hilgard's pessimistic diagnosis notwithstanding, any hint of contradiction here can be dissipated by the Two-Levels View. James is saying that it may be possible to make a case for the existence of the soul, for instance as conceived by Descartes, as an overbelief about the self, ultimately to be reduced to its cash value in pure experience; such overbeliefs are an important fact about the history of reflection about the self, to be given their due in the full empirical-level view of the self, just as James enjoins the philosopher in *The Principles* to take into account the "many worlds," including supernatural and pathological ones, while holding that they all bottom out in what he called objective sensation, what would become pure experience when he came to write *Essays in Radical Empiricism.*

However, for scientific purposes overbeliefs such as Cartesian speculations are superfluous, since the passing Thought can account for every empirical, verifiable aspect of personhood and personal identity. This is a perfectly consistent line of thought, while Hilgard's concern is properly diagnosed as a failure to apply a two-levels analysis to the passage he quotes. James makes the diagnosis himself, nearly enough, when he says that "our reasonings have not established the non-existence of the Soul; they have only proved its superfluity for scientific purposes" (Hilgard 1987, 331). And the two-levels structure is implied by James's qualifying the admission that the soul may exist by adding:

> So, in the present instance, we ought certainly to admit that there is more than the bare fact of coexistence of a passing thought with a passing brain-state. But we do not answer the question "What is that more?" when we say that it is a "Soul" which the brain-state affects. This kind of more explains nothing; and when we are once trying metaphysical explanations we are foolish not to go as far as we can. For my own part I confess that the moment I become metaphysical and try to define the more, I find the notion of some sort of an *anima mundi* thinking in all of us to be a more promising hypothesis, in spite of all its difficulties, than that of a lot of absolutely individual souls. (PP, 328)

An instrumentalist about scientific theory, James expects a proposition to pay its own way in the coin of prediction, verification, and control at the scientific level, and references to the soul fail to pay their way, he concludes. It is from this perspective that James judges that Kant's transcendental ego, for instance, is "simply nothing." It is explanatorily and predictively impotent. At the metaphysical level on the other hand a proposition's function is to make as much sense as possible of one's experience and the human condition generally. Kantian or Cartesian claims about the soul must be freshly examined by this metaphysical standard, to which James is implicitly appealing in the quoted passage. The unity amongst us afforded by the world-soul's "thinking in all of us" is more satisfactory, James proposes, than the stubborn isolation from each other implied by other notions of the soul. James tentatively explores this possibility in *The Varieties*, where he entertains the idea that God is not an infinite being but "something larger" than us. The "something larger" God "need not be infinite, it need not be solitary. It might conceivably even be only a larger and more godlike self, of which the present self would then be but the mutilated expression, and the universe might conceivably be a collection of such selves, of different degrees of inclusiveness, with no absolute unity realized in it at all. Thus would a sort of polytheism return upon us—a polytheism which I do not on this occasion defend" (VRE, 413). James's polytheism will seem preposterous if measured by the instrumental standard of science, but not necessarily so if it is related to its proper metaphysical domain, where a sentence's truth conditions relate not to predictive power but to its capacity to make satisfying sense of things.

In emphasizing this difference in truth conditions between scientific and metaphysical propositions, I am following Ayer's interpretation of James's pragmatic theory of truth (Ayer 1968, 186–209). True beliefs are those that "work," according to James, "but they work in different ways," as Ayer observes, different types of proposition having different functions in our total system of beliefs:

> The equation of true beliefs with those that work is intended to apply to beliefs of every kind. What he [James] should have made much clearer than he does is that true beliefs are not treated by him as being all of a pattern. They all work, but they work in different ways. The criteria by which we have to assess a belief which related to a matter of empirical fact are different from those which apply to a belief which is concerned only with relations between ideas: and these are different again from the criteria which apply to beliefs whose function is to satisfy our moral and emotional requirements. These distinctions are implicit in James's writing, but he does not draw attention to them. In my view, it is his failure to set them out explicitly that has been mainly responsible for the extent to which his position has been misunderstood. In particular, the notion that a belief is to be accounted true if it gives one satisfaction to hold it is applied by him only to beliefs of the third class, and to them only with reservations. It has, however, been almost universally assumed by James's critics that he puts this forward unconditionally as a general criterion of truth. (Ayer 1968, 191)

This interpretation contrasts with Gale's, which stipulates that beliefs work when they maximize desire-satisfaction. Scientific propositions work by being reliable instruments for prediction of sensory experience, and metaphysical and religious propositions work by satisfying our emotional needs.

James's Shoehorn

Hilgard objects that there is a contradiction between Chapter 9 of *The Principles*, "The Stream of Thought," and Chapter 10, "The Consciousness of Self." The former "assigned a place for a personal self as adding something to the thought as the thinker" (Hilgard 1987, 61), whereas the latter dispenses with any sort of soul substance in favor of the passing Thought. Noting that thoughts in James's sense come as something personal, as *my thoughts*, Hilgard quotes James as though to clinch the point that there is a contradiction between the two chapters: "On these terms the personal self rather than the thought might be treated as the immediate datum of psychology. . . . No psychology, at any rate, can question the existence of personal selves. The worst psychology can do is to interpret the nature of these selves as to rob them of their worth" (Hilgard 1987, 64). If that is so, if the personal self rather than the thought is psychology's fundamental datum, Hilgard is asking, how can James also say that the passing Thought is the only thinker? The answer to Hilgard's question is that the relevant passing Thought must be specified as my thought or your thought. The quoted passage belongs to a discussion of the isolation of personal minds from each other, about which James observes that "everyone will recognize this to be true, so long as the existence of something corresponding to the term 'personal mind' is all that is insisted on, without any particular view of its nature being implied" (PP, 226). So for all the quoted passage says, the something corresponding to the term "personal mind" could be identified by what Hilgard calls the strange doctrine that the judging Thought is the only thinker that psychology needs to recognize, as long as it is added that the judging Thought contains the sense of personal possession, of being my thought. One of James's contemporaries objected to this addition, saying James had made the Cartesian blunder of personifying the stream of consciousness. James replied: "[I]t could only be a blunder if the notion of personality meant something essentially different from anything to be found in the mental procession. But if that procession be itself the very 'original' of the notion of personality, to personify it cannot possibly be wrong. It is already personified" (PP, 226–27). Personification must be distinguished from privacy. The privacy of personal consciousness is a deep fact but not a logically required feature of consciousness:

> The definitively closed nature of our personal consciousness is probably an average statistical resultant of many conditions, but not an elementary force or fact; so that, if one wishes to preserve the Soul, the less he draws his arguments from that quarter the better. So long as our self, on the whole, makes itself good and practically maintains itself as a closed individual, why, as Lotze says, is not that enough? And why is the being-an-individual in some inaccessible metaphysical way so much prouder an achievement? (PP, 350)

James is helping himself to an instant solution to the problem of transverse identity (identity-at-a-time), as opposed to longitudinal identity-through-time. There is no need to show how the various mental elements come together at a given time to become my consciousness, because they natively, primitively belong to my consciousness. This personifies the stream of consciousness, but it does not "entify" a person as an entity in or behind the stream of consciousness. This is an application of what I dub James's Shoehorn; the self, or rather a sense of selfhood, is shoehorned into the immediately introspectable thought. Accepting Hume's critique of the self, James shoehorns the sense of selfhood into thoughts in order to make less of a break with appearances than Hume, while nonetheless following Hume in denying the independent existence of the self.

The Spiritual Self

Consider a third and final objection from Hilgard. As noted earlier, James has a conception of the empirical self as having three components, a material self, a social self, and a spiritual self. His discussion of the material self, for instance, expands on the old joke that the human person is composed of three parts — soul, body, and clothes; and it ventures the speculation that "there are few of us who, if asked to choose between having a beautiful body clad in raiment perpetually shabby and unclean, and having an ugly and blemished form always spotlessly attired, would not hesitate a moment before making a decisive reply" (PP, 292). Then there is "a man's Social Self," as James says with unthinking nineteenth-century sexism; this self is "the recognition which he gets from his mates," for "we have an innate propensity to get ourselves noticed, and noticed favorably, by our kind" (PP, 293). Finally there is the spiritual self, which is "felt by all men as a sort of innermost center within the circle, a sanctuary within the citadel, constituted by the subjective life as a whole" (PP, 297). Hilgard is puzzled by how "this palpitating inward life" can turn out to be nothing more than a collection of cephalic motions, as James suggests in the following passage: "In a sense, then, it may be truly said that, in one person at least, the 'Self of selves,' when carefully examined, is found to consist mainly of the collection of these peculiar motions in the head or between the head and throat" (PP, 298). This hypothesis works well with James's view that a human being is, from an outward point of view, a reflex physiological mechanism. It challenges the perennial idea that we are inwardly aware of something spiritual which is in principle inaccessible to nonintrospective empirical observation. The nuclear part of the self, as he notes, "would be a collection of activities physiologically in no essential way different from" overt acts, and the self's activities "would obey the reflex type," being the result of sensorial and ideational processes discharging either into each other within the brain or into muscles and other parts. But Hilgard reasonably asks, "What has become of the palpitating inward life that James had made the basis for describing the spiritual self as empirically experienced?" (Hilgard 1987, 50). And what has become of the active, welcoming and rejecting, presiding agency which James associates with the spiritual self? James invites such questions in passages like this one:

> Probably all men would describe it [the Spiritual Self] in much the same way up to a certain point. They would call it the active element in all consciousness; saying that whatever qualities a man's feelings may possess, or whatever content his thought may include, there is a spiritual something in him which seems to go out to meet these qualities and contents, whilst they seem to come in to be received by it. It is what welcomes or rejects. It presides over the perception of sensations, and by giving or withholding its assent it influences the movements they tend to arouse. (PP, 298)

James solves this puzzle in two steps. First, he offers a partial physicalistic reduction of the spiritual self, identifying it with brain movements rather than with something nonphysical, as common sense and Cartesian theory are inclined to do. He supposes that a physicalistic reduction of the spiritual self could go sufficiently far to discredit references to mental ego substance in empirical psychology, and far enough indeed to imply that all we are introspectively aware of in awareness of our spiritual selves is a collection of motions in the brain. That the physicalistic reduction can go quite far is suggested by such remarks as, "whenever my introspective glance succeeds in turning around quickly enough to catch one of the manifestations of spontaneity in the act, all it can ever feel distinctly is some bodily process, for the most part taking place within the head" (PP, 300). However, and this is the second step, he leaves it a live option that the spiritual self represents something more than cephalic motions, namely, an original force in the stream of thought which intervenes in the physiological mechanism, making for a more robust freedom than can be conjoined with reflex physiological mechanism. Let me distinguish three forms that this intervention might take. First, there is the free-floater form, in which the will has no physical correlate and is caused by no antecedent physical event; I argued in Chapter 3 that James's considered view, or the view that makes the best sense of his theory of mind, is that free-floaters don't exist. Second, there is the will with its physical correspondent, its simultaneous nomic equivalent, and no antecedent physical event standing to its correspondent as cause to effect. Will which is an original force in this sense is an exception to his view of the body as a reflex mechanism, but I believe it is an exception he was willing to make. Third, there is the will which is consistent with reflex mechanism, but in which the brain is serving as a medium of filtration for the influence of some form of teleology, as James speculated in *The Principles* (PP, 21). A proponent of "the mechanical philosophy" could adopt a stance toward the body as nothing more than a reflex mechanism, but someone who saw purpose in the world could see mental states, in their simultaneous nomic equivalence with cerebral states, as expressions of "the life of souls as it is in all its fullness."

The Original Force

The second step is very clearly taken in James's chapter on attention, immediately following the one on the self. There he asks whether voluntary attention is a resultant or a force—whether we are pure effects or causes:

> When we reflect that the turnings of our attention form the nucleus of our inner self . . . we must admit that the question whether attention involve such a prin-

ciple of spiritual activity or not is metaphysical as well as psychological, and is
well worthy of all the pains we can bestow on its solution. It is in fact the pivotal
question of metaphysics, the very hinge on which our picture of the world shall
swing from materialism, fatalism, monism, towards spiritualism, freedom, pluralism, — or else the other way. (PP, 447–48)

James concludes that the two theories of attention—the effect theory, which
thinks of attention as an epiphenomenon of brain processes, and the cause
theory, which thinks of it as an "original psychic force"—are equally congruent
with the empirical facts. However, he adds that our pretheoretical commitment to the cause theory is responsible for "our sense that in it things are really
being decided from one moment to another, and that it is not the dull rattling
off of a chain that was forged innumerable ages ago" (PP, 453). This sense could
be an illusion, as the effect-theory implies, but one is entitled to resolve the
issue, "incline the beam" as James says, by reference to one's general philosophy. James inclines the beam with ethical reasons for believing in a spiritual
force, confessing this without explanation because these reasons "are hardly
suited for introduction into a psychological work" (PP, 454).

What clinches the reconciliation of James's physicalistic reduction with
his belief in the original psychic force is his distinction between the condition
of an experience and the thing experienced (PP, 304). So the thing experienced in experience of one's spiritual self may be nothing but cephalic motions, and not at all a soul substance, James submits; but the condition of that
experience need not be a brain process, as the effect theory would have it, but
may be what the cause-theory says it is: an original psychic force. This original
force would be responsible for initiating James's disappointed introspective
searches for a Cartesian soul substance, for example, which yielded instead
only cephalic motions. The conclusion should not be drawn that the spiritual
self is entirely physical. Rather, it should be concluded that we do not know
what more there is to it, if anything, and cannot know the "something more"
without leaving scientific psychology behind. The importance of separating
these two possible conclusions becomes apparent in solving Myers's mystery.
That mystery is generated by accepting the first conclusion without qualification, as in Myers's judging that "for James the self seemed to be a collection of
movements in the head" (Myers 1986, 347). This judgment yields an exclu-

sively bodily self, which would be unfit for service in the metaphysical and religious roles James later created for it.

So it would indeed be a mystery that James should have thought those later roles to be quite compatible with the earlier claims about the self. The Two-Levels View solves the mystery by stopping short of equating the self with something bodily, holding instead that James creates a theoretical place-holder in his psychology for a description of the self at the metaphysical level, a description which would detail the nature of the original force hypothesized by the cause theory of attention in Chapter 11 of *The Principles*. Compatibility with James's later religious and mystical speculations follows naturally from this view, since there is complete methodological freedom at the metaphysical level to entertain religious and mystical descriptions of the original force. This remains a possibility even if there is no mystery about the self that psychology studies, the empirical, introspectable self. Psychology need not concern itself with Cartesian and Kantian mysteries, for example, because they have no empirical, introspectable content; but there may be more to the self than psychology can study, as the Two-Levels View implies, and this "more" may be mysterious. The body is central to the psychological self, the self as introspected; it is not, and need not be, central to the metaphysical self, the ultimate referent of "I," which may be nonbodily as well as mysterious. Nothing nonbodily is introspected, and that is reason to follow Hume in banishing the Cartesian ego and other nonphysical entities from psychology; but something nonbodily might still be the metaphysical self. James's radical empiricism will declare finally that the minimal metaphysical self is sciousness, the passing Thought construed as a pure-experiential fact. And anything about the metaphysics of the self that goes beyond this is either false metaphysics, or *anima-mundi*-style speculation about a pure-experiential structure that goes beyond the passing Thought and its empirical appropriations.

Use of the word *I* does not commit us to mysterious referents, since there might be nothing more to the self than what can be said at the psychological level. Yet I might be more mysterious than psychology can possibly know, and in saying this I am no misusing the word *I*. The notion of an original force functions as a cipher in *The Principles*, or more precisely as a variable which might take any metaphysical object as its value. This is what makes it a natural ally of metaphysics. As well as admitting metaphysical mysteries as values, it may accept metaphysical austerities such as James's radical empiricist doctrine that neither the mental nor the physical, but rather pure experience, is fundamental to the world. The self might be an item or items of pure experience, perhaps those constituting a particular human perspective that, in normal adult experience, would yield experience of a particular continuing body and a stream of consciousness. So the incredulity of James's contemporary James Ward is misplaced when he says, "I find it hard to believe that the same man has written such opposite and seemingly incompatible statements as some of yours on this topic are to me. . . . I shall some day perhaps play off James the psychologist against James the metaphysician, moralist, and humanist." (Myers, 354–55). If the Two-Levels View is correct, this attitude toward James's writing is bound to be a mistake, overlooking as it does the theoretical interaction between James the psychologist and James the metaphysician.

Empirical and Metaphysical Thinkers

Foreshadowing the doctrine of pure experience, James asserts in *The Principles* that "sciousness" is more basic than consciousness, sciousness being the stream of consciousness as a stream of knowing, "including and contemplating its 'me' and its 'not-me' as objects which work out their drama together, but not yet including or contemplating its own subjective being" (PP, 304). By making the knowing function of the stream of thought a fundamental datum for psychology, as he announced at the outset of *The Principles*, and by construing the knowing function as operating at a more basic level than consciousness, as implied by his distinction between consciousness and sciousness, James is keeping the door open for entry into a metaphysics which will ground both "me" and "not-me"; he is anticipating here the radical empiricism of his later writing. James proposes that the content of associating a thinker with the stream of thought is just the activity of "sciousness" at any given time: the sciousness in question would be the tinker, and the existence of this thinker would be given to us rather as a logical postulate than as that direct inner perception of spiritual activity which we naturally believe ourselves to have. But who the thinker would be, or how many distinct thinkers we ought to suppose in the universe, would all be subjects for an ulterior metaphysical inquiry. I suggest that this proposal commits James to two conceptions of the thinker or spiritual self, corresponding to his two conceptions of attention. The effect theory views the thinker not as a logical postulate but simply as the temporally present stage of the stream of thought; this may be called the empirical thinker, or ET for short.

The cause-theory conception views the thinker as not only the present stream stage but also as an original force motivating the voluntary activity of the ET; this may be called the metaphysical thinker, or MT. By virtue of its second component, the MT is a logical postulate in the sense of the quoted passage: our freedom is not a phenomenological given, a direct inner perception. It is the MT James had in mind when he wrote Bergson, "I send you a little popular lecture of mine on immortality. . . . It may amuse you to see a formulation like your own that the brain is an organ of filtration for spiritual life" (Myers 1986, 354). Clearly the self whose spiritual life is James's topic here is being presented as an original force, not simply an effect of brain activity. It is equally clear, in the light of the two-levels analysis, that there is no contradiction between the claim about filtration and James's position in *The Principles* that one cannot introspect a nonphysical subject of spiritual life and that awareness of the spiritual self turns out to be awareness of motions in the brain, mainly.

Two Conceptions of Self-Synthesis

If James requires the two thinkers, he also requires two conceptions of the self-synthesis he describes in the following passage, in which he is refining his simile of the herd of cattle in order to bring it more into line with the intuition that one doesn't arbitrarily "brand" something as belonging to oneself but rather discovers that it so belongs:

> For how would it be if the Thought, the present judging Thought, instead of being in any way substantially or transcendentally identical with the former owner of the past self, merely inherited his "title," and thus stood as his legal representative now? It would then, if its birth coincided exactly with the death of another owner, find the past self already its own as soon as it found it at all, and the past self would thus never be wild, but always owned, by a title that never lapsed. We can imagine a long succession of herdsmen coming rapidly into possession of the same cattle by transmission of an original title by bequest. May not the "title" of a collective self be passed from one Thought to another in some analogous way? (PP, 339)

As discussed in Chapter 1, James is gesturing here toward a theory of self-synthesis comparable to one of those that Robert Nozick explores in developing his Closest-Continuer theory of personal identity. Nozick tries to account for what he calls reflexive self-awareness—awareness of oneself subjectively, or from the inside—without supposing the existence of a preexisting I. His theory is that there are two ways in which this entity might articulate itself. First, "an agent as doer of the reflexively self-referring act A is postulated," and then its extent in space and time is delineated (Nozick 1984, 88). Second, alternatively, the act A somehow synthesizes an entity around itself, and then the I is that entity. The second conception of self-synthesis is more thoroughgoing, doing without any "doer" of the act A, and Nozick favors it.

But the MT's self-synthesis should be thought of in the first way, as a delineation of empirical contours guided by a postulated or hypothesized transemperical I, James's pure force. So James's empirical "passing Thought" delineates its material, social, and spiritual dimensions in a way that can be construed as self-synthesis in Nozick's second sense. But separate from this delineation, the passing Thought may have a metaphysical dimension as an original force, even if this dimension is impenetrable by introspection, and this metaphysical "I" will be guiding my delineation of the empirical self. The ET's more thoroughgoing self-synthesis on the other hand is a live option for empirical psychology if there is no further story to be told about the self at the metaphysical level. It creates itself totally in the process of acts of delineation by passing Thoughts, which "round up" their material, social, and spiritual constituents so as to make a purely empirical self. It is guided in this delineation not by its anterior metaphysical dimension as an original force, but by brain activity. In either case the delineation takes place, for James, according to the standard of warmth and intimacy: "Each thought, out of a multitude of other thoughts of which it may think, is able to distinguish those which belong to its own Ego from those which do not. The former have a warmth and intimacy about them of which the latter are completely devoid, being merely conceived, in a cold and foreign fashion, and not appearing as blood-relatives, bringing their greetings to us from out of the past" (PP, 331).

The judging Thought—The I in James's sense—fuses the stream of consciousness into a whole, into a person, by virtue of looking backward to past sections of the stream and perceiving in them a "warmth and intimacy" which makes them *mes* in James's sense. ("Hereafter let us use the words *me* and *I* for the empirical person and the judging Thought" [PP, 350]). What produces this warmth and intimacy? Paramountly, there is the possession of the same memories, since "however different the man may be from the youth, both look back on the same childhood, and call it their own" (PP, 351). And generally James appeals to resemblance and continuity, as in the passage quoted above. For the ET the delineation of the warmth-and-intimacy zone, the contour of the person through time, is entirely a matter to be determined by the judgments of warmth and intimacy entertained by the passing Thoughts. The self takes shape after and in consequence of those judgments. Conjoining the ET with the effect conception of attention and voluntary activity, we get the result that the shape of the self is entirely a function of cerebral activity, since the ET's judgments will be effects of cerebral causes. For MT however the thinker is an original force, so it has some "shape"—whether (say) that of a soul-substance, or an anima mundi, or simply a neutral force different on each occasion of its intervention in the mind-body nexus—which must be independent of antecedent cerebral activity, by definition of what James intends by the phrase "original force" and by way of conjoining the MT to the cause theory of attention and voluntariness; however, it may still have a cerebral event as a simultaneous nomic equivalent, as hypothesized in Chapter 3, as opposed to being a "free-floater." Still, the logically postulated MT could perhaps be wildly different from the ET, as would be the case, for instance, if the world spirit were responsible for the original force thinking in each of us, the ET's judgments to the contrary notwithstanding.

Self-Definition and the Closest-Continuer Theory

There is a modest freedom available in James's account of the self which is available to the ET as well as the MT. This is the freedom of having the parameters of one's empirical identity determined by oneself, by what one's judging thought chooses to feel the requisite "warmth and intimacy" toward. So I might identify in this sense with recent stages of the stream of consciousness that are causally continuous with my present state of consciousness but not with earlier ones; myself yesterday would be one of my past *mes*, in James's terminology, but not myself as an infant. ("Myself" in the preceding sentence is used in the ordinary, un-Jamesian way, of course.) But the freedom to appropriate to oneself is much broader than this, as the following passage implies, with its attempt to assign weight to different dimensions of one's identity, anticipating the widely held Closest-Continuer conception of personal identity:

> The *body* is the innermost part of the material me in each of us; and certain parts of the body seem more intimately ours than the rest. The clothes come next. The old saying that the human person is composed of three parts—soul, body, and clothes—is more than a joke. We so appropriate our clothes and identify ourselves with them that there are few of us who, if asked to choose between having a beautiful body clad in raiment perpetually shabby and unclean, and having an ugly and blemished form always spotlessly attired, would not hesitate a moment before making a decisive reply. Next, our immediate family is a part of ourselves. Our father and mother, our wife and babes, are bone of our bone and flesh of our flesh. When they die, a part of our very selves is gone. If they do anything wrong, it is our shame. If they are insulted, our anger flashes forth as readily as if we stood in their place. Our home comes next. Its scenes are part of our life; its aspects awaken the tenderest feelings of affection; and we do not easily forgive the stranger who, in visiting it, finds fault with its arrangements or treats it with contempt. (PP, 280)

In this way my longitudinal identity would be "up to me," even if there are sufficient cerebral conditions for my choices. The same holds true of transverse identity. I might identify now with my clothes or my children, but not with my pineal gland or my reputation. (In a related vein Nozick remarks, "In its self-synthesis, the self incorporates a (partial) metric of closeness; does bodily continuity have greater weight for basketball players than it does for philosophers?" [Nozick 1981, 106].) This freedom is implied by a latent message in the simile of the herd of cattle, the message that the judging Thought is related to the constituents of the self as a herdsman is related to his cattle. The thought's perception of something's warmth and intimacy corresponds to the herdsman's seeing his brand on the cattle. The message comes out when James acknowledges a limitation of his simile. As for the cattle and their herdsman, "They are not his because they are branded; they are branded because they are his" (PP, 320). But it is the opposite for the Thought and its *mes*, the *mes* being mine in James's sense because they are perceived as having warmth and intimacy, rather than being perceived as having this quality because they are mine. This Jamesian freedom of self-definition is echoed in contemporary philosophical literature by Nozick in his Closest-Continuer theory of personal identity. In place of

James's notion of perceiving warmth and intimacy, Nozick speaks of selecting and weighting dimensions of closeness:

> I suggest that there is not simply one correct measure of closeness for persons. Each person's own selection and weighting of dimensions enters into determining his own actual identity, not merely into his view of it. . . . Only with selves, reflexively self-referring beings with conceptions of themselves, is the closeness relation fixed in this way. Since their images of what constitutes their identity (partially) fixes which their closest continuer is, such beings partially choose themselves. I have a special authority in fixing who I am—it is my view of closeness that (partially) specifies my identity. (Nozick 1981, 50)

The Closest-Continuer theory may be welcomed as an evolutionary branch of a Jamesian trunk. It even accommodates James's tolerance for metaphysical possibilities like the *anima mundi* thinking in all of us. Although we may not view the world soul as our closest continuer, it may view us, collectively, as its closest predecessor. Although the MT can have parameters quite different from the ET, as has been noted, it is also possible that they should be the same, except of course that the MT's choices would not be cerebrally determined, as they would be free original forces. There would be no further story to be told, however, at the metaphysical level of description. The sense of one's choices as free would be entirely justified but incapable of further explanation, whether empirical or metaphysical. This negative characterization of the MT would easily fit within the limitations of the radical empiricist tenet that nothing exists in the final analysis other than pure experience.

If interpreting James in the light of the Closest-Continuer theory is correct, then a person's various selves are weighted dimensions of a person's identity, and consequently Richard Gale's criticism is misplaced when he writes: "The reconciliation among the different selves and their corresponding different worlds is of a first-I-am-this-sort-of-self-and-then-I-am-that-sort-of-self nature. . . . While this 'taking turns' strategy might work in preventing conflicts in a nursery school between children, all of whom want to use the swing, it does not succeed in enabling each of us to become an integrated self" (Gale 1999, 195). This is part of Gale's critique of James as guilty of Poohbahism, the mistake of "wearing many hats" without regard to coherence among them. But first, when James speaks of one's clothes, family, and home as elements of the empirical self, or as among one's empirical selves, he does not mean that one steps through them in a series. Rather, they each make a contribution to one's personal identity, as the Closest-Continuer theory spells out. And second, although the unity of the self falls short of the unity provided by what James derided as the "soul-pellet theory" of personal identity, namely the Cartesian view, that sort of integration is well worth abandoning, and James deserves credit for being among the first to challenge it and offer an alternative. We do wear many hats, especially in these busy "postmodern" days, and integrating our various roles into our lives in a coherent and honest way can be a chore, but acknowledging various weighted dimensions of personal identity doesn't imply that the chore can't be managed; rather, it reminds us of how complex the task is.[1]

The Active Self

Although James makes common cause with Hume in his attack on the substantial self, it would be a mistake to exaggerate what the New Englander has in common with the Scotsman by following Sir Karl Popper and J. C. Eccles in thinking that James, like Hume, presents an essentially passive model of selfhood. "The self is almost always active," they say. "It is not, as David Hume and William James suggested, the sum total, or the bundle, or the stream of its experiences: this suggests passivity" (Popper and Eccles 1977, 20). Surely James says enough in *The Principles*, especially in the chapters on epiphenomenalism and attention, to dispel any such suggestion. In Chapter 5, "The Automaton-Theory," James characterizes consciousness as a "fighter for ends" which "loads the dice" of the brain so that its inherent instability is overcome in the pursuit of its owner's ends. This is not unlike Popper and Eccles's speaking of "the self and its brain" in order to suggest, as they say, "that the brain is owned by the self, rather than the other way round" (Popper and Eccles 1977, 120). Popper and Eccles go on to compare the relationship between self and brain to that between programmer and computer, writing that "the active, psycho-physical self is the active programmer to the brain (which is the computer), it is the executant whose instrument is the brain." James's analogy of a gambler and his loaded dice speaks just as vigorously of the self's activity as Popper and Eccles's analogy of the programmer and his computer. But the most telling evidence against the passivist reading is James's commitment to the cause theory of attention and the idea of the self as an original force. It is James after all who describes the sense of our will's being an original force as responsible for "the whole sting and excitement of our voluntary life" (PP, 453).

James's Radical-Empiricist Mysticism

James has principled reasons to say very little about the "original force," which are at the same time reasons for saying very little about pure experience generally. The original force is the preconceptual subject of conceptualization, through which each of us constructs his or her empirical self and the physical world, according to the cause theory.

If the predicate "smiths" be the story of Mr. Smith's life, then "There is something x such that x smiths" is as much as one can say without introducing what James would call overbeliefs about x, such as its being a pure-experiential *anima mundi*. This overbelief was congenial to James, keeping close as it does to that of which one is unmediatedly aware. But in the final analysis it attempts to say what cannot be said (but only experienced in mystical states?). As pure experience, x is an object of unmediated awareness. But all conceptualization, even use of austere concepts like *anima mundi*, *original force*, and the like, introduces mediation.

Since one of the themes of this book is the continuing relevance of James's thought, and one of the variations on this theme is that his thought resonates with contemporary philosophical work, I will close by noting the similarities between James's two-levels approach to the self and Colin McGinn's "mysterianism" about it, focusing on the chapter "Secrets of the Self" from his recent *The Mysterious Flame*. He rehearses the myriad of puzzle cases that have been discussed in the literature, such as brain fission and fusion, brain transplants, various teleportation scenarios (*two* copies of Captain Kirk get beamed down by Scotty), radical amnesia, split-brain experiments, and so on:

> The point I am driving at is that we don't know enough about what the self is to resolve these kinds of puzzles. We don't know enough about what *makes* a self exist. And this means that there are facts about selves that we are not grasping. The ancients exhorted us to "Know thyself!" That is all very well as a piece of practical advice about being aware of one's motivations and talents and foibles, but we do not know ourselves in a very fundamental way. According to the central thesis of

this book, this ignorance is not going to be remedied. We are deeply puzzled about the kinds of questions about the self that I have been raising, precisely because we understand to little of what a self is. To answer those questions we would need to know the secrets of the self, but the very existence and intractability of the questions shows how far we are from unearthing those secrets. Maybe, then, we cannot know ourselves, not all the way down. We can know that we exist all right, but we cannot grasp our intrinsic nature.

I suggest that our ignorance here is an ignorance of a hidden architecture of the self. Something about the hidden structure of the self determines its unity and identity, but we do not grasp this hidden structure, which is why we cannot answer questions about unity and identity with any reliability. It is not that we know the essential nature of the self but fail to understand under what physical conditions it exists; rather, we are ignorant of what the self intrinsically is. This is why we tend to picture the self as a kind of extensionless point, an ethereal peg on which mental states can hang. We have no positive substantive conception of what kind of item a self is. We are apt to think of the self simply as what "I" refers to. The thinness of our notion of the self is an indication of how little we grasp about its nature. Of course, we know many properties of selves—biographies are full of such properties; what I am saying is that we don't know what the essential inner nature of the self is. (McGinn 1999, 162–63)

James's Two-Levels View, distinguishing as it does empirical questions about the self from metaphysical ones, requires less emphasis on the "thinness" of our understanding of the self. At the empirical level, James is an early exponent of the Closest-Continuer theory of the self, which yields a rich picture of its empirical nature, though not a *substantive* conception. At the metaphysical level, on the other hand, James acknowledges the possibility of various substantial conceptions of the self, including ones that would vindicate our conception of our free agency in a more profound manner than the empirical self can deliver on its own. James is not so resolutely "mysterian" as McGinn, holding out more hope that the metaphysical truth is not, as McGinn likes to say, "cognitively closed" to beings with mental equipment like ours. One might well find the optimism and open-endedness in the Two-Levels View preferable to rigid mysterianism.

Finally, although the metaphysical level of James's system is large enough to accommodate many suggestions about the nature of the self, his radical empiricism leads him to favor *austere*, pure-experiential conceptions, which are *naturalistic* in that they posit a self that can be experienced but *nonnaturalistic* in that the posited self is not empirical, in the sense that it is the preconceptual source of the conceptual activity of "the human serpent," in particular the activity that takes the form of constructing the various facets of "the empirical self." This distinction, an expression of the Two-Levels View of James's system, should be kept in mind when evaluating Richard Gale's chiding James for playing down his commitment to a metaphysical self, in the following passage:

> James sometimes found it convenient to overlook the nonnaturalistic commitments of his theory of free will, as for example when he made this disclaimer in his 1904 "The Experience of Activity":
>
> > "I have found myself more than once accused in print of being the assertor of a metaphysical principle of activity. Since literary misunderstandings retard the settlement of problems, I should like to say that such an interpretation of the pages I have published on effort and on will is absolutely foreign to what I meant to express. . . . Single clauses in my writing, or sentences read out of their connexion, may possibly have been compatible with a transphenomenal principle of energy; but I defy anyone to show a single sentence which, taken with its context, should be naturally held to advocate such a view." [ERE, 93]
>
> The sentences that I have just quoted from *The Principles of Psychology* on effort as an "original spiritual force, as originating *ex nihilo* [as] . . . from a fourth dimension," more than meet James's challenge. James is not alone in overlooking his nonnaturalistic account of the will in this work. . . . It is almost as if there were a conspiracy among naturalistically inclined historians of American philosophy to remake James in their own image no matter how much of his writings they must overlook. (Gale 1999, 77)

I take it that James's denial of a transphenomenal principle of energy is the same thing as his affirming a pure-experiential self, rather than a more exotically metaphysical, transcendental one. So his challenge does not ignore his nonnaturalistic commitments, if that means his commitment to a world of pure experience rather than the empirical world of mind and body. But James's metaphysics of the self is still the theory of a radical empiricist.

James therefore should not be charged with "going back" on the notion of a spiritual force that he introduced in *The Principles*, as Gale does:

It might be conjectured that the reason for James going back on his earlier "meta-physical" account of the will is that the 1904 paper was his presidential address to the American Psychological Association, and he wanted to impress the "brethren" that he was as tough-minded as they. James was not above playing to his audience like a barnstorming politician. He knew that they thought he was too tender-minded and gullible because of his interest in the paranormal and made a ritual throughout his career of allaying their suspicions by taking an outwardly hard-headed stance to the field. (Gale 1999, 77)

Such psychologizing, quite invidious to James, should be an interpretive last resort, and given the pragmatic solution of distinguishing one sense in which James's metaphysical self is naturalistic (it is a construct out of pure experi-ence) and another in which it is not (it is not reducible to the brain/body), the psychologizing isn't necessary.

6

God: Imminent Purpose

Slipping into Pure Experience

> At last he caught a branch which stopped his fall, and remained clinging to it in misery for hours. But finally his fingers had to lose their hold, and with a despairing farewell to life, he let himself drop. He fell just six inches. If he had given up the struggle earlier, his agony would have been spared. As the mother earth received him, so, the preachers tell us, will the everlasting arms receive us if we confide absolutely in them, and give up the hereditary habit of relying on our personal strength, with its precautions that cannot shelter and safeguards that never save. It is but giving your little private convulsive self a rest, and finding that a greater Self is there. (VRE, 96)

In this passage from *The Varieties of Religious Experience*, James is repeating a revivalist preacher's story about a man who found himself at night slipping down the side of a precipice. I hope to show that this story is especially well suited to James's conception of God. To believe in God is to fall just six inches, neither to earth nor to a transcendent heaven, but into a world of pure experience motivated by good purposes, including the purposes of the good people who participate in shaping the direction of this world, and also including purposes of the world as a whole, which might be called the purposes of God or the *anima mundi*.

I shall assume the continuity and coherence of James's thought in the psychological writings, especially *The Principles of Psychology*; the metaphysical writings, especially *Essays in Radical Empiricism*; and the religious and epistemological writings, especially *The Varieties of Religious Experience* and *Pragmatism*. I believe that this requires that one should give full weight to James's radical empiricist metaphysics, particularly the doctrine of pure experience, which is the medium of construction of mind and body in *The Principles*, and is furthermore, as I shall now try to show, essential for understanding his conception of God.

Otherwise, for example, it is hopeless to show that the superficially materialistic ("cerebralistic") work of James's early psychological period contributes to a philosophical system that, in his later writings, concedes truth to religious claims about a nonphysical God. I follow Marcus Ford in holding that James was a realist about pure experience. This realism doesn't disappear when James embraces pragmatism, and it is nascent in his discussion of sensation in *The Principles*. I will be assuming also that we can at least make sense of the view that the physical world and the stream of consciousness both are constructs out of "sensation," as James expressed it in *The Principles*, or out of "pure experience," as expressed in *Essays*.

There is a school of "ordinary language philosophy" inspired by a certain reading of Wittgenstein which purports to find unintelligible the family of views, including Berkeley's idea-ism and Mach's phenomenalism, to which James's belongs. (But see John Cook's *Wittgenstein's Metaphysics* for a controversial reading of both the early and late Wittgenstein as an empiricist and neutral monist.) Here I follow Ayer in holding that we can make sense out of the view that the world as ordinarily experienced is a construct out of pure experience, even if we finally reject the view as false. Although I simply assume here the pivotal role of James's radical empiricism and the intelligibility of his constructivism about the stream of consciousness and the physical world, I hope to answer the questions raised about James's conception of God in Gerald Myers's biography of James: "As James was the first to acknowledge, his religious notions were vulnerable to many objections. How, for instance, is the concept of consciousness as something preexistent or eternal, as a reservoir or mother-sea with which individual consciousnesses are somehow mingled, consistent with James's denial of consciousness as an entity in his metaphysics of radical empiricism? Is his religion consistent with his metaphysics?" (Myers 1986, 477). I accept Myers's question as a challenge to retrieve as coherent and plausible an interpretation of James's philosophy of religion as is compatible with fidelity to the texts. I do not doubt that there are passages in James's oeuvre which resist my interpretation, but I recommend it as bringing the main ideas into a unified whole. And I shall suggest at the end of this study that James's conception of God has the same sources of plausibility as contemporary philosophies of mind that talk about "the intentional stance" and deny intrinsic intentionality.

God's Place in the Two-Levels View

The philosophy of religion in James's writings such as *The Varieties of Religious Experience* is continuous with the psychology and metaphysics that preceded it in writings such as *The Principles of Psychology* and *Essays in Radical Empiricism*. The following passage from *The Principles* exhibits the general form of James's religion-tolerant scientific positivism:

> Just so we form our decision upon the deepest of all philosophic problems: Is the Kosmos an expression of intelligence rational in its inward nature, or a brute external fact pure and simple? If we find ourselves, in contemplating it, unable to banish the impression that it is a realm of final purposes, that it exists for the sake of something, we place intelligence at the heart of it and have a religion. If, on the contrary, in surveying its irremediable flux, we can think of the present only as so much mere mechanical sprouting from the past, occurring with no reference to the future, we are atheists and materialists. (PP, 21)

James's God, specifically, fits comfortably into what I have called the Two-Levels View in James's system, a view which stipulates a scientific and a metaphysical level of truth. The posits of scientific psychology, for instance, and particularly psychology's fundamental data about the stream of consciousness and correlated physical states, are justified by their instrumental value in predicting and controlling the flow of experience. But human beings have interests which cannot be satisfied simply by this instrumentality, an interest for instance in living meaningful and important lives, raising questions such as "Is there a God?" which get answered at the metaphysical level. What knits this system together is the metaphysical notion of pure experience, which looks in both directions. It is present in psychology, for instance, as sensation logically prior to its conceptualization as "inner" or "outer"; sensation in this sense belongs neither to the stream of consciousness nor to the physical world. And it is present in religious belief as the element of pure experience that grounds every pragmatically meaningful conception of God. This feature of looking in both directions is what justifies James's boast, "You see by this what I meant when I called pragmatism a mediator and reconciler. . . . [I]n the religious field she is at a great advantage both over positivistic empiricism, with its anti-theological bias, and over religious rationalism, with its exclusive interest in the remote, the noble, the simple, and the abstract in the way of conception" (P, 43). The intermediary role of pure experience is also connected to James's fascination with the noetic quality of mystical experience, as in his description of mystical states as "windows through which the mind looks out upon a more extensive and inclusive world," to which he adds, "The supernaturalism and optimism to which they would persuade us may, interpreted in one way or another, be after all the truest of insights into the meaning of this life" (VRE, 339). Mystical states in James's sense are to be understood as achievement of a mode of experience uncolored by the conventional separation of experience into the stream of consciousness or the physical world, permitting an unblinkered view of the metaphysical terrain.

Purposive Structure

James always thought of himself as a philosophical friend of sensation, unlike his idealistic contemporaries and their rationalist predecessors. Whereas they doubted its authority as a guide to knowledge and looked beyond it, he affirmed its authority and explained knowledge by reference to it. This friendship matured into a radical empiricist metaphysics, notably an ontological doctrine of pure experience. The concept of sensation in *The Principles* as neither mental nor physical becomes the centerpiece of James's metaphysics, labeled pure experience in *Essays in Radical Empiricism*. Ultimately the world is not dualistic but monistic; there are no minds and bodies, no streams of consciousness and physical objects, but rather a pluralistic monism of pure experiences in all their variety, in the various stages of organization that give us the experience of a more or less ordered cosmos. We are the agents of this organization, we classifiers. This is a mystery at the heart of James's system, the mystery of how we create ourselves out of pure experience, as opposed to our being spiritual or material substances behind experience.

My present aim is to explore a different but related mystery of God's place in a world of pure experience. The general answer must be that God is the purposive structure of pure experience—that is, the variety of pure experience brought together under a description which reveals it as cooperating in the achievement of a purpose that makes our experience meaningful and important. This is our description, of course, and there is a question about what justifies us in inflicting it upon the cosmos, answered by James's pragmatic conception of meaning and truth. That conception requires not simply that a religious belief should tend to make our lives go better, but also that it should fit without unacceptable dissonance into a larger scheme of belief, much of it tied to experience more directly than the concept of God, and liable to clash with implications of belief in God. This serves as a constraint upon the subjectivity of religious belief, but the subjective element remains and raises the question of whether there is any truth about God which is not relative to the individual's purposes and standards of conceptual harmony.

At this juncture it is important to note that James's pragmatism floats on a bed of realism about pure experience. Although it is "the pragmatistic view that all our theories are instrumental, are mental modes of adaptation to reality, rather than revelations or gnostic answers to some divinely instituted world-enigma," they are precisely modes of adaptation to reality, namely, to pure experience (P, 87). Pure experience in his view was given, although as soon as we try to say something about it we enter the realm of conceptualizations, which must be put to the tests of the pragmatic theory of meaning and truth. For this reason it is probably not possible to have a religion without what James called "overbelief," but it is possible to have a conception of God which keeps overbelief to a minimum, and this will recommend itself to an empiricist philosopher whose metaphysics espouses realism about pure experience and nothing else. I shall be arguing that James was inclined toward a minimal interpretation of the world of pure experience, such that in a distributive sense God is everywhere, in each pure experience, and in a collective sense God is a world soul or *anima mundi* constituted by pure experience.

Dogmatic versus Pragmatic Theology

Pure experience is present in metaphysics as the pragmatic meaning ("cash value") of materialistic or religious claims, such as "the mind is the brain" or "God exists." Cash value and Pragmatic meaning are crucial ideas. I anchor them here with two quotes from James's *Varieties*. According to the first, to track the cash value of God (or truth, etc.) is also to reject as meaningless the alleged noncash remainder:

> The guiding principle of British philosophy has in fact been that every difference must make a difference, every theoretical difference somewhere issue in a practical difference, and that the best method of discussing points of theory is to begin by ascertaining what practical difference would result from one alternative or the other being true. What is the particular truth in question known as? In what facts does it result? What is its cash-value in terms of particular experience? . . . All further ideas about it, such as the oneness or manynesss of the spiritual substance on which it is based, are therefore void of intelligible meaning; and propositions touching such ideas may be indifferently affirmed or denied. (VRE, 350)

And according to this second quote, cash value is to be sought by looking toward sensation:

> To attain perfect clearness in our thoughts of an object, we need then only consider what sensations, immediate or remote, we are conceivably to expect from it, and what conduct we must prepare in case the object should be true. Our conception of these practical consequences is for us the whole of our conception of the object, so far as that conception has positive significance at all. (VRE, 351)

Understanding James's God is, before all else, understanding how pragmatic meaning works in the context of religious belief. Pragmatic meaning may be contrasted with what I shall call dogmatic meaning or, alternately, purported or notional meaning.

For example, the dogmatic meaning of "the Absolute" in transcendental idealism is given in the arcane and voluminous writings of Hegelian philosophers. But its pragmatic meaning, its value for experience in concrete life, is relatively simple and straightforward. It affords religious comfort "to a class of minds," as James writes in *Pragmatism*, and consequently it has just that amount of cash value; it performs, for such minds, the life-enhancing function suited to religious belief. "As a good pragmatist," James concludes, "I myself ought to call the Absolute true 'in so far forth' [as it provides this comfort] then; and I unhesitatingly now do so" (P, 41).

The phrase "true in so far forth" negotiates the difference between dogmatic and pragmatic meaning, which, James strongly insinuates, is an enormous chasm in this case. There are many aspects of the dogmatic meaning of the Absolute that "the ordinary lay-reader in philosophy . . . fails to follow," James writes with uncharacteristic understatement. But the pragmatic meaning is plain enough. Applying the pragmatic method, seeking out "his [the Absolute's] cash value when he is pragmatically interpreted," James concludes that what the believers in the Absolute mean is that, since "in the Absolute finite evil is 'overruled' already, we may, therefore, whenever we wish, treat the temporal as if it were potentially eternal, be sure that we can trust its outcome, and, without sin, dismiss our fear and drop the worry of our finite responsibility. In short, they mean that we have a right ever and anon to take a moral holiday, to let the world wag in its own way, feeling that its issues are in better hands than ours and are none of our business" (P, 41).

Although the lay reader in philosophy can use the Absolute for moral holidays, and can find it precious on this account, James finds it less easy to restrict the notion of the Absolute to its "bare holiday-giving value." He is not able to free it from its "supernumerary features," the ones that have no cash value. "And these it is that clash so" (P, 43).Belief in the Absolute fails to "run the gauntlet of all [his] other beliefs," clashing with his convictions about logic, evil, and freedom and creativity (P, 43).

About logic, James reminds us that even its principles are feats of human constructivity, and that different constructs are vying for adherents: "[The Absolute] happens to be associated with a kind of logic of which I am the enemy" (P, 43).

About evil, James's empiricism insists that even so august a concept as that of God must conform itself to the coerciveness with which some experience bespeaks evil:

> Truly there is something a little ghastly in the satisfaction with which a pure but unreal system will fill a rationalist mind. Leibniz was a rationalist mind, with infinitely more interest in facts than most rationalist minds can show. Yet if you wish for superficiality incarnate, you have only to read that charmingly written "Théodicée" of his, in which he sought to justify the ways of God to man, and to prove that the world we live in is the best of possible worlds. (P, 18)

About freedom and creativity, James ties his meliorism to related ideas about freedom, dignity, and responsibility:

> Does our act then create the world's salvation so far as it makes room for itself, so far as it leaps into the gap? Does it create, not the whole world's salvation of course, but just so much of this as itself covers of the world's extent?

Here I take the bull by the horns, and in spite of the whole crew of rationalists and monists, of whatever brand they be, I ask why not? Our acts, our turning-places, where we seem to ourselves to make ourselves and grow, are the parts of the world to which we are closest, the parts of which our knowledge is the most intimate and complete. Why should we not take them at their face-value? Why may they not be the actual turning-places and growing-places which they seem to be, of the world—why not the workshop of being, where we catch fact in the making, so that nowhere may the world grow in any other kind of way than this? (P, 138)

His disbelief in the Absolute, then, means disbelief in those supernumerary features that are allegedly justified by Hegelian logic. "I personally just give up the Absolute," James writes. "I just take my moral holidays; or else as a professional philosopher, I try to justify them by some other principle." In terms of the pragmatist vocabulary of "The Will to Believe," belief in the Absolute is a dead hypothesis for James:

Let us give the name of hypothesis to anything that may be proposed to our belief; and just as the electricians speak of live and dead wires, let us speak of any hypothesis as either live or dead. A live hypothesis is one which appeals as a real possibility to him to whom it is proposed. . . . Next, let us call the decision between two hypotheses an option. Options may be of several kinds. They may be—1, living or dead; 2, forced or avoidable; 3, momentous or trivial; and for our purposes we may call an option a genuine option when it is of the forced, living and momentous kind. (WB, 14)

For James, the Absolute is not a live option for serving the function of religious belief, that of making deep and satisfying sense of life, though it may be otherwise for others, like the lay reader.

Pragmatic Toleration of Overbelief

Is the lay reader's susceptibility to belief deplorable? Just as the variety of feline, canine, human, and higher forms of experience enhances the purposive structure of pure experience, according to James, so too the variety of religious belief may be presumed to be functional, as James speculates in the following passage:

Or are different functions in the organism of humanity allotted to different types of man, so that some may really be the better for a religion of consolation and reassurance, whilst others are better for one of terror and reproof? It might conceivably be so; and we shall, I think, more and more suspect it to be so as we go on. And if it be so, how can any possible judge or critic help being biased in favor of the religion by which his own needs are best met? He aspires to impartiality; but he is too close to the struggle not to be to some degree a participant, and he is sure to approve most warmly those fruits of piety in others which taste most good and prove most nourishing to him. . . . Expressing myself thus abstractly and briefly, I may seem to despair of the very notion of truth. (VRE, 384)

I want to try to define now a sense in which James might have sustained the notion of truth despite the functional variety of belief that his speculation calls for. Briefly, just as Berkeley had it right in his criticism of material substance as something somehow underneath experience, James will have it right in criticism of God as something somehow over and above experience. "The fact of the bare cohesion [of experience] itself is all that the notion of substance signifies," James writes in *Pragmatism*, emphasizing that "Behind that fact is nothing." By parallel reasoning James will be critical of overbeliefs about God which take the believer beyond experience. This criticism takes its harshest form in connection with what James calls intellectualism.

"The intellectualism in religion which I wish to discredit," James writes in *Varieties*, "assumes to construct religious objects out of the resources of logical reason alone, or of logical reason drawing rigorous inferences from non-subjective facts" (VRE, 342). On the other hand the criticism is muted, and is even transformed into endorsement, when belief in a transcendent God makes life go best. In this case the notion of a transcendent God has pragmatic meaning: belief in a God beyond experience makes experience go best. This points out an asymmetry between Berkeley's critique of matter and James's critique of spirit (including God), namely, the fact that nonintellectualist spiritual beliefs can make life go better, whereas a naturalistic, materialistic world view does not have this potential. As James puts it: "a little cooling down of animal excitability and instinct, a little loss of animal toughness, a little irritable weakness and descent of the pain-threshold, will bring the worm at the core of all our usual springs of delight into full view. . . . [T]he purely naturalistic look at life, however enthusiastically it may begin, is sure to end in sadness. This sadness lies at the heart of every merely positivistic, agnostic, or naturalistic scheme of philosophy" (VRE, 119).

This asymmetry explains why James is more open to religious hypotheses than Berkeley was to materialistic ones. James did not profess certainty that his experiential God was the true God, for he made pragmatic note of the fact that "the most striking practical application to life of the doctrine of objective certitude has been the conscientious labors of the Holy Office of the Inquisition" (WB, 23). Nevertheless he felt that his conception of God was recommended to a tough-minded and enlightened empiricist temperament, on the grounds that it contains the experiential grounding for any and every theology, without the various incompatible "overbeliefs" that they contain:

> But if you are neither tough nor tender in an extreme and radical sense, but mixed as most of us are, it may seem to you that the type of pluralistic and moralistic religion that I have offered is as good a religious synthesis as you are likely to find. Between the two extremes of crude naturalism on the one hand and transcendental absolutism on the other, you may find that what I take the liberty of calling the pragmatistic or melioristic type of theism is exactly what you require. (P, 144)

James's God is, so to speak, the lowest common experiential denominator of all gods. At the same time, his God contains those overbeliefs within Himself, since by James's speculation about the functional character of variety in religious belief, pure experience is best structured so as to include those beliefs; the purpose of the Cosmos's unfolding is best served by this variety:

> The obvious outcome of our total experience is that the world can be handled according to many systems of ideas, and is so handled by different men, and will each time give some characteristic kind of profit, for which he cares, to the handler, while at the same time some other kind of profit has to be omitted or postponed. Science gives to all of us telegraphy, electric lighting, and diagnosis, and succeeds in preventing and curing a certain amount of disease. Religion in the shape of mind-cure gives to some of us serenity, moral poise, and happiness, and prevents certain forms of disease as well as science does, or even better in a certain class of persons. (VRE, 105)

This is not so much subjectivism about God as a sort of "metasubjectivism": God is the temporally unfolding structure of experience that is guided by religious belief.

Analogizing to a Higher Purpose

What counts as a live religious hypothesis for James? Let us be clear that we are thinking for the moment about James the fin-de-siècle cosmopolitan American man who happens to be an empiricist, not James the pragmatist who happened to be writing philosophy at the turn of the century. For the latter, the pragmatist, all pragmatically meaningful hypotheses are live. This James has no preference among religious hypotheses, so long as they have life-affirming pragmatic meaning. On the other hand, James the man, because he is an empiricist philosopher, demands that the gap between dogmatic meaning and pragmatic meaning should be as small as possible. As Quine's forefather, he wants the least possible metaphysical foliage to sully the desert landscape of pure experience. So the ratio of dogmatic meaning to pragmatic meaning will be small. His God will not be transcendent to experience, and consequently his God will not have transcendental resources for denying the reality of evil, for instance.

James's God will not be omnipotent and perfectly good, for this assumption not only clashes with the reality of evil but leaves no role for us to play in deciding the fate of the cosmos. His path to God is not the rationalist's a priori path but the empiricist's a posteriori path, specifically arguments from analogy that suggest we are contributing to a direction in history guided not only by our efforts but by the efforts of beings superior to us in the way that we are superior to dogs and cats: "I firmly disbelieve, myself, that our human experience is the highest form of experience extant in the universe. I believe rather that we stand in much the same relation to the whole of the universe as our canine and feline pets do to the whole of human life" (P, 143). The point of the analogy is not that God is to be found only elsewhere in the universe, but rather that the world of pure experience has a richer, better, and more powerful texture than we could infer on the basis of human, canine, and feline experience alone.

A Pantheistic Theism

So James's God is to be found in two places, yielding one sense in which James is a pantheist and another sense in which he is a theist. God is found both within the landscape of pure experience, in our experience and higher forms of experience as well, and also as the structured landscape of pure experience itself, under a suitably purposive and meaningful description. The purpose and meaning go beyond the bare description of pure experience, for it is possible to see only a material universe unfolding according to mechanical laws, and even with insight into the fundamentality of pure experience it is possible to see only chaos. But for those who are capable of the gestalt switch of seeing the ocean as purposive, and as drawing on its purposive components such as ourselves for achieving larger goals, James's God is a live and momentous option. The meaning and importance introduced by the purposive interpretation of pure experience is the dogmatic meaning of James's philosophy of religion, and it makes a claim to truth by virtue of not clashing with experience, as many dogmatic theologies do, and by virtue of enhancing our experience, making our lives go better.

God is the total world of pure experience understood purposively, as guided by loci of experience that are aiming to create good. In this sense, collectively speaking, James's philosophy of religion is a theism, or a polytheism: "It need not be infinite, it need not be solitary. It might conceivably even be only a larger and more godlike self, of which the present self would then be but the mutilated expression, and the universe might conceivably be a collection of such selves, of different degrees of inclusiveness, with no absolute unity realized in it at all. Thus would a sort of polytheism return upon us—a polytheism which I do not on this occasion defend" (VRE, 413). But distributively speaking, James's God is a pantheism. Pantheism is arrived at as follows: In the sense that I am a human body, each part of my body is me. And in the sense that the world is God, each part of God is God. The evil that we observe in the world is part of the world soul, just as the evil that we experience within ourselves is part of ourselves. And just as we can fight the evil within and become better persons, so too we constituents of the world of experience can make the cosmos unfold in a better way than it would in the absence of our efforts. So the collective notion of God is fundamental. If you see God in the totality, you will see God in the parts. If you see God not in the totality, the world of pure experience will seem a mere plurality. This reasoning makes us witness to James's *via media* between monism and pluralism. We live in a pluralistic universe, but by virtue our ancestors we have unified it (to the extent of their virtue), and perhaps we can unify it further. We can aim at monism, unity, in such a way that "total oneness would appear at the end of things rather than at their origin. In other words the notion of the 'Absolute' would have to be replaced by that of the 'Ultimate'" (P, 72).

A Real God?

I conclude by responding to an important objection to the foregoing, one that leads to a clearer perspective, I think, on what is at stake in James's philosophy of religion. It is objected that there is, in James's account, no genuine purpose in the universe, and accordingly there is no real God whose purpose makes sense of it. There is only a world of pure experience, the objection continues, over which people like James may superimpose a comforting fiction, "God" or the *anima mundi*. The purposes of this Being are merely as-if, like the as-if ascription of intentionality to inanimate objects and forces ("the wind is angry," etc.), whereas our purposes, by contrast, are genuine; not "as-if" but intrinsic. There is a striking similarity between this objection to James and an objection in contemporary philosophy of mind, leveled by realists about intentionality, such as John Searle, against instrumentalists about it, such as Daniel Dennett. (The distinction between realism and instrumentalism is a convenient expository device, but I don't suppose that it would be welcomed by all those whom I would classify as one or the other. Dennett, specifically, has attempted to challenge the classification of his position as a form of instrumentalism [Dennett 1991]).

The parallels are sufficiently illuminating, I feel, that there is value in drawing them out. "The Great Divide" is Dennett's phrase for the issue. Searle holds that "intrinsic intentionality is a phenomenon that humans and certain other animals have as part of their biological nature. It is not a matter of how they are used or how they think of themselves or how they choose to describe themselves" (Searle 1995, 79). But intentionality for Dennett is a function of taking a certain stance toward ourselves, the Intentional Stance, because of the heuristic (especially predictive) power we gain by so doing. As for intrinsic intentionality, Dennett writes, "I have never believed in it and have often argued against it. As Searle has noted, 'Dennett . . . believes that nothing literally has any intrinsic intentional mental states'" (Dennett 1987, 288). Dennett believes that we are artifacts of evolution, and that no artifact has anything but derived intentionality (Dennett 1987, 298). As he explains, "If anything deserves to be called intrinsic intentionality, at least in the sense of being derived from no other, ulterior source, it is Mother Nature, or more exactly natural selection: . . . the intentionality of natural selection deserves the honor. What is particularly satisfying about this is that we end the threatened regress of derivation with something of the right metaphysical sort: a blind and unrepresenting source of our own sightful and insightful powers of representation" (Dennett 1987, 318).

And even this blind and unrepresenting intentionality has a fragile existence, dependent on our needs for a heuristic stance towards a mechanical, nonintentional universe, fully describable in the extensional language of the physical sciences. Pending completion of our mechanical knowledge, we need the intentional characterizations of biology to keep track of what we are trying to explain, and even after we have all our mechanical explanations in place, we will continue to need the intentional level against which to measure the bargains Mother Nature has struck.[1] The objection against James's God can be answered by separating Dennett's instrumentalism from his physicalism, taking the instrumentalism as James's defense against the objection, while replacing Dennett's Mother Nature with James's *anima mundi*, or better by subserving the blind and unrepresenting forces of natural selection to the purposes of God.

Part of the strength of James's philosophy of religion is its willingness to give full value to Darwinian and other naturalistic explanations within their proper domain, while rejecting physicalism (as well as mentalism) in favor of the doctrine of pure experience and the radical empiricist metaphysics it crowns. The crucial aspect of the appropriation of contemporary instrumentalism in James's defense is the idea that the attribution of purpose to God is no more dubious than the attribution of purpose to human beings.

When James's pragmatism is taken into account, his God is a more satisfying ultimate object of belief than a physicalistic metaphysics, even if physicalism of Dennett's sort can do without it for purposes of explaining our intentionality. God is not competing with Mother Nature in this contest, and therefore it is inappropriate to invoke Ockham's razor. James's God is more capable of investing our lives with meaning and importance, and therefore, even if it loses the explanatory contest, it wins the contest to offer a credible life-enhancing metaphysics, one that does not founder by requiring antiscientific premises that are beyond belief for modern minds.

So if one can bring oneself to believe in such a God, in addition to the blind and unrepresenting physical processes that mechanical knowledge provides, it is arguable that only *Schadenfreude*, a delight in the ultimate meaninglessness of our existence, prevents one from so doing. Although I do not pretend to have offered that argument here, it is at least a start to note that James's God does not explain too much too quickly, for his philosophy of religion accepts the limits imposed by the problem of evil rather than purporting to explain it away, and it accepts that the function of religious belief in human life is different from that of belief in what the physical sciences tell us about the world. Religious belief loses to the physical sciences in the predictive contest simply because it does not compete; it has other work to do.

The great divide between proponents and opponents of intrinsic intentionality finds James siding with the opponents. Not only does this make for the most plausible account of James's God, if the foregoing is correct, but it is fully harmonious with James's total philosophical system, particularly with his insistence in *The Principles of Psychology* and elsewhere on the instrumental character of ascriptions of psychological states. In Dennett's parlance, these ascriptions issue from a stance which is ultimately justified, not because it picks out brute intentional facts, but because it has the capacity to serve human needs. In scientific psychology, the intentional stance is justified fundamentally by its capacity to predict and control human behavior, and in religion it is justified by its capacity to invest our lives with as much meaning as is consistent with the credibility of the religious hypothesis and our intellectual integrity in entertaining it.

But the realist replies that God without intrinsic intentionality is no God at all, merely an as-if projection. If belief in God and God's purpose is a matter of taking a stance toward nature, this "God" lacks the degree of intentionality that even animals possess. Whether the instrumentalists are right about the intentional stance, or whether instead their realist critics such as Searle are right in supposing that original intentionality is a stance-independent objective fact, turns out to be the key question for a full assessment of James's God. However this assessment turns out, James's projective conception of God harmonizes perfectly with his doctrine of pure experience and his constructivism; pure experience, I have tried to show, is the medium in which we construct facts about mind, body, self, and God.

7

The Mystical:
Its Role in the Two-Levels View

Poohbahism Redux

I am presenting the view that James's mysticism is fundamental to his philosophical system, both because it is associated with a teleological conception of the world (his God, in effect) and because of its association with the subsymbolic ineffability of pure experience, the medium in which the world is constructed. I do not see his mysticism as a response to the evils of science, nor as an expression of a self that is divided by Promethean pragmatism on one hand and anti-Promethean mysticism on the other hand, so I will take this opportunity to detail the role of mysticism in the Two-Levels View, by contrasting it with Gale's conception, according to which it is a "panacea for the evils of scientifically based bifurcationism," an antidote to the impersonal character of science. Gale quotes James from *Essays in Psychical Research*:

> The only form of thing that we directly encounter . . . is our own personal life. The only complete category of our thinking . . . is the category of personality, every other category being one of the abstract elements of that. And this systematic denial on Science's part of personality as a condition of events, this rigorous belief that in its own essential and innermost nature our world is a strictly impersonal world, may . . . be the very defect that our descendants will be most surprised at in our own boasted Science. (Gale 1999, 221)

Gale interprets this passage by reference to his idea that James is committed to a scientific bifurcation between a real world of atomic microstructure and the remainder, which is illusion and delusion. James's Promethean-pragmatic self exults in the manipulative power of science, while his anti-

Promethean mystical self cherishes values for which science leaves no space. His self is divided, and this particular conflict between the two selves is one of the chief fissures.

A gestalt switch leads however to the two-levels account of these matters: James's Promethean pragmatic self, or, as I prefer to say, James's pragmatism, is prominent at the empirical level, where it guides the human serpent in conceptualizing experience so as to serve its interests. James's mysticism on the other hand is prominent at the metaphysical level, where it explores possibilities left open or underdetermined by empirical facts as well as the "leakage" of metaphysical issues into the empirical world, such as questions about free will that remain unanswered even after science has made its best case that the world operates according to physical mechanisms.

Just as dramatic as the leakage of free will is that of the pure-experiential, subsymbolic "bottom" of physical objects and the stream of thought. Gale puts the point nicely when he writes that "the most fundamental assumption of James's philosophy [is] that the true nature of reality is to be ascertained not through the employment of symbols or concepts but rather through personal experience" (Gale 1999, 221–22). I would prefer to speak of the metaphysical nature of reality in this context, for it is to be contrasted with the empirical world of physical and psychological facts, which, though not ultimate, is no less part of the true nature of reality than the pure-experiential sea on which it floats.

Gale goes on to quote the following passages from *The Varieties of Religious Experience*, underscoring this point on which we agree:

> So long as we deal with the cosmic and the general [as does Science], we deal only with the symbols of reality, but *as soon as we deal with private and personal phenomena as such, we deal with realities in the completest sense of the term*. . . . Individuality is founded in feeling; and the recesses of feeling, the darker, blinder strata of character, are the only places in the world in which we catch real fact in the making, and directly perceive how events happen, and how work is actually done. (Gale 1999, 222, quoting VRE, 393)

We are used to thinking that ultimate explanations come in the form of setting out physical mechanisms mediating the causal relationship between one event and a later one, but such explanations are not ultimate in James's account, and they are compatible with mental and cerebral events being simultaneous nomic equivalents in the sense described in Chapter 3, so that a teleological conception of the mind/brain is a live option, an option that James is taking when he speaks of the recesses of feeling in which we catch real fact in the making. This is nothing more nor less than the cause theory of the will, from *The Principles*, dressed in the emotional tones of the *Varieties*. The will is freely at work in these recesses of feeling, and each of us is privy to it, as we shape ourselves and the world. Our wills are not being determined by antecedent events, nor does their associations with simultaneous nomic equivalents rule out the possibility that the self's teleology rather than mechanism is at play in these equivalencies.

Why should one adopt the gestalt shift that leads from the divided-self interpretation of James's mysticism to the Two-Levels View, given that both organize the textual materials plausibly? I argued in Chapter 1, while criticizing Wilshire's protophenomenological interpretation, that James's comments about science should be read with the science/scientism distinction in mind: science is *separable* from philosophical/ideological projections onto it, no matter how popular these latter may be. I now want to take profit from that discussion by proposing that Gale's conception of the passive anti-Promethean mystic depends too much on viewing the Promethean pragmatist's science as scientism: it is plausible only if, contrary to James's radical-empiricist metaphysics, science is inseparable from a philosophy that interprets the world in exclusively scientific terms, as material and mechanistic. As long as science doesn't collapse into scientism, there is no reason that scientific thinking can't cohabit an integrated personality with the variety of humanistic trains of thought and modes of feeling that James cherished.

With James's mysticism theorized in this way, I turn to a relational analysis, examining now its connection to Wittgenstein's.

Self, Subjectivity, and Privacy

John Cook's *Wittgenstein's Metaphysics* makes a serious case that Wittgenstein, both in his earlier and latter work, assumed a broadly empiricist and neutral-monist outlook that, according to Cook, was much like James's. In Cook's words,

> Wittgenstein, if I am right, never rejected the empiricist metaphysics that forms
> the basis of the *Tractatus*. By 1916 he had embraced that version of empiricism
> that William James called "radical empiricism" and Bertrand Russell later called
> "neutral monism." From that date until his death his fundamental views changed
> very little. In his later writings he did revise the *Tractatus* account of language, but
> beyond that he merely tinkered with empiricism, adjusting both it and ordinary
> language until he could bring them to a conformity that suited him. (Cook 1994,
> xv)

In what follows I touch upon a few points about the relationship between
James's neutral monism and Wittgenstein's, assuming for the sake of argument
that Cook's account is correct.

There are several differences between James's and Wittgenstein's versions
of neutral monism. Above all, in the *Tractatus Logico Philosophicus* period
Wittgenstein's version was meant to eliminate the self and reduce the mental
to the physical, neither of which was James's intention. As Cook records, Wittgenstein said in the 1914–1916 *Notebooks*, for instance, that "All experience is
world and does not need the subject," and in the *Tractatus* itself that "There is
no such thing as the subject that thinks or entertains ideas," and in conversation with Friedrich Waismann recorded in *Philosophical Remarks* that "The
word 'I' belongs to those words that can be eliminated from language" (Cook
1994, 15). Although Wittgenstein and James have common cause insofar as they
both reject the Cartesian conception of the self, I showed in Chapter 4 that
James has a *constructive* theory of the empirical self, centering on the present
Thought's "lassoing" past thoughts, and that he leaves theoretical space, at the
metaphysical level of his system, for the self as an "original force." He gives a
particular account of the self's nature rather than denying that there is a nature
of it to be dealt with.

Cook credits Wittgenstein's neutral-monist ontology with enabling him "to
combine phenomenalism and behaviorism, i.e., to hold that the thoughts and
feelings of others are definable in terms of their bodily behavior and that their
bodies are definable in terms of sense-data" (Cook 1994, 121). This is dramati-
cally at variance with James's doctrine. For one thing, James's theory is not
about definitions. (It is no part of his radical empiricism to show that statements of ordinary language are really truth functions of atomic propositions.)
But putting that aside, James "defines" both "thoughts and feelings" and be-

havior in terms of pure experience, directly. They are correlated constructs out of pure experience, and consequently the mind is not a candidate for the behaviorist reduction that Wittgenstein intended.

Nor did James's theory aim at elimination of the subjectivity and privacy of mind. On the contrary, he provides a famous account of it in "The Stream of Thought," Chapter 9 of *The Principles*. The breaches between personal minds are "the most absolute breaches in nature," according to James (although he paves the way for a metaphysical *arrière-pensée* when he notes elsewhere that this breach may be an empirical regularity rather than a necessity).

Therefore Cook is mistaken in the passage that follows, insofar as it is a report on James's form of neutral monism, however it may be with Wittgenstein's appropriation of it:

> Wittgenstein turned for a solution to a radical form of empiricism which was much in vogue at the time: neutral monism. This theory, which originated with William James and Ernst Mach, holds that the world consists, not of mind and matter, but of "pure experience." Or as Mach put it, "the world consists of our sensations." The radical feature of neutral monism is that, unlike idealism, it does not hold that everything is mental or *in* a mind. On the contrary, it claims to eliminate altogether the (Cartesian) mind or ego, thus doing away with the subjectivity of experience. In this view, then, there is nothing that is subjective (or private) and therefore there is nothing that is unknowable: not only are such things as tables and chairs given in immediate experience, but so, too, are the thoughts, feelings, desires, etc. of other people. This, then, was the view Wittgenstein adopted in the *Tractatus*. (Cook 1994, 8)

I trust that the confusion about James is evident, but for emphasis I quote what James has to say in "The Stream of Thought" when he is discussing the first of the five "characters" of thought, namely, "Every thought tends to be part of a personal consciousness." It might be objected that evidence from *The Principles* isn't probative with regard to James's metaphysical views, since they were arrived at later in his intellectual life. However, as I argued in Chapter 1, there really isn't good textual evidence to suppose that he changed his mind about the basic ideas in *The Principles*, and on the contrary I am making a case for the unity of his thought and for continuity between the sensationalism of *The Principles* and the pure experience of his radical empiricism. Here, then, is a passage which undercuts Cook's view of James's neutral monism as eliminating self, subjectivity, and privacy:

> Each of these minds [in this classroom] keeps its own thoughts to itself. There is no giving or bartering between them. No thought even comes into direct *sight* of a thought in another personal consciousness than its own. Absolute insulation, irreducible pluralism, is the law. It seems as if the elementary psychic fact were not *thought* or *this thought* or *that thought*, but *my thought*, every thought being *owned*. Neither contemporaneity, nor proximity in space, nor similarity of quality and content are able to fuse thoughts together which are sundered by this barrier of belonging to different personal minds. The breaches between such thoughts are the most absolute breaches in nature. Everyone will recognize this to be true, so long as *something* corresponding to the term "personal mind" is all that is insisted on, without any particular view of its nature being implied. On these terms the personal self rather than the thought might be treated as the immediate datum in psychology. The universal conscious fact is not "feelings and thoughts exist," but "I think" and "I feel." (PP, 221)

Mysticism and Science

As I argued in Chapter 1, pure experience is protomental; it is objective before becoming internalized in the stream of thought; it is that which we apprehend without mediation in sense perception of the physical world; and so on. So in this respect James's neutral monism, to call it that, is different from other versions of neutral monism which assign a more completely theoretical role to the neutral "stuff," and his expectation is different too from that of functionalists about the mind, whose official view is that we have no idea in the first instance what the nature of mental items might be, having to wait for science to reveal what fills their nature-defining causal roles. Rather, we know so well what we are talking about that conceptualization gets in the way; *that* is what Ramsey-sentence analysis reveals in James's neutral monism. It invites a sort of mysticism about pure experience, a Wittgensteinian "What we cannot speak about we must pass over in silence" (Wittgenstein 1963, 151). Indeed, James's research into telepathy, clairvoyance, mediumship, and even demonic possession was not simply an extension of abnormal psychology, but was also fascination with the thought of "crossing over" to conceptually unsullied pure experience. A fitting coda to the foregoing Ramsey-sentence analysis of the doctrine of pure experience is his concluding in 1909, "I find myself believing that there is 'something in' these never ending reports of psychical phenomena, although I haven't yet the least positive notion of the something" (Myers 1986, 10).

James is a bit more expansive in the passage quoted at the top of this chapter, from the essay "Human Immortality," which I read as grounding the brain and its activity in pure experience, such that although the mind is dependent on the brain, as James's cerebralism stipulates, the brain is also dependent on the mind qua pure experience. The veil or "dome" is conceptualized experience, the physical world and our streams of consciousness. The supersolar blaze whose rays cut through the veil at certain cephalic points is the world of pure experience. The empirical upshot of the mutual dependence is the "correspondence" between mental and physical, which, interpreted in terms of simultaneous nomic equivalence, avoids epiphenomenalism. One of the attractive features of James's Two-Levels View is that it balances tough-minded naturalism at the empirical level with openness to possibilities, such as immortality, at the metaphysical level.

Note that the supersolar blaze of pure experience is imminent in ordinary experience, unlike the sun in Plato's allegory of the cave. This mysticism of the imminent sets James's neutral monism apart from others which have scientific analysis, e.g. chemical analysis, as a model for their metaphysics. Arguably Russell's and Mach's neutral monism were of this form. James would not have aspired, as Russell did to use analysis to get down in theory, if not in practice, to the ultimate simples of which the world is built. If one "got down" there at all, it would be via mystical experience, perhaps of oneness with the *anima mundi* in which the veil of concepts was stripped away, rather than by analysis in the mode of Russell's logical atomism. James would have agreed with Wittgenstein's diagnosis of Russell's error, and of his own in the *Tractatus*, as follows: "Philosophers constantly see the method of science before their eyes, and are irresistibly tempted to ask and answer questions in the way science does. This tendency is the real source of metaphysics, and leads the philosopher into complete darkness" (Cook 1994, 28). James rings the same note when he writes:

> The aspiration to be "scientific" is such an idol of the tribe to the present generation, is so sucked in with his mother's milk by every one of us, that we find it hard to conceive of a creature who should not feel it, and harder still to treat it freely as the altogether peculiar and one-sided subjective interest which it is. But as a mat-

ter of fact, few even of the cultivated members of the race have shared it; it was invented but a generation or two ago. In the middle ages it meant only impious magic. (PP, 921)

According to the evidence that John Cook has assembled, Wittgenstein was defending neutral monism not only in his early work, but also as late as 1938, after much of *Philosophical Investigations* had been written, when he wrote:

> It is not a question here at all whether the name of the physical object signifies one object and the name of the impression signifies another, as if one successively pointed to two different objects and said, "I mean this object, not that one." The picture of the different objects is here used entirely wrongly. Not, the one name is for the immediate object, the other for something else [that's *not* given in immediate experience]; but rather, the two words are simply used differently. (Cook 1994, 15)

This certainly does look very much like the sort of theoretical structure James attempted to build up in *Essays in Radical Empiricism*, when he tried to reduce the dualism of knower and thing known to different roles that pure experience plays in different contexts. James asks us, for instance, to consider paint:

> In a pot in a paint-shop, along with other paints, it serves in its entirety as so much saleable matter. Spread on a canvas, with other paints around it, it represents, on the contrary, a feature in a picture and performs a spiritual function. Just so, I maintain, does a given undivided portion of experience, taken in one context of associates, play the part of knower, of a state of mind, of "consciousness"; while in a different context the same undivided bit of experience plays the part of a thing known, of an objective "content." In a word, in one group it figures as a thought, in another group as a thing. And, since it can figure in both groups simultaneously we have every right to speak of it as subjective and objective both at once. (ERE, 7)

Evidence like this supports the hypothesis that James and Wittgenstein had at least this much in common under the rubric of "neutral monism": that the physical world is a construct out of pure experience or sense-data. This is compatible with supposing that they differed on selves, subjectivity, and privacy, and compatible too with supposing that Wittgenstein changed his mind about the valorization of science in the *Tractatus*, about its definitional behaviorism, about its view of ordinary language as truth—functionally related to more elementary propositions, and so forth.

The philosophies of James and Wittgenstein both have a dimension of mysticism. In James this is bound up with the empirical and metaphysical levels, and particularly the gap between conceptualized experience and pure experience. With this gap in mind, which we each traverse with every experience, one might say that pure experience "shows itself," thinking of *Tractatus*: "There are, indeed, things that cannot be put into words. They *make themselves manifest*. They are what is mystical" (Wittgenstein 1963, 151). But this gap can't be what Wittgenstein has in mind, of course, because for him the gap is closed by the correspondence of elementary propositions to facts in the world. Wittgenstein is a correspondence theorist, whereas James is not. Wittgenstein has the mirroring relationship to span the gap, James does not.

Wittgenstein's mysticism certainly had something to do with a sense of the contingency of the world ("It is not how things are in the world that is mystical, but that it exists" [Wittgenstein 1963, 151].) Cook diagnoses this as the result of his phenomenalism:

> [W]e must bear in mind that Wittgenstein thought he inhabited a phenomenal, and hence an indeterministic, world—a world in which whatever happens "just happens." In the *Tractatus* Wittgenstein makes this clear when he says: "The world disintegrates [*zerfallt*] into facts" (TLP, 1.2), meaning that no fact has any connection with any other fact. He adds: "Each item can be the case or not the case while everything else remains the same" (1.21). He is saying here that in order for a state of affairs to come into being no *other* state of affairs is required, i.e., states of affairs come into being *ex nihilo*. This comes to the same as Hume's claim that we can "conceive any object to be non-existent this moment and existent the next, without conjoining to it the distinct idea of a cause or productive principle" (*Treatise* I, III, iii). (Cook 1994, 216)

But Cook is treating Hume's phenomenalism as though it uncontroversially represented phenomenalism generally, and patently it does not, as James's phenomenalism shows. James's universe was purposive, for one thing, and James regarded the alleged simple ideas that collect themselves into

Humean objects as so much mythical mind dust. James championed the view of thought as continuous rather than granular. The "un-Humean" aspects of his phenomenalism contribute significantly to his mysticism, as for instance in his conception of God as an evolving structure of pure experience.

Another expression of James's mysticism, linking the "half-truths" of the present to the "absolute truths" of a future human consensus, is his confidence that there is a direction in history toward that ultimate consensus. This movement is not historical inevitability, depending on the contributions that good people make; but it is not the indeterministic, disintegrated world that Cook speaks of either. This linkage should be borne in mind when assessing Barry Allen's critique of James's social or community idealism (his humanism), which arrives at a harsh conclusion from the following premise:

> For his part, James never doubts that the pragmatic method will confirm that it is always good to have the truth, the more truth the better. In private correspondence he is "in favor of the eternal forces of truth which always work in the individual and immediately successful way [*sic*], underdogs always, till history comes, after they are long dead, and puts them on top." In public oratory, for example in his "Address on the Philippine Question" (1903), he is in solidarity with "the long, long campaign for truth and fair dealing which must go on in all the countries of the world until the end of time. . . . Everywhere it is the same struggle under different names—light against darkness, right against might, love against hate. The Lord of life is with us, and we cannot permanently fail." (Allen 1993, 68)

The harsh conclusion is this:

> "The trail of the human serpent is thus over everything." Yet James evades an implication of this which Nietzsche might insist on. This serpent's trail *divides* truth's value differentially among groups and individuals, because this serpent is itself riven by history and politics, by differences of power. James thinks of the production of knowledge as if it were happily situated in a community where what passes for true cannot fail to be empowering, or as if a more particular social identity (female, disabled, aboriginal, indigent, HIV-positive) is irrelevant to the good of the occasional truth. But there is no pragmatic difference between the truth and what passes for true, and there is no reason not to suspect that the good of the occasional truth depends on who more particularly you are. (Allen 1993, 69)

Keeping in mind the "half-truth/absolute truth" distinction is important here. Without it, Allen can make James seem like a Pollyanna about current events, a veritable Leibniz. Plainly for James not every half-truth is going to be absolutely true. Moreover, not every half-truth need be instrumental toward absolute truth, "what passes for true" in a particularly benighted community having no redeeming value whatsoever, not even by way of a better community's reaction to it. Bringing these points to bear on Allen's interpretation that "the superior good of truth is instead a guaranteed result," we see that it is simply an ungrounded reading of James, if Allen is implying that the superior good of every half-truth is a guaranteed result. On the other hand, although Allen doesn't acknowledge James's notion of absolute truth, surely he would agree that an unforced, fully informed consensus among human beings about the truth would be a good thing? James's faith is that there are many half-truths in many good communities that will, if we do our part, ultimately prevail in creating absolute truth.

This faith underpins James's theory of truth in a profound way, as Putnam has observed. The true opinion for Peirce is the one which we would converge to if inquiry were indefinitely continued, the counterfactual possibility being sufficient for truth. But for James truth must "happen" to an idea for it to be true: "Like the half-truths, the absolute truth will have to be *made*, made as a relation incidental to the growth of a mass of verification experience, to which the half-true ideas are all along contributing their quota" (P, 107).

James's idealism about a single human community should be understood in terms of the distinction between the present and the future, half-truths and absolute truths. Failing to do so distorts James's views about the Philippines, among other things. He did not think that there was a single empowering voice of truth regarding that situation, whether that of Roosevelt and Taft or any other. Rather, he had this to say, displaying a keen sense for the invidious effect of differences of power on the course of the serpent's trail:

> The real obstacle to a promise of independence by our Congress is the old human aversion to abdicating any power once held. When love of power and desire to do good run in double harness, the team is indeed a difficult one to stop. Cant and sophistry then celebrate their golden wedding. It is then that we have to kill thousands in order to avert the killing of tens or hundreds by one another. It is then

that the boss-ruled Yankee finds the sacred duty laid upon him of preserving alien races from being exploited by their own politicians.

If after twenty years or so we let the Filipinos part in peace, it is likely that some American commandments will be broken. But the situation will have this much of good about it, that it will then have become endogenous and spontaneous. It will express native ideals, and natives will be able to understand it. Continuity is essential to healthy growth. Let the Filipino leaders try their own system — no people learns to live except by trying. We can easily protect them against foreign interference; and if they fail to be good exactly according to our notions, is not the world full even now of other people of whom the same can be said, and for whose bad conduct towards one another we agree that it would be folly to make ourselves responsible?

Any national life, however turbulent, should be respected which exhibits ferments of progress, human individualities, even small ones, struggling in the direction of enlightenment. We know to our cost how strong these forces have been in the Islands. Let them work our their own issues. We Americans surely do not monopolize all the possible forms of goodness. (179–80)

These are surely not the words of a man for whom, according to Allen, "History disappears as significant difference; differences of class, race, gender, or historical experience are reduced to individual psychological phenomena" (Allen 1993, 60). I do not detect this particular reductionism in James.

Gale's Critique of Absolute Truth

The question of the nature of truth, for James, should be separated from the question of whether there is a world external to the knower. The latter is a metaphysical question, the answer to which is: Yes, the world external to the knower is the world of pure experience. The former is a question in the philosophy of language, and I take it that James's theory here is: A sentence p is half-true (true in context) if p works (in this context). A sentence p is absolutely true if it will work at the ideal limit of inquiry: if there will be a universal consensus that p in a future ideal limit of inquiry.

Gale does not separate these questions, and as a result he is disposed to reject the idea of absolute truth because it allegedly gives bad metaphysical results. He writes,

"James's attempt to capture the realist's intuition that there is a reality independent of the knower and of which there are true and false propositions implicitly
makes use of Peirce's definition of the absolutely true as an ideal limit of *properly* conducted inquiry, for a proposition that is virtually true one that would be
verified if the appropriate tests or inquiries were properly conducted" (Gale
1999, 142). But he sees this, in line with his basic charge of Poohbahism, as
James's "attempt to throw a bone to his realist opponent," a matter of "lip service to the ideal limit account of absolute truth (I say 'lip service' because it is
dubious that James was deeply committed to it" (Gale 1999, 143). Although he
does not directly explain why James's commitment to it is dubious, Gale does
give two reasons for skepticism about absolute truth, but not before he sets out
considerable textual evidence that James really was committed to it:

> "The 'absolutely' true, meaning what no farther experience will ever alter, is that
> ideal vanishing-point towards which we imagine that all our temporary truth will
> some day converge" [P, 106–7]. There is a convergence toward a limit with respect
> to both agreement and the content of our scientific theories. This is clearly brought
> out by his claim that there is "an ideal opinion in which all men might agree, and
> which no man should ever wish to change" and "Truth absolute . . . means an
> ideal set of formulations towards which all opinions may in the long run of experi-
> ence be expected to converge" [MT, 142–43]). That there is an ultimately true
> solution to the casuistic rule also makes use of the ideal limit doctrine: "Actual-
> ized in his [God's] thought already must be that ethical philosophy which we seek
> as the pattern which our own must evermore approach" [WB, 161]. (Gale 1999,
> 143)

Gale's two reasons for skepticism are, first, that James "could not consis-
tently combine it with his deep-seated, career-long commitment to fallibilism,
which holds that *every* proposition admits of the possibility of being revised or
rejected in the light of *future* experience," and, second, "his Kuhnian account
of scientific theories precludes the very possibility of it," since "any given phenomenon will be equally well explainable by more than one scientific theory"
(Gale 1999, 145).

But Gale's reasons for skepticism aren't compelling. As for the first, the
consensus theory requires universal agreement about a theory of things *T*, including belief that no further experience will upset *T*, but that is compatible
with the fallibilist view that, for any actual historical consensus, the parties to it

might be mistaken, and compatible too with the parties' accepting the view that they might be mistaken. The consensus theory of truth is not a consensus recipe for truth.

And as for the second reason for Gale's skepticism about absolute truth, the possibility of explaining things through more than one theory doesn't count against the historical possibility that human beings might converge on *T* rather than the equally good theory *R*. More fundamentally, parties to the consensus might divide about *T* and *R*, perhaps for aesthetic or even tribal reasons, while agreeing that the two theories have the same predictive implications, and in such an eventuality that would be agreement enough for James to secure the relevant consensus. The truth is given by both *T* and *R*, just as the truth about weight can be given in kilos and pounds.

Pure Experience Revisited

James's relationship to Russell is more straightforward than his relationship to Wittgenstein, at least as far as the doctrine of pure experience is concerned, and focusing on the Russell of 1921, the author of *The Analysis of Mind*. Russell accepts James's doctrine in broad outline and in most detail, holding that "psychology and physics are distinguished by the nature of their causal laws, not by their subject matter" (Russell 1921, 287). There is no proprietary subject matter for physics, because matter is a logical construction of the "particulars" or "appearances" out of which it is built, and there is no proprietary subject matter for psychology either, because the substantial self, such as Descartes's *I*, is a myth, and mental phenomena are logical constructions out of the same particulars, the same "neutral stuff," as matter.[1]

This neutral stuff is what James called pure experience, but Russell has scruples about that term. Alluding to the two essays at the beginning of *Essays in Radical Empiricism*, "Does 'Consciousness' Exist?" and "A World of Pure Experience," he writes: "The use of the phrase 'pure experience' in both essays points to a lingering influence of idealism. 'Experience,' like 'consciousness,' must be a product, not part of the primary stuff of the world. It must be possible, if James is right in his main contentions, that roughly the same stuff, differently arranged, would not give rise to anything that could be called 'experience'" (Russell 1921, 24). This is a valid point, as far as it goes. It reminds us that the term "experience" is often used in such a way that it presupposes consciousness. (But can't one experience a good night's sleep?) However the implications of ordinary language use work themselves out, James is certainly free to stipulate that he will use the term to denote something which has some features of consciousness but not all, such that it is fit for its dual role in the construction of matter and consciousness. I argued for this stipulation in Chapter 2, as capturing the spirit of James's doctrine of pure experience. Pure experience is not private, inner, and subjective, although it is capable of being related to other experience in such a way as to give rise to these features, in a stream of consciousness. However, pure experience is purposive, and as such it presupposes a subject that imbues it with purpose; this is the "owned" or personal character of pure experience. The term "personal" in this context must be construed quite broadly, so that it can refer to experience that subserves the consciousness of nonhuman animals, alien sentient beings, and God, and the world as perceived from these different perspectives. If this is the lingering influence of idealism, so be it, though it could also be viewed as the lingering influence of materialism, since pure experience in this sense is fit to serve as a *tertia*, a common ground for mind and matter.

A more substantial departure from James's doctrine is Russell's insistence on distinguishing mental images from sensations, the former being denizens of the mental world *essentially*, because they are subject only to psychological laws, not to physical ones, whereas sensations, as caused by external objects of perception, figure in physical laws about the relationship between external objects and the brain states that subserve them. Russell considers the option of viewing mental images as centrally caused sensation, but rejects it as an unconfirmed hypothesis, whereas James's guiding assumptions, including his cerebralism, and particularly his idea that for every mental event there is a corresponding physical event (the Correspondence Thesis), lead him away from treating mental images as special in the way that Russell stipulates. Here is how Russell sees the matter:

> But I should say that images belong only to the mental world, while those occurrences (if any) which do not form part of any "experience" belong only to the physical world. There are, it seems to me, *prima facie* different kinds of causal laws, one belonging to physics and the other to psychology. The law of gravitation, for example, is a physical law, while the law of association is a psychological law. Sensations are subject to both kinds of laws, and are therefore truly "neutral" in

Holt's sense. But entities subject only to physical laws, or only to psychological laws, are not neutral, and may be called respectively purely material and purely mental. (Russell 1921, 26)

This passage brings out another difference between James's and Russell's versions of neutral monism. James does not define neutrality by reference to causal laws, but rather by phenomenology: apart from relations to other experiences and the overlay of conceptualization, no experience is self-intimatingly mental or physical. So even if mental images are not subject to physical law, they will count as neutral by this criterion. A mental image of an orange patch could be, for all that introspection tells the subject apart from the image's relata, a glimpse of an orange patch in the physical environment. And similarly, seeing an oasis could be, apart from relata, a hallucinatory image of an oasis.

8

Pragmatism I: Pragmatism and Radical Empiricism

> There is only one primal stuff of material in the world,
> a stuff of which everything is composed. (ERE, 4)

In the next few chapters I will be interpreting James's pragmatism by reference to the Two-Levels View. In this chapter I explore the close relationship, usually ignored by contemporary adherents of James's pragmatism, between his pragmatism and his radical empiricism, specifically his doctrine of pure experience. In Chapter 9 I interpret the pragmatic theory of meaning by appeal to James's account of meaning in *The Principles*, showing how it helps to make sense of what he wants to say about pragmatic meaning and the pragmatic method in *Pragmatism* and elsewhere. In Chapter 10, I examine James's theory of belief, separating it from the reading that leads to Richard Gale's "Master Syllogism" and his divided-self interpretation. And in Chapter 11 I consider the intimate relationship between rationality and truth.

The Serpent's Trail

> I believe that James's considered position on separating the phenomenologically given from its conceptualization is that, on theoretical grounds, we must postulate a given—"baby's first sensation"—for otherwise our epistemological wheels would spin idly in a frictionless void, but that in practice we cannot make any absolute discrimination between the two, only a context-relative one. . . . There is no more difficult problem in philosophy than that of separating the phenomenologically given from the way it is conceptualized, and until it is adequately addressed, James's "common denominator" strategy will not amount to much. (Gale 1999, 329–30)

In this chapter I take up Richard Gale's challenge, in the passage quoted above, to work out the strategy of separating the phenomenologically given from its conceptualization; the result will also be a neutral-monist solution to the problem of the relationship between mind and body.

The trail of the human serpent is over everything, James famously wrote in *Pragmatism*. I will attend to an implication of this dictum, namely, that there is something over which the serpent's trail lies. The upshot will be a thorough integration of James's pragmatism and his radical empiricism, in particular his doctrine of pure experience. His philosophical system includes a quite general form of functionalism, not just about the mind but also about the physical world. I will call this *global functionalism*, and I will try to make a case for it, not only as capturing the spirit of James's radical empiricism, but also as having as much plausibility as functionalism about the mind. Functionalism in the narrower sense, about the mind, quantifies mental events, so it has a mental *ontology*. But it restricts itself to physical predicates about them, and so it has a physical *ideology*. Global functionalism, on the other hand, has a *neutral* ontology, and both a mental and a physical ideology.

My argument will have reference to what *The Philosophical Lexicon* calls "carnaps":

> **carnap,** n. (1) A formally defined symbol, operator, special bit of notation. "His prose is peppered with carnaps" or "the argument will proceed more efficiently if we introduce a few carnaps." n. (2) Loss of consciousness while being taken for a ride.

The following case for James's global functionalism may be carnap-inducing, and in my conclusion I will suggest how this might be so. But the soporific carnap was brought to the party by functionalism itself, which employs a technique of definition-exploiting Ramsey sentences to explain how mental events can be defined solely by their holistic causal role with respect to physical input, physical output, and one another.

The basic idea behind Ramsey-sentence analysis can be expressed without carnaps. It is to treat mental terms as theoretical terms. The sentences with mental terms that express "the platitudes of folk psychology" ("A person who *wants* something will *try to get it*, other things being equal"; "If someone believes that an action is lethal, he or she will *choose not to perform it*, other things being equal"; and so forth) are assembled into a very long conjunction. This will include a description of the causal roles of the referents of these terms, linking the referents (the "mental events") to sensory stimuli, each other, and behavior. (The inclusion of this causal role in the Ramsey sentence is what distinguishes functionalism from logical behaviorism.) Each mental term is replaced by an appropriate free variable, creating an open formula and draining our regimented folk psychology of its "psychological" look. Then the Ramsey sentence will just be the existential closure of the open formula, declaring that there exist in the world just those things that folk psychology says there are, but without introducing explicitly psychological terminology. For all that folk psychology implies, according to the Ramsey-sentence analysis, a mental event is simply *something* that occupies a certain causal role in the physical world. Logically regimented folk psychology can be expressed in terms of bound variables, physical concepts, and topic-neutral relationships (especially causal relationships). This is *compatible* with affirming that everything that exists is physical. What exists, according to the Ramsey sentence, may turn out to be physical, roughly in the way that the gene, the "something" responsible for heredity, turned out to be DNA.

I agree with Colin McGinn that the invention of the Ramsey-sentence definitional technique is largely responsible for the confidence of many functionalists, and I will be tracking his demonstration that the technique is equally available to "a certain kind of neo-phenomenalist about physical objects and their properties" (McGinn 1991, 191). I want to suggest that James's radical empiricism, and specifically his doctrine of pure experience, belongs to this kind, and that it has advantages that McGinn's argument overlooks.

McGinn's intent is to undermine the confidence of functionalists by using their carnap to reveal that phenomenalism can be presented in the same way. He is appealing to the prevailing view that phenomenalism is a nonstarter, enshrined in *The Philosophical Lexicon*'s definitions of "mach" and "davidsonic," where phenomenalism is characterized as going nowhere but somehow staying in the air.

> **mach,** n. A measure of speed; *mach one*, the speed at which a research program (e.g. phenomenalism) becomes superdavidsonic.

davidsonic, adj. Of speed: minimum forward velocity required to keep a research program in the air. *Superdavidsonic,* of research program for which this speed is zero. Hence, *davidsonic boom,* the sound made by a research program when it hits Oxford.

My intent is to give phenomenalism, especially in its Jamesian form, some forward velocity. My strategy is to follow McGinn's argument just far enough that the parallel between functionalism and phenomenalism is in place, and then to jump off before it becomes a *reductio ad absurdum.*

Ramsifying Pure Experience

James's doctrine of pure experience could use the clarity of formulation that Ramsey-sentence analysis affords. I will try to rehabilitate the verb "to ramsify" here, saving it from the meaning assigned to it in *The Philosophical Lexicon*:

ramsify, v. To simplify, e.g. ramsified theory of types.

Ramsifying pure experience in the present sense will mean showing how Ramsey-sentence analysis applies to James's doctrine. I hope it will be a remedy for a perceived lack of clarity in James's writings about experience and consciousness. Gerald Myers expresses this perception in his intellectual biography of James: "James wanted to hold that in one way consciousness does not exist, but that in another way it does; yet he was never able, even to his own satisfaction, to define the two ways clearly enough to show that they are consistent rather than contradictory" (Myers 1986, 64). Myers will be satisfactorily answered if James's doctrine of pure experience allows us to say: We quantify pure experience, which is neither mental nor physical, neither consciousness nor matter. In this respect consciousness does not exist; it does not belong to our ontology. But both the mental and the physical, both consciousness and matter, do exist in the sense that mental and physical predicates are true of what exists, in the way that theories can be true about their subject matter.

Talk of "quantification" of pure experience does no violence to James's doctrine, for it simply expresses the requirement that, in order to be able to say that *this* item of pure experience is the same as or different from *that* item, one should be able to specify what condition of the world makes for identity or difference. Items of pure experience are distinguished by the different mental and physical predicates that are true of them, the predicates that describe the holistic causal roles which are, according to global functionalism, definitive of the mental and physical properties. Their identity is given in relational terms, rather than absolute, nonrelational properties. This is, in a Jamesian phrase, the "cash value" of structuring the doctrine of pure experience in terms of the logic of quantification, and there will be occasion below to trace its connection to James's mysticism of the imminent.

This answer to Myers introduces the idea that *both* mental and physical terms are semantically like theoretical terms. Having Ramsified mental terms in an informal way, above, let us do the same now for physical terms, with a bit more attention to formal detail.[1] First, the platitudes are rewritten in property-name style, so that physical terms occur in property position. "If a basketball is dropped, it will bounce when dropped, other things being equal" becomes "If something has the property of being a basketball, it will bounce when dropped, other things being equal," and so forth. Then these rewritten platitudes are assembled into a long conjunction, which can be represented as a relational predicate P which is true of the various physical properties, while the property of being a basketball and so forth are represented by the letters a, b, c, and so on. So the conjunction will have the form

$$P[abc \ldots]$$

The next step is to strip out each mention of a property-name of a physical property and replace it with a free variable, like so:

$$P[xyz \ldots]$$

With this much accomplished, it follows that if there are any physical properties, then there is a unique set of properties which are in fact related to each other and to the world in just the way that the long conjunction of platitudes said; or in formalism,

$$'x'y'z \ldots P[xyz \ldots] \ \& \ (x^*)(y^*)(z^*) \ldots P[x^*y^*z^* \ldots] \ \text{iff} \ (x = x^*, y = y^*, z = z^* \ldots)$$

Moreover, if the variable *x* replaced the property of being a basketball in the stripping-out step, the property of being a basketball could be defined in terms of the network of relations it stands in to other physical properties, and to all the other things that are mentioned in the platitudes of folk physics, including causal properties such as bouncing when dropped, looking in such and such way to a normal observer under certain lighting conditions, and so forth; in formalism, the property of being a basketball *is* the *x* such that

$$\exists y z \ldots P[xyz \ldots] \mathbin{\&} (x^*)(y^*)(z^*) \ldots P[x^*y^*z^* \ldots] \text{ iff } (x = x^*, y = y^*, z = z^* \ldots)$$

When all of folk physics is treated in this way, the upshot is a set of definitions of physical objects that mentions no physical terms at all. The phenomenalist is emboldened to claim that these definitions reveal the nature of the physical world.

The next step, moving beyond physicalism and idealistic phenomenalism to the Ramsification of pure experience, involves redirecting the reference of the theoretical terms in each of the two previous processes, so that the theoretical terms in the Ramsey sentence for folk psychology refer not to physical states but to pure-experiential states, and those for folk physics refer not to mental states but to pure-experiential states. N-tuples of pure-experiential states are what realize both the regimented theories, rather than *n*-tuples of physical and mental states. After all, the Ramsey sentences are entirely topic-neutral with respect to the nature of the referents that actually occupy the causal roles they specify. Functionalists believe the roles are occupied by physical states; phenomenalists believe they are occupied by mental states. But they are wrong. The roles are occupied by pure experience, and the radical empiricist's Ramsey sentence helps to show this happens. It is a conjunction of the two conjunctions given by folk psychology and folk physics, quantifying pure experience.

That, at any rate, is the general picture. I proceed to fill in some detail and to integrate it with the bigger picture of James's philosophical system.

The Tightly Wedged Mind

When James wrote the preface to *Pragmatism* in April 1907, he concluded it by emphasizing that the new pragmatism and his earlier radical empiricism were not, from a logical point of view, a package deal; pragmatism didn't entail radical empiricism: "To avoid one misunderstanding at least, let me say that there is no logical connexion between pragmatism, as I understand it, and a doctrine which I have recently set forth as 'radical empiricism.' The latter stands on its own feet. One may entirely reject it and still be a pragmatist" (P, 6). With that final sentence James seems to have anticipated posterity's selective appropriation of his philosophical system, which rejects radical empiricism while counting many pragmatists among its followers. But are the two so loosely related?

Consider an argument that the connection is tighter. Understand pragmatism as a theory of truth according to which the practical cash value of truth is the guidance that true beliefs afford us in the course of our experience. And understand radical empiricism as a doctrine of *pure experience* according to which the mental and physical are constructs out of stuff that is neither mental nor physical but capable of becoming either by virtue of the constructive activity of the human subject, as described for instance in *The Principles of Psychology* and interpreted metaphysically in *Essays in Radical Empiricism*, where the sensations of *The Principles* become pure experience.

When pragmatism guides us "in the course of our experience," the experience in question is to be interpreted either as pure experience in the technical sense of James's radical empiricism, which would make the connection between pragmatism and radical empiricism extremely tight, or else it is to be construed as experience of the familiar world of physical and mental facts. This latter assumption fits the hypothesis of a loose connection, as well as fitting the deafening silence about radical empiricism and pure experience in *Pragmatism*. But the world of physical and mental facts is a constructed world, the cash value of truths about it to be found in "the function of giving human satisfaction in marrying previous parts of experience with newer parts," such that "the trail of the human serpent is thus over everything" (P, 37). Now either this constructive activity is grounded in unconstructed pure experience, which tightens the connection between pragmatism and radical empiricism, or it is grounded in something nonexperiential, which offends against James's empiricism, active in *Pragmatism* for instance in his pragmatic gloss on Berkeley's refutation of "material substance." Or else, absurdly, the constructive activity goes on without end, which amounts to a vicious regress.

The first alternative in this trilemma is the most attractive interpretation, not only because the second is so un-Jamesian and the third so illogical, and not only because it harmonizes with the constructive accounts in James's psychology and radical-empiricist metaphysics, but also because it brings out the idea of nonpragmatic constraints on pragmatic activity, an idea that is put to service in *Pragmatism* when James writes, "Between the coercions of the sensible order and those of the ideal order, our mind is thus wedged tightly. Our ideas must agree with realities, be such realities concrete or abstract, be they facts or be they principles, under penalty of endless inconsistency and frustration" (P, 101). Such facts and principles may be generated in part by the past constructive activity of the human race, as James observes when he writes, "But how plastic even the oldest truths nevertheless really are has been vividly shown in our day by the transformation of logical and mathematical ideas, a transformation which seems even to be invading physics" (P, 37). However, James's appeal to the sensible and abstract orders would not have the argumentative force he plainly intends for it, were these orders totally rather than in part constructed, for in this case there would be no nonpragmatic constraint on pragmatic activity, nothing to enforce contradiction and frustration when it gives satisfaction to a subject to free himself from the coercions of the sensible and ideal orders; but this freedom is just the invitation to believe in fantasies that James hoped to rescind by deploying the argument from "the tightly wedged mind."

Functionalism, Global Functionalism, and Ramsey Sentences

The foregoing argument for a close connection between James's pragmatism and his radical empiricism doesn't categorically bind a pragmatist to pure experience. There are many ways to be a pragmatist. Ignoring James's constructivism, for instance, one can suppose that pragmatic considerations operate within parameters set by physical and mental facts, and it may even be possible to square this with the "human serpent" theme in *Pragmatism*, of relativity of concepts to human needs and satisfactions.

But is there anything to be said for the close connection, apart from preserving unity in James's philosophical system among its psychological, metaphysical, and epistemological elements? It is widely thought that his doctrine of pure experience is not a live option for belief, because it belongs to a philosophically discredited family of "phenomenalist" ("neutral-monist," "sense-data") theories. The critiques of such theories over the past hundred years pose a Gordian knot, not to be untied but cut through, and the sword is at hand in

Ramsey-sentence analysis of both folk psychology and folk physics. This affects the reduction of mental and physical terms that the doctrine of pure experience requires, in a clear and convincing manner, while saying nothing about such entities as sense data that might trigger the old debates.

A Ramsey sentence, in summary, is a sentence generated from the sentences of a theory after they have been conjoined together, by replacing the theoretical terms with variables and existentially quantifying the result, reproducing the structure of the theory and its empirical consequences without the implication that anything is known about the theoretical items themselves. In the present application, it will allow James to respond to the following demand, from "Does 'Consciousness' Exist?": "First of all, this will be asked: 'If experience has not "'conscious'" existence, if it be not partly made of "'consciousness,'" of what then is it made? Matter we know, and thought we know, and conscious content we know, but neutral and simple "'pure experience'" is something we know not at all. Say *what* it consists of—for it must consist of something—or be willing to give it up!'" (ERE, 14). The way James chose to respond to this question is not entirely satisfactory, leaning too hard on the word *that* to do what might be called, skeptically, magical reference:[2] "Although for fluency's sake I myself spoke early in this article of a stuff of pure experience, I have now to say that there is no *general* stuff of which experience at large is made. There are as many stuffs as there are 'natures' in the things experienced. If you ask what any one bit of pure experience is made of, the answer is always the same: 'It is made up of *that*, of just what appears, of space, of intensity, of flatness, brownness, heaviness, or what not'" (ERE, 14). The problem is that the conceptualizations having to do with space, intensity, flatness, brownness, heaviness, or whatnot do not belong to "just what appears" but are rather our conceptual artifacts, leaving the demonstrative *that* with too much work to do. One is invited to answer the question, "What are you referring to?" a request for a concept, and to answer the question is to falsify pure experience, which is preconceptual. This is the crucial point for James's austere, radical-empiricist mysticism of the imminent.

Ramsey-sentence analysis shows how to remove this burden from the demonstrative and transfer it to mental and physical predicates in existential quantifications.

David Lewis and others have shown how Ramsey-sentence analysis works for mental terms, yielding "functionalism," and Colin McGinn has shown that it is equally applicable to physical terms, yielding idealistic phenomenalism. This is not to be construed as necessarily vindicating the doctrine of pure experience. Indeed, McGinn views the Ramsification of the physical as an argument against functionalism about the mental, a *reductio ad absurdum*. But since functionalism is certainly a live option for belief in the philosophical community, amounting perhaps to the received view about the nature of mind, surely the family of theories to which James's doctrine of pure experience belongs is entitled to the same level of credibility.

Mentalistic and Nonmentalistic Phenomenalism

Should both functionalism and phenomenalism be accepted on the basis of this parallel, or should functionalism be rejected? McGinn recommends the latter because he assumes that the two analyses eat each other's lunch, so to speak. They are mutually incompatible theories, he reasons:

> Perhaps some people will find themselves persuaded by the parallel but react, not by rejecting functionalism, but by accepting both it and functionalistic phenomenalism. A moment's reflection shows, however, that this way is blocked, at least if such definitions are to have the metaphysical significance usually accorded them. For the two doctrines are mutually incompatible. This is because, taken as programs of definitional elimination, the *definiens* concepts of the one are the *definiendum* concepts of the other: they propose competing reductions, since behavior is physical and experiences are mental. (McGinn 1991, 195)

This is the crucial juncture, of course, where my strategy dictates jumping off before McGinn calls it a tossup between functionalism and phenomenalism; he deplores the implausibility of the idea that our ultimate theory might be basically idealist in its ideology, and he concludes that functionalism is no more plausible. I have introduced the idea that the reductions needn't be competing but may be, rather, complementary. They are not eating each other's lunch but rather a third party's, so to speak—namely, a world of pure experience that the mental and physical organize in different ways.

Phenomenalism analyzes the physical in terms of the mental, and functionalism defines the mental in terms of the physical, but that is all right because neither the mental nor the physical has to stake a claim to existence; in particular, neither has to stake a claim that trumps the other's. James's neutral monism of pure experience shows how this can be.

McGinn's point invites a distinction between two forms of phenomenalism, namely, that form of it which posits that the theoretical terms of the Ramsey sentence for folk psychology refer to something mental, and that which posits something neither mental nor physical. The first form leads to McGinn's dilemma, "Shall we mentalize the behavioral or behavioralize the mental? We can't do both." But James's phenomenalism is definitely of the latter form. When I seem to see an apple in front of me, in his account, there is not something self-intimatingly mental about that experience. If this were the case, the path would be blocked for Ramsification of pure experience, since this involves attaching the reference of the theoretical terms in folk physics, as well as the theoretical terms in folk psychology, to something nonmental as well as nonphysical, and conjoining the result.

An experience's mental character is for James a function of its relationship to other experiences in the stream of thought; similarly, something's physical character is a function of its relationship to other physical things in the physical world. Both these functions can be spelled out by reference to pure experience, via functionalist and phenomenalist Ramsey sentences. So functionalism and phenomenalism will not be mutually incompatible under a Jamesian interpretation of the latter, but rather they will describe different relationships that pure experience can enter into, namely, constructive relationships that generate the physical world and those that generate the mental, as detailed in *The Principles*, relationships articulated in the appropriate Ramsey sentences.

The Ramsey sentences for folk psychology and folk physics will have different realizations, different *n*-tuples of pure experience which coexist with each other. Their coexistence is at the bottom of the fact that we live in a physical world in which some physical objects are associated with streams of consciousness.

Intermediary and Nonintermediary Phenomena

In addition to this distinction between mentalistic and neutral versions of phenomenalism, it is helpful to divide the "phenomenalist" family of theories into those that regard the phenomena (sense data, ideas, etc.) as intermediaries between the subject and the external world, on one hand, and those theories which do not regard them as intermediaries on the other. As Hilary Putnam notes, James's theory is of the latter sort:

> The most striking aspect of James's radical empiricism is its intention to be close to "natural realism" [ERE, 63ff]. In perception I am *directly acquainted* with external reality—indeed, to speak of my "sensations" and to speak of the external realities the sensations are "of" is to speak of the same bits of "pure experience," counted "twice over" (with two different "contexts"). I have argued that James was the first post-Cartesian philosopher to completely reject the idea that perception requires *intermediaries*. (Putnam 1997, 174)

The foregoing Ramsey-sentence analysis of the mental and physical shows how this realist dimension of James's theorizing can be meshed with his pragmatic constructivism. The trail of the human serpent is over everything, as the latter requires, but there is *something* under the trail, some pure experience which constraints the direction that the trail takes, as the realism requires. The serpent's influence on conceptualization is acknowledged by the austerity of reference to pure experience in the Ramsey analysis: the bare subject of existential quantifications, where the predicates record the meanderings of the serpent's trail. Interpreters of James like Richard Rorty, who read antirealism into his thinking (Rorty 1986, 86), cannot account for this theoretical integration of pragmatism and empiricism.

James's pragmatism and radical empiricism, although not logically connected, constitute a theoretical organic unity, which Ramsey-sentence analysis brings to fullest light. His radical empiricism mounts just as sharp a challenge to materialism about folk physics as functionalism does to dualism about folk psychology, and just as defensibly. Radical empiricism stands for a directly perceived *tertium quid* more basic than the physical or the mental, and explanatory of both. By parity of reasoning, as McGinn's argument reveals (when turned on its head), functionalists about the mind should be radical empiricists about everything mental and physical. And Jamesian pragmatists, should they want to maintain the idea that we live in one world despite the diversity of conceptualizations, may wish to give "a world of pure experience" a second look.

Either that, or I have badly "bubered."

> **buber,** v. To struggle in a morass of one's own making. "After I defined the self as a relation that relates to itself relatingly, I bubered around for three pages." Hence buber, n. one who bubers. "When my mistake was pointed out to me, I felt like a complete buber."

I will consider two objections before declaring the present argument buber-free.

Phenomenalism can easily consort with a mentalistic form of behaviorism, the mind reducing to patterns of (experiences of) behavior. John Cook argues that Wittgenstein was defending this form of phenomenalism-cum-behaviorism in the *Tractatus*:.

> [T]o avoid skepticism regarding the "'external world," Wittgenstein had opted for a reductionist account of material objects, and this left him with an ontology of sense-data. But sense-data, as typically conceived of, are themselves "in the mind" and so would seem to be irreconcilable with behaviorism, which aims to eliminate things "in the mind."
>
> We have already seen how Wittgenstein avoided this difficulty: he traveled from idealism to solipsism and finally to pure realism, i.e., neutral monism, which rejects the idea that sense-data are "in the mind." The ontology of the *Tractatus*, then, is nondualistic: it rejects both unknowable "external" objects and "inner" or ("private") contents of the mind. This ontology enabled Wittgenstein to combine phenomenalism and behaviorism, i.e., to hold that the thoughts and feelings of others are definable in terms of their bodily behavior and that their bodies are definable in terms of sense-data. (Cook 1994, 121)

Isn't this what is happening with the Ramsification of James's doctrine of pure experience?

I reply that James's phenomenalism is different. Ramsification would lead to behaviorism if it reduced *only* folk physics and then tried to configure the mind within the resulting reduction. But Jamesian Ramsification, I have emphasized, requires the conjunction of reduced folk physics *and* reduced folk psychology. Psychology is functionally linked to behavior, as Ramsification of folk psychology reveals, but that is crucially different from thinking of the mental as nothing more than a pattern of behavior within Ramsified folk physics. It is simply the difference between behaviorism and functionalism, transposed into a phenomenalist key—more exactly, a pure-experiential key. Jamesian

Ramsification, unlike behaviorism and its phenomenalistic variant, does not undermine the status of the mental as inner and private.

Cook recognizes the difference between Wittgenstein's and James's formulations of neutral monism, although he does not explicitly refer to James:

> The two most important features of neutral monism were developed by Berkeley (the elimination of matter) and Hume (the elimination of the self as an entity), but the neutral monists made significant additions. Their aim was to dispatch dualism by doing away with (Cartesian) minds as well as matter, which is why the view came to be called *neutral monism*, which distinguishes it from the "mentalistic" monism of idealists such as F. H. Bradley. Accordingly, they sometimes stated their view by saying that the world consists of a neutral stuff, a stuff which, in itself, is neither mental nor physical but which may, in some of its relations, be called "mental" and, in other relations, "physical." This formulation did not interest Wittgenstein, and I will therefore ignore it. (Cook 1994, 14–15)

The formulation that did not interest Wittgenstein, James's formulation for present purposes, profits from the parity of functionalism about the mind and phenomenalism about the physical world, without the taint of behaviorism.

McGinn is not satisfied. Commenting on a strategy like the one adopted here, he writes:

> Suppose you form the conjunction of our (common-sense) theories of the mental and physical realms. Now consider how you would carry out Lewis's Ramsification technique on this combined theory. You might start by eliminating the mental terms, in the prescribed way, from the conjunct expressing your psychological theory; you then eliminate the physical terms, in parallel fashion, from the conjunct expressing your physical theory. But then, of course, the resulting open sentence still contains terms—behavioral and experiential—to whose definition and elimination you are, as a global functionalist, committed. To implement both doctrines you need to eliminate these terms too. But if you take the elimination to its conclusion, then the resulting Ramsified theory will contain *only* topic-neutral vocabulary. There seems little to be said for the suggestion that this colorless ideology suffices to confer the intended content upon the original mental and physical terms—to capture what the concepts essentially involve. Besides, what would have become of the original motivation to vindicate a basically physicalist or phenomenalist (ideological) metaphysics, as the case may be? So there seems no hope of accepting both doctrines. (McGinn 1991, 195–96)

I have two replies. First, James's metaphysics of pure experience simply does not share the motivations of either physicalism or phenomenalism, when the latter is understood, as McGinn intends it to be, as a project of reducing the physical to the mental. Its motivation is to reduce both to a third category, pure experience. So this part of his reason for rejecting the conjunctive strategy is simply irrelevant. Second, the really big step toward "colorlessness" is taken by functionalism about the mental. Once that step is taken, functionalism about the physical, spelled out in terms of sensory experience, requires only the idea that the sensory properties themselves, as distinguished from their relationships to each other, are topic-neutral. There is nothing self-intimatingly mental (or physical, for that matter) about the visual experience of a blue expanse, for instance. There *is* something to be said for this. It seems correct about the phenomenology or what-it-feels-like of the experience in isolation, and it is plausible to suppose that the experience's status as hallucinatory or as veridical "of a blue wall" (say), is a function of context, of the character of the experience's relationship to other experiences, such as that of bumping into a wall. Indeed, much of James's *Principles* is given over to analyses of perception of the physical world in such "colorless" terms, i.e., in terms of sensations (understood in a topic-neutral way) and their relationships to each other. In short, the conjunctive strategy survives McGinn's objection because it is motivated by a radical-empiricist metaphysics, in which both mental and physical events bottom out in pure-experiential ones, the latter comprising a topic-neutral subset of mental events, the subset that figures in the reduction of folk physics.

Embracing a Reductio?

I conclude that I haven't bubered, but it might still be objected that I have outsmarted McGinn in the technical sense of *The Philosophical Lexicon's* tribute to J. J. C. Smart's defense of utilitarianism:

> **outsmart,** v. To embrace the conclusion of one's opponent's *reductio ad absurdum* argument. "They thought they had me, but I outsmarted them. I agreed that it *was* sometimes just to hang an innocent man."

McGinn wants to conclude that functionalism is false. That may well be correct. I have assumed the truth of functionalism *arguendo*, however, in order to use his argument for the parity of functionalism and phenomenalism in defense of James's doctrine of pure experience. Instead of rejecting both, as McGinn proposes, I integrated them both by means of a global-functionalist Ramsey sentence. But I embraced these two forms of functionalism guardedly, in order to interpret James's doctrine of pure experience in what I take to be its most defensible form. I have not tried to show that functionalism of either sort is true. To settle this hash, as James might say, other arguments are needed. I have attempted reconstruction and retrieval of radical-empiricist metaphysics and its central doctrine of pure experience. Like functionalism about the mind, James's metaphysics is a live option for belief, not a discredited relic in the history of philosophy.

The mind-body problem has been approached recently with the presumption that naturalism is true, which means, at a minimum, that the canonical notation for our theory of the universe, including the mind, should quantify over physical events. The foregoing argument suggests that this presumption is wrong. We should be quantifying pure experience. The implications are, for philosophy, enormous. The various identity theories, reducing the mind to the brain, are revealed as provincial, as well as those versions of functionalism that anticipate that the occupants of the relevant causal roles are physical. Behaviorism is a nonstarter. Eliminative views warrant a second look, since they object to reduction of mind to brain, and global functionalism does so as well. But to the extent that eliminative theories anticipate vindication of physicalism, they too are mistaken.

Let me conclude by responding to the objection that the subjectivity of mental events prevents a pure-experiential reduction. First, if the objection derives from Cartesian assumptions about the self-intimating character of mental events, such assumptions are to be rejected, as I have argued earlier. Second, bearing the Two-Levels View in mind, it is quite possible to insist on the introspectable difference between mental and physical events while saluting the doctrine of pure experience. One does not have to "feign anesthesia" to accept global functionalism. Qualia are real but reducible, not to physical events but to pure experience. Qualia will lose, not their subjective feel, but rather the alleged introspective flag that marks them as irreducibly mental. This loss is painless.

What is it like to be a bat? A hard question, no doubt. But the difficulty of conceiving bat subjectivity, or ours, in physical terms should not be a barrier to radical empiricism, which does not demand such a conception. It demands a conception of subjectivity as pure-experiential, but that is not an objection. At any rate, it is not an objection presumed by the standard responses to physicalist reductions.

One more objection: What are the criteria of identity for translation of theory about mind and body to theory about pure experience? At one level, I answered this question earlier by holding that the identity conditions for an item of pure experience are just the predications of it in the Ramsey sentence which quantifies it. But if the question is a request to justify quantification over pure experience, on the grounds that it is comparable to bad theoretical entities like phlogiston, I answer that this is a *wrong* question, because, unlike typical theoretical reductions, radical empiricism expects not a reduction of one theory to another, but reduction of the theoretical to the given, which is not theoretical at all but something imminent in ordinary experience. On this view of the mysticism of the imminent, we all know what this mysticism is about, just as certainly as we know we are in pain, or some other subjective mental state. The difference is that the given is preconceptual, not identifiable with its conceptual labels, such as pain, searing pain, and so on.

Finally, the request for identity conditions might be made in hope of learning the ultimate *nature* of pure experience, a question that James wrestled with till the end of his life, notably in *Manuscript Essays and Notes*, particularly his responses to the Miller-Bode objections. He had basically two concerns. First, there is a problem raised by the continuity of pure experience, in view of the fact that my experience and yours are patently discontinuous. Does the continuity of experience extend itself to *our* experience, or does it not? If not, here is an exception to the continuity principle. If so, the experiencer must be subconscious or transcendent to our consciousnesses, forcing a significant qualification to the principle that the essence of pure experience is precisely to-be-experienced, since we do not (consciously) experience the hypothesized continuity. Second, there is a problem about perspectives, yours and mine on the same pen (for example). How can they be perspectives on the same pen? In a world of pure experience, it would seem that there should be just the experiences from our various perspectives, rendering problematic the commonsense notion of a pen which we all experience. The radical empiricist wants to solve the first problem without invoking a transcendental subject of all our experiences, an *I* beneath experience; and the second problem should be solved without calling upon an object transcendent to experience, an *it* beyond experience. James's reflections in the Miller-Bode notebook confirm that the problem is hard, but not that it's insoluble. Philosophy in his view is continuous with science, and it is not surprising that there should be a horizon of unsolved problems for a radical-empiricist metaphysics. The notebooks should be read as James's preliminary and inconclusive scouting of this horizon rather than a virtual deathbed recantation of radical empiricism.

James's Blues Dispelled

One form that the blues take for James, according to Richard Gale's recent interpretation, is "The Many Selves Blues," which he sings because of inadequate time to realize the many empirical selves within him, "numerous potential selves each crying out for full self-actualization" (Gale 1999, 2). A parsing of selves that had reference to James's philosophical system would, in my view, distinguish only two selves, the metaphysical and empirical selves, corresponding to the two levels of James's system. But Gale thinks that James's "Divided-Self Blues" poses his many empirical selves against his mystical self, creating a fundamental ontological problem: "The underlying thesis of this book is that the primary clash was between James's Promethean and mystical selves, and the ultimate aim was to find some way in which he could unify them, or at least reconcile them with each other so that they could lie down together in peace" (Gale 1999, 7). For my part, I would understand James's empirical/pragmatic self, the Promethean one, as conceptualizing experience differently at different times, constructing different elements of the empirical self, while acknowledging the metaphysical/mystical self implies that there is one world, a world of pure experience, which the different conceptualizations are of. Gale, on the contrary, interprets conceptual relativism as ontological relativism, which he describes as "the Big Aporia" in James's philosophy, "consisting in a clash between his pragmatic self's metadoctrine of Ontological Relativism"—that all reality claims must be relativized to a person at a time—and the absolute, nonrelativized reality claims he based on mystical experiences" (Gale 1999, 19). If the foregoing Ramsey-sentence interpretation of James is correct, the Big Aporia is no clash at all: James's pragmatic self, or rather the many empirical selves, are predicatively related to the absolute, nonrelativized reality of that pattern of pure experience that gets structured in a human life, and which, if James is right about free will, structures that life.

The accusation of Poohbahism has two principle foci, one having to do with the self, the other with reality. The Pooh-Bah self lacks the integrity of personal identity, and Pooh-Bah reality unravels into a motley of different belief clusters. But neither sort of Poohbahism is at work in James's system. The self has the integrity that the Closest-Continuer account reveals, and reality has the unity of the world of pure experience, that which our folk-physical and folk-psychological conceptualizations are conceptualizations *of*. It remains a mystery why conceptualization gets channeled as it does, at least for us, into streams of consciousness and a physical world. Why does experience take this shape? Radical empiricism does not answer this question, but on the other hand it resolves philosophy's traditional "world knot," the problem of the relationship between mind and body, by analyzing mind and body as predicative of pure experience, in the manner of this chapter's Ramsey-sentence analysis. It eliminates *this* mystery, just as thoroughly, and more plausibly, than reductive physicalism. And it obviates the mystery recently recommended by McGinn, whose "mysterianism" or transcendental naturalism would premise the existence of mind and body as given by the philosophical tradition and hold that there is a perfectly *natural* but unknowable-by-human-beings property of our minds, which connects them to our bodies in an intelligible way. Radical empiricism on the other hand premises that we have knowledge by acquaintance with that which connects mind and body, namely, pure experience. The special features of mind and body, which create the appearance of a mysterious explanatory gap, are features of *experience-as-constructed*. Traced back to the experience that gets constructed, as in a Ramsey sentence that quantifies pure experience and predicates mental and physical properties of it, the mystery dissolves.

Conclusion

If functionalism about the mind is true, then functionalism about the physical is also true. But the only way for both of these functionalisms to be true is for them to be about something else, which is neither mental nor physical. Moreover, this "something else" should be something that neither physicalists nor antiphysicalists ("qualia freaks" and others) have reason to question. *Experience* in the sense of James's doctrine of pure experience meets these requirements for a *tertium quid*. Physicalists don't deny that there is an experience of a blue expanse, say, when you look up at the sky. They deny rather that this experience is irreducibly mental, and Jamesian global functionalism confirms this. But equally it confirms the antiphysicalists' intuition that the experience is not reducible to a brain state. They need only concede that the subjectivity of a mental state is a function of the *relationship* it has to other mental states rather than a self-identifying feature of each mental state. Of course, this is what functionalists about the mind have said all along. But it makes all the difference that the state that has these mental-making relationships is an item of pure experience rather than a brain state. That confirms the antiphysicalists' intuition that something immediately given in experience, as brain states are not, is what they are talking about when they talk about a visual experience of a blue expanse.

9

Pragmatism II: Meaning

Pragmatic Meaning

Pragmatic meaning in the sense of James's *Pragmatism* is meaning in the sense laid out in Chapter 12 of *The Principles*, "Conception." Meaning has the function of relating a person—strictly speaking, the passing Thought—to patterns and regularities in experience. Being able to think "the same X" allows the thinker to avoid chaos and isolation, by constructing a continuous self, including a stream of consciousness, and a physical world and a coherent perspective on it. Pragmatic meaning is the application of meaning in this sense to the clarification of our ideas, especially ideas in philosophy that tend to get detached from their function of relating the subject to experience. One is not forced to accept the idea that there is a contradictory or incoherent conception of meaning for James, which requires shuttling between two sub-conceptions. This is Gale's view, however:

> We shall see him shuttling back and forth between two species of empiricism: One is the exclusively future-oriented operationalistic or pragmatic empiricism that he officially endorses as his pragmatic theory of meaning, according to which the whole meaning of an idea is a set of conditionalized predictions stating what experiences would be had in the future upon performing certain actions, and the other that of classical British empiricism, which finds the meaning of an idea in terms of the sensory or experiential contents that its analysis comprises, regardless of whether they are future or not. The latter species of empiricism will be called "content empiricism" and the former "operationalist or pragmatic empiricism." (Gale 1999, 152)

A first problem for Gale's "shuttling" interpretation is that pragmatic meaning, in his construal of it, is constantly changing, since the conditionalized predictions a meaning sanctions will change with every passing moment, for the simple reason that passing moments will no longer be available for the (conditionalized) predictions that can *now* be made. Not only does such a churn in meanings seem absurd on the face of it, but there is plainly a flat contradiction between hypothesizing such churn and the doctrine of the sameness of meanings in *The Principles*, to which I now turn.

Meaning or Conception

James begins the chapter on "Conception" by reminding the reader that he has acknowledged the phenomenon of *bare acquaintance* in an earlier chapter, "The Relation of Minds to Other Things":

> *There are two kinds of knowledge* broadly and practically distinguishable: we may call them respectively *knowledge of acquaintance* and *knowledge-about.* . . . I am acquainted with many people and things, which I know very little about, except their presence in the places where I have met them. I know the color blue when I see it, and the flavor of a pear when I taste it; I know an inch when I move my finger through it; but *about* the inner nature of these facts or what makes them what they are, I can say nothing at all. I cannot impart acquaintance with them to anyone who has not already made it himself. I cannot *describe* them, make a blind man guess what blue is like, define to a child a syllogism, or tell a philosopher in just what respect distance is just what it is, and differs from other forms of relation. At most, I can say to my friends, Go to certain places and act in certain ways, and these objects will probably come. . . . In minds able to speak at all here is, it is true, *some* knowledge about everything. . . . The two kinds of knowledge are, therefore, as the human mind practically exerts them, relative terms. That is, the same thought of a thing may be called knowledge-about it in comparison with a simpler thought, or acquaintance with a thought of it that is more articulate and explicit still. (PP, 217)

The acquaintance terminus of the acquaintance-description continuum is, on the interpretation presented in this essay, pure experience. No matter how profoundly conceptualized by knowledge-about, there is pure experience at bottom, the given. What allows the mind to rise above sheer acquaintance with pure experience is conception or meaning: "The possibility of two such knowledges depends on a fundamental psychic peculiarity which may be entitled '*the principle of constancy in the mind's meanings*,' and which may be thus expressed: '*The same matters can be thought of in successive portions of the mental stream, and some of these portions can know that they mean the same matters which the other portions meant.*' One might put it otherwise by saying that '*the mind can always intend, and know when it intends, to think of the Same*' (PP, 434).

This sense of sameness, the very keel and backbone of our thinking, as James phrases it, fixes sameness of a subject of discourse, such as the dog Fido, through a function he calls conception, the vehicles of which he calls concepts, by which he means a particular state of mind, such as a mental image of a dog, which subserves the conception of Fido, and perhaps other conceptions. "It is plain," he writes, "that one and the same mental state can be the vehicle of many conceptions, can mean a particular thing, and a great deal more besides" (PP, 436). So the concept/image of a dog could figure in a person's conception of Fido but also his conception of the canine species, his conception of loyalty, and so forth. Such vehicles of conceptions can change, and new conceptions can replace them, but the conceptions themselves are just the meanings they are, particular functions relating mental states to the subjects of discourse of which they are the conceptions: "Each conception thus eternally remains what it is, and never can become another. The mind may change its states, and its meanings, at different times; may drop one conception and take up another; but the dropped conception can in no intelligible sense be said to *change into* its successor" (PP, 437). Meanings are a profound exception to James's empiricist penchant to see flux everywhere. They *function* to lift the subject out of the unique immediacy of the stream of thought at a given time, allowing her to relate herself, by the meaning of the word "pen" (for instance) to pens everywhere ("All pens are a nuisance") or a particular pen that is not now the object of her experience or anyone else's ("There might be pens on Mars"). James's view that meanings are vague and "fringey" is not to be confused with Willard van Orman Quine's views about the indeterminacy of meaning, as for James what someone means on a given occasion by "rabbit" (say) is quite particular, even if evanescent and vague. He does not take the Quinean view associated that the objective reality of meaning consists entirely of correlations between external stimuli and dispositions to verbal behavior. Rather, meanings are a third factor, correlated with neural processes and available to the subject's awareness. So the Quinean idea that there can be different and incompatible "translation manuals" correlating verbal dispositions to external stimuli is not to the point; whatever the correlations and whatever the translation manuals, meaning is a third item, a particular fact of mind:

> *The sense of our own meaning is an entirely peculiar element of the thought.* It is one of those evanescent and "transitive" facts of mind which introspection cannot turn round upon, and isolate and hold up for examination, as an entomologist passes round an insect on a pin. In the (somewhat clumsy) terminology I have used, it pertains to the "fringe" of the subjective state, and is a "feeling of tendency," whose neural counterpart is undoubtedly a lot of dawning and dying processes too faint and complex to be traced. (PP, 446)[1]

Moreover, to know Fido, my conception of Fido need not mirror, copy, or duplicate Fido. My conception can have a particular perspective on Fido, what Fido means for me or us, or what John Searle calls an "aspectual shape," although, contrary to Searle's view, not all knowledge is knowledge-about; there is a role for resemblance and sheer acquaintance in James's commitment to a world of pure experience, whereas Searle, who accepts a scientific world-view in which everything has microstructure, has no use for the notion that states of mind resemble the external world, since mental states don't resemble physical microstructure.

What James requires is that my conception should lead to states of mind in which I am acting on Fido (e.g., serving him chow), or in which I am considering which states of mind resemble Fido (e.g., visual sensations of Fido's healthy golden coat this resemblance is not sheer acquaintance, involving as it does knowledge-about healthy coats, etc., but it approximates to such acquaintance as to an ideal limit). As James puts it, "[I]deas, in order to know must be cast in the exact likeness of whatever things they know, and . . . the only things that can be known are those which ideas can resemble. . . . All that a state of mind need do, in order to take cognizance of a reality, or intend it, or be 'about it,' is to lead to a remoter state of mind which either acts upon the reality or resembles it" (PP, 445). Call this the *leading-to* account of what conceptions do, what function they perform in the relationship between mental states and their subjects of discourse.

Shuttling Again

A second problem for Gale's "shuttling" interpretation is that James never shuttles *to* classical British empiricism, which located the meaning of complex ideas in their pedigree, the simple ideas they could be traced back to. James always reckoned that the continuity of consciousness was a very fundamental difference from the "granular" conceptions of consciousness in Hume and the classical empiricist tradition. And it is clear from *The Principles'* treatment of conception that meaning has a leading-to function, rather than decomposing into the simple ideas that comprise its history.

Gale evidently supposes that the only live options about pragmatic meaning are either his view or the view that pragmatic meaning is only one species of meaning, the latter expressed as the notion that James had a theory of pragmatic meaning rather than, as Gale holds, a pragmatic theory of meaning. But there is a third alternative: pragmatic meaning is the meaning of *The Principles* as applied to the resolution of problems, especially philosophical problems. If one Bears in mind what James writes in *Principles* about the leading-to relationship and interprets his remarks in *Pragmatism* about ideas as guides to experience in this light, the "applied theory of meaning" view of pragmatic meaning is quite plausible.

As a test, consider James's resolution in *Pragmatism* of the dispute among his camping friends about whether a man walks around a squirrel or not when he circles a tree where a squirrel keeps the tree trunk between itself and the man. This anecdote, which James sets out at length in order to introduce the pragmatic method, must be dismissed in Gale's reading as a basic mistake, the error of using the classical British empiricist account of meaning instead of his conditionalized-prediction theory:

> James attempts to resolve the dispute by deploying his pragmatic theory of meaning, but what he actually does is to apply the content empiricist theory to the rival claims to show that, in spite of their differences in language, they mean the same thing, because they describe the same experiences or experiential contents. That he is using this species of empiricism is manifest in his confining his experiential rendering of the "rival" claims to the experiences an observer would have had *at the time of the circling*, not those which would be had at some future time if cer-

tain steps were taken, such as subsequently checking the tree for tiny claw marks
and the ground for human footprints and squirrel droppings. (Gale 1999, 153)

But what James does is to show that both formulations, "'the man goes around
the squirrel" and "the man does not go around the squirrel," would lead to the
same experience (of man-and-squirrel-in-motion); and it is immaterial whether
the experience in question is in the future, or in the past, or hypothetical. Presumably James's camping friends *saw* (past tense) the episode in question, so
the pragmatic method operates in this case on the past. The man is not going
around the squirrel (because the squirrel keeps its stomach facing the man)
and the man is going around the squirrel (because he moves to its north then
its west then its south and then its east) have the same pragmatic cash value;
the formulations lead to the same experience. It may well be that most of the
interesting problems relate to the future, since our need for guidance from our
ideas is most pronounced with respect to the future, but accepting this point
doesn't require Gale's theory of pragmatic meaning and its attendant paradoxes,
such as the following: "But James fails to realize that, according to his exclusively future-oriented pragmatic or operationalist theory of meaning, his claim
that "Caesar *had* effects" or that "we lend and borrow verifications" has as its
whole meaning a set of conditionalized predictions that report what experiences
we will have in the future if we perform certain operations. The apparently
retrospective meanings get converted into exclusively future-directed ones"
(Gale 1999, 173). The paradox is resolved by interpreting pragmatic meaning
in the light of the treatment of meaning in *Principles*, notably its leading-to
relation, which isn't tethered to conditionalized predictions about the future.
Consequently, we can accept the tale of the squirrel for what it is, an easy introduction to a method for resolving metaphysical disputes in which the contesting theories have the same cash value, despite their verbal appearance of in-
compatibility. When two metaphysical views have the same experiential
consequences, the conflict between them is illusory. (And when there are no
experiential consequences on either side, as in the dispute between the "elf-
theory" of why yeast rises and the "brownie-theory," the dispute is also illusory.
The method reveals the same cash value in the case of the squirrel, and no
cash value in the case of the yeast.)

Attention to *The Principles'* account of conception may dissolve what Gale
regards as a "deep aporia in James's philosophy," between beliefs and meanings

being normative and their being causal (Gale 1999, 160). He writes that James usually characterizes the disposition of the believer in purely causal terms, as when an idea provides the "impulse" to action, or in the stricture that the Absolute is meaningful if it can be shown to have "any consequences" for our life. But Gale favors the normative account that James sometimes gives, in terms of which conduct is to be "recommended" or "required." On the other hand, Gale doesn't explain why the two accounts should be mutually exclusive. The leading-to relation that conception mediates between consciousness and action is clearly a causal one. Yet James writes at the end of Chapter 12 that conceptions are teleological instruments: *"This whole function of conceiving, of fixing, and holding fast to meanings, has no significance apart from the fact that the conceiver is a creature with partial purposes and private ends"* (PP, 456). And it is not hard to see how conceptions, and through them beliefs, could have both causal and teleological roles. Importantly, there could be background teleology and foreground habit: we are habituated into meaning certain things by our words and by acting in certain ways when beliefs in which those conceptions figure. In the foreground, the meaning of "fire" leads me to fire, and the belief that there is a fire in the theater causes me to run for the exit. In the background, the salience of fire in human life makes it important in our societies to have a word for it, so that the causal relationship between individuals and their environment is mediated by this conception; in particular, the harm that fire can do makes it important that someone who grasps the conception that there is a fire in the theater, and believes it, will take steps to protect himself, and the conception of fire contributes to practices of making children aware of such dangers, conditioning them so that when the dangers arise, belief leads to action immediately, without an internal rehearsal of the purpose of doing so. This notion of background teleology and foreground causality seems to fit James's theorizing about leading-to quite well, and consequently it is an important alternative to thinking that one or the other must be the whole story, and that James unwittingly conflated the two.

10

Pragmatism III: Belief

The "Master Syllogism"

The Principles' treatment of belief holds that belief is a type of feeling rather than an action; it exhibits the indirect malleability of the emotions, to which it is akin, rather than the direct voluntary control of a free action like raising or lowering one's arm at will. The malleability of belief does not give rise to a form of justification, "pragmatic justification," which aims at desire-satisfaction rather than truth; instead, it offers a revisionary notion of epistemic justification, which acknowledges some weight for noncognitive reasons in rational belief that aims at the truth. James's doctrine of the will to believe should be read in *this* light, rather than creating an interpretive schema from the materials in some of his later writings that does violence to *The Principles'* account of belief.

When James writes about belief in *The Principles*, he emphasizes that "*In its inner nature belief, or the sense of reality, is a sort of feeling more allied to the emotions than to anything else*" (PP, 913) and he is clear about covering a broad range of cases, from the lowest to the highest possible certainty and conviction. This view that belief is a feeling akin to the emotions is a far cry from the master-syllogism imputation that belief is a free action. And although, as Gale notes, James goes on to say that belief "resembles more than anything what in the psychology of volition we know as consent" (PP, 913), it is clear from the context, about emotion and range of cases, that there are beliefs that amount to *forced consent*, such as the torture victim's absolute conviction that he is in pain, my certainty that I have one and only one head, and so forth. James also says that "Consent is recognized by all to be a manifestation of our active nature," but it should be kept in mind that our active nature is expressed not only in free choice but also in our vulnerability to being compelled by our emotions and feelings. According to James's identification of will and belief, as when he writes that *"Will and Belief, in short, meaning a certain relation between objects and the Self, are two names for one and the same psychological phenomenon,"* it is imperative to understand will in a broad sense, to include feeling and emotion as well as free choice (PP, 424).

From this perspective, Richard Gale must be engaged in an interpretive red herring when he imputes to James, as a premise in "James's master syllogism," the view that *belief is a free action.* This syllogism, which is the keel of Gale's reading, runs as follows, in its first-shot statement:

1. We are always morally obligated to act so as to maximize desire-satisfaction over desire-dissatisfaction.
2. Belief is an action.
3. We are always morally obligated to believe in a manner that maximizes desire-satisfaction over desire-dissatisfaction.

Subsequently, Gale replaces 2 with 2′, "Belief is a free action," since unfree beliefs wouldn't generate obligations (because *Ought* implies can), and then qualifies 2* as "Belief is a free action or inducible by free actions."[1] These are not small changes, so I propose to take the trio one at a time.

With regard to 2, there are two ranges of cases to consider, namely (i) those in which belief is alleged to be comparable to free consent, and (ii) those in which it is compared to forced consent. As Gale appreciates, the ii-range of cases threatens his syllogism, since consent that is forced tends to remove responsibility, so the inference to the conclusion, 3, becomes invalid. Since I take *The Principles* to be unequivocal about the significance of the ii-range of cases, the "master syllogism" is already hopelessly compromised. There are some extreme cases in category ii, such as the belief that one is in pain while being tortured, and at one point Gale asks that his interpretation not to be taxed with such cases (Gale 1999, 97) on the grounds that James had little concern with merely possible cases and was more concerned with the way things are; but I don't think this will help him, because the extreme cases are not merely possible. People get tortured too often, for instance. Besides, category ii includes most of our perceptual beliefs, such as my visual belief that when I put my hand in front of my face I see my hand in front of me. (Possible exceptions include the "duckrabbit" drawing that one can see as a duck or a rabbit; one is able to "direct" oneself to see it either way.)

But there is worse to come, turning to type-i cases, around which Gale might hope to reconstruct his syllogism with scope limited to them. These lead from 2 to 2′, "Belief is a free action," where the beliefs in question are now only the type-i beliefs. The original ambition of the master syllogism has been left behind. So consider directing oneself to see a duckrabbit first as a duck, then as a rabbit. The voluntarism in this kind of case surrounds the directing, rather than the belief (that one sees an image of a duck, that one sees an image of a rabbit). Although I don't know exactly what items Gale would put into 2′, the duckrabbit item suggests that 2′ *is empty*; there are no i-items. Instead, there are cases where belief is induced by the will, as in directing oneself to see a duck, then a rabbit. This is the master syllogism with 2* instead of 2 or 2′, although it might as well be 2, "Belief is inducible by free actions." This is true, whether the case be duckrabbit attention-directing, I-think-I-can power of positive thinking, or hanging with friends who share an infectious belief you want to acquire.

My diagnosis is that Gale, using suggestions in James's later writings as an interpretive springboard, is arriving at an implausible interpretation of James's philosophical system as a whole. Does James hold that belief is an action, as Gale maintains, *in the sense of something that is done intentionally or at will?* Given James's background thoughts about belief-as-emotion and range-of-cases, it seems he does not hold this but rather: belief is sometimes inducible by one's action. It is sometimes brought into existence indirectly, as 2 affirms. But it was obvious to James, as it is obvious to everyone else, that not all cases are like this; premise 2 of the master syllogism is a nonstarter. The discussion of belief in *The Principles* should be a bulwark against the strong voluntarist notion of belief that Gale imposes on James.

Gale is so adamant about imposing 'Belief is a free action' on James that he becomes vexed when James resists, in the following passage from *The Will to Believe*: "Does it not seem preposterous on the very face of it to talk of our opinions being modifiable at will? Can our will either help or hinder our intellect in its perceptions of truth? Can we, by just willing it, believe that Abraham Lincoln's existence is a myth, and that the portraits of him in *McClure's Magazine* are all of someone else? . . . We can *say* any of these things, but we are absolutely impotent to believe them" (WB, 15–16). Gale comments:

> This is a disastrous response that leads right into the creating-discovering aporia. We are supposed to be able to create some of our beliefs by making the effort to attend, but now we are told that the cause of all beliefs is passional, and since we cannot control our passions at will neither can we control at will our beliefs. This makes us into passive registerers or discoverers of our beliefs.
>
> Why, for heaven's sake, did James not avail himself of his earlier causal recipe for indirectly inducing belief by acting as if we believe? (Gale 1999, 68)

But is not the "aporia" dissolved in the quoted passage, by the phrase "by just willing it"? Rational belief formation, including instances when it is rational to induce belief indirectly, is more complex than "just willing." James's epistemology is not *simply* "based on" an ethical principle of utility and the premise that "all belief is a free action."

Maximizing Desire-Satisfaction

Gale notes that his syllogism has as its conclusion, "We are always morally obligated to believe in a manner that maximizes desire-satisfaction over the other available belief options," and he observes that "for the argument to work," the premise about belief "must be beefed up" to assert that "Belief is a *free* action." And this sets up a rule he attributes to James: "We are always morally obligated to act so as to maximize desire-satisfaction over the other options available to us." I have approached this syllogism in one way, by directly challenging its presumptions about belief. But approach it differently, by asking whether any remotely charitable reading of James's basic ideas would imply that, *given* my not believing that I am in pain would maximize desire-satisfaction (since I very much desire not to be in pain, and if I did not believe I was, I wouldn't be), I should believe that I am not in pain, at will. Gale has much sport with James, by crucifying him on his "master syllogism," but James's treatment of belief in *The Principles* and a modest principle of charity in interpretation require that we bring him down from the crucifix. Gale sometimes suggests that problems such as the one I just raised, in the case of pain, are nitpicking, because we can always indirectly change belief in conformity with the demands of desire-satisfaction, by the familiar mechanisms of the power of positive thinking and the like. But how are these mechanisms going to be effective in the range of beliefs where consent is forced consent? Should my torturer visit me every day, no amount of positive thinking is going to produce a session in which I am blessedly free of the belief that I am in pain. Gale applies a principle of charity in interpretation a different way. He writes, "This [Master Syllogism] attempt to base epistemology in general on ethical principles, even if it should not ultimately prove to be fully defensible, is one of the boldest and most original contributions to philosophy of all time and secures a permanent place for James in the Philosophical Hall of Fame" (Gale 1999, 25). This is hard to read without thinking that Gale is being disingenuous. After all, the divided-self interpretation assesses James's work as riven with muddles ("aporia," as Gale styles them) as a result of James's internalizing both philosophical satyrism ("Prometheanism") and a belletrist's notion of oneness with humanistic values ("anti-Promethean mysticism"), an evidently pathological and certainly incoherent desire to have it all and merge with all. In this assessment James's "Master Syllogism" should secure for him a permanent place in the Philosophical Hall of Muddled Tender-Minded Satyrs.

Although the alleged Master Syllogism is sufficiently discredited by the failure of the second premise to support the conclusion, the first premise is defective as well, as the preceding line of thought shows. I believe its attraction can be traced to remarks like the following one, from "The Dilemma of Determinism," where James is rehearsing two suppositions he makes when addressing the issue of determinism: "first, when we make theories about the world and discuss them with one another, we do so in order to attain a conception of things which shall give us subjective satisfaction; and, second, if there be two conceptions, and the one seems to us, on the whole, more rational than the other, we are entitled to suppose that the more rational one is the truer of the two" (WB, 115). Note that the first supposition could be read in two ways, as stating that (A) subjective satisfaction is the *only* virtue of a theory, or (B) despite its often being deemed irrelevant, subjective satisfaction *is* a virtue of a theory, albeit one among many. The distinction is vitally important. Construed in the first way, Gale's first premise acquires support; construed in the latter, it does not. I argue for the latter, on the basis of a principle of interpretive charity which attempts to read James's first supposition from the 1884 paper in a manner that is consistent with *The Principles'* discussion of free will and determinism in 1890, where it clearly serves in a B-type role. First, James states in "The Stream of Thought" that "An act has no ethical quality whatever *unless* it be chosen out of several all equally possible," (PP, 276, my emphasis). Free choice is being characterized, reasonably, as a necessary condition for an action's having an ethical quality, whereas in Gale's interpretation, it is a sufficient condition: if an act is freely chosen, according to his syllogism, then it has the ethical quality of being right just in case it maximizes desire-satisfaction, and otherwise wrong.

Second, there is James's deployment of his Tie-Breaker, as I dubbed it in Chapter 1. His most important use of it in *The Principles*, already referred to in Chapters 3 and 5, is at the end of the chapter "Attention," after many pages of *sifting evidence* on both sides of the issue between those who favor the effect theory of attention, which implies freedom-defeating determinism in James's view, and the cause theory, which implies free will (PP, 428–30). Sifting evidence would seem to be unnecessary if only desire-satisfaction were at stake, but James makes it plain that the sifting is basic to science and that his ethical reasons for preferring the effect theory "are hardly suited for introduction into a psychological work." Note that he does not say that proponents of the effect theory are wrong; nor does he say that they are *morally* wrong, as he would have to say if he were committed to Gale's syllogism. Rather, "one can leave the question open whilst waiting for light" (PP, 429) allowing one's opponents to adhere to the effect theory without opprobrium, on the basis of their general mechanistic philosophy, while one takes advantage of "a similar privilege" to construe attention as an original force, for ethical reasons.

A third objection to the first premise of Gale's syllogism is obvious from James's writing that ethical reasons "are hardly suited for introduction into a psychological work." Works of psychology express a large number of beliefs, and if they are *hardly* liable to ethical critique for failing to maximize desire-satisfaction, they constitute an expansive field of counterexamples to the syllogism; indeed they represent the thin end of a wedge, which becomes thicker as the irrelevance of ethical reasons in physics and other natural sciences is taken into account, and thicker still as stock is taken of their irrelevance to all sorts of mundane beliefs.

Of course it is evident to virtually everyone that the Master Syllogism is preposterous. But on the basis of the foregoing discussion of its major and minor premises I am inclined to assert that the syllogism is also a preposterous interpretation of James. I anticipate rejoinders such as "But putting *The Principles* aside and focusing on admittedly ambiguous statements in popular lectures and unfinished manuscripts . . . ," but these presuppose an interpretive methodology which, judged by the fruit I have been inspecting, is itself preposterous. (For a more tempered discussion of methodological considerations, see the final section of Chapter 1.)

One World or Many?

The Two-Levels View of James's philosophy counts many worlds at the empirical level, but one world, a world of pure experience, at the metaphysical level. This contrasts with the divided-self reading, which counts many worlds and diagnoses James as unable to bring them into a unity. James's emphasis on many worlds starts from *The Principles'* treatment of belief:

> Suppose a new-born mind, entirely blank and waiting for experience to begin. Suppose that it begins in the form of a visual impression (whether faint or vivid is immaterial) of a lighted candle against a dark background, and nothing else, so that whilst this image lasts it constitutes the entire universe known to the mind in question. Suppose, moreover (to simplify the hypothesis), that the candle is only imaginary, and that no "original" of it is recognized by us psychologists outside. Will this hallucinatory candle be believed in, will it have a real existence for the mind? (PP, 917)

James answers that the candle has a real existence (*Any object which remains uncontradicted is ipso facto believed and posited as absolute reality* [PP, 918]), but he goes on to note that "A dream-candle has existence, true enough; but not the same existence (existence for itself, namely, or *extra mentem meam*) which the candles of waking perception have" (PP, 920). James reckons himself entitled to some profligacy about the worlds of the mental candle and the physical candle, not to mention the candle that figures in the novelist's tale, because they all bottom out in what he calls *sensation* in *The Principles*, sensation in an objective sense that can be *imported* into the stream of consciousness or *exported* into the physical objects you are aware of; they are all perspectives on the world of pure experience (objective sensation). So there are many grades of "real existence." "The total world of which the philosopher must take account," James writes, "is thus composed of the realities *plus* the fancies and illusions" (PP, 920). His reference to "the realities" acknowledges the habitual and practical sway of the ordinary person's beliefs.

Indeed, he distinguishes various "sub-universes" which "the complete philosopher" will recognize: the world of sense, the world of science, the world of ideal relations, the world of "idols of the tribe," the various supernatural worlds, the various worlds of individual opinion, and the worlds of sheer madness and vagary. The complete philosopher traces the relations among these worlds, and classifies her opinions as pertaining to this or that world. But each and every world on his list is a perspective on pure experience, even if, for the individual thinker, his world is "for him the world of ultimate realities," revealing "the everlasting partiality of our nature" (PP, 923).

It is helpful to recall that the chapter on different realities is positively surrounded by *sensationalist* accounts, including theories according to which physical objects and space itself are constructs out of sensation. (James's Shoehorning voluminousness into the spatial quale, in order to pave the way toward sensationalist construction of three-dimensional space, was noted in Chapter 1.) The accusation of Poohbahism about reality either ignores this fact or betrays skepticism about pure experience or unconceptualized sensation.

Such skepticism is common in contemporary philosophy. Fred Dretske had to resist it when he defended the notion that our experience of the world, the sensory dimension of our mental life, should not be confused with cognitive phenomena, with possession and deployment of concepts. Responding to critics of his *Seeing and Knowing*, he pleads that surely, as philosophical commitments go, commitment to sense experience involves a tolerable level of risk. But the pendulum swings, he observes, and his critics deem that the burden of proof falls on him to justify talk about such exotica. He does so by showing that a human being or other animal can see an object without thereby having beliefs about it. Seeing a bug, in this fundamental nondoxastic sense, is like stepping on it: "Whether we have—whether we *always* have—beliefs about the bugs we see (or step on) is *not* the issue. If bugs emitted a deafening roar when molested, we should doubtless notice their presence when we stepped on them. This would be no reason to advance a doxastic or cognitive theory of *stepping on*" (Dretske 1991, 183). James evidently thought there were episodes in the early life of everyone in which there was such simple seeing, but that isn't the crucial point, as Dretske notes: "the claim is, and has always been, not that simple seeing of X occurs *only* (or, indeed, *ever*) when one has *no* beliefs about X, but that its occurrence is *compatible* with no such beliefs" (Dretske 1991, 182).

   In holding that James's sensationalism can be rationally reconstructed using Dretske's resources, I do not mean to imply that Dretske would want to
endorse James's doctrine of pure experience. He would want to replace the
idea of how things *look*, nonepistemically, with an information-theoretic account of the processing of sensory information that is made available to cognitive centers for conceptual utilization.[2] Such replacement would fit the "look"
of something for physicalistic reduction, not pure-experiential reduction. (This
may be too strong, since there may be a way of wedding James's radical empiricism to information theory, but Dretske's information-theoretic account of the
way things look certainly allows him to be noncommittal, at least, about James's
view.) But the defense of nonepistemic experience is something that James's
and Dretske's theories have in common.

11

Pragmatism IV: Rationality and Truth

There are conflicting opinions about the relationship between James's pragmatism and truth. In one view he dispenses with truth altogether; in another, his theory of truth is really a theory of rational belief, according to which it may be rational, when the practical benefits are sufficiently great, to believe something one knows to be false. In another view pragmatic justification aims at desire-satisfaction while epistemic justification aims at truth; pragmatic and truth-oriented considerations operate differently. Against such opinions, I will argue here that pragmatic considerations are an element of epistemic justification, aiming at the truth, understood as distinct from practical benefits.

Consider the following passage from *Pragmatism*:

> Let me now say only this, that truth is *one species of good*, and not as usually supposed, a category distinct from the good, and co-ordinate with it. *The true is whatever proves itself to be good in the way of belief, and good, too, for definite, assignable reasons.* Surely you must admit this, that if there were *no* good for life in true ideas, or if the knowledge of them were positively disadvantageous and false ideas the only useful ones, then the current notion that truth is divine and precious, and its pursuit a duty, could never have grown up or become a dogma. In a world like that, our duty would be to *shun* truth, rather. But in this world, just as certain foods are not only agreeable to our taste, but good for our teeth, our stomach, and our tissues; so certain ideas are not only agreeable to think about, or agreeable as supporting other ideas that we are fond of, but they are also helpful in life's practical struggles. If there be any life that it is really better we should lead, and if there be any idea which, if believed in, would help us to lead that life, then it would be really *better for us* to believe in that idea, *unless, indeed, belief in it incidentally clashed with other greater vital benefits.* (P, 42)

Remarks like this tend to support interpretive projects like Rorty's, which prescind from the moments when James said something constructive about truth and follow up instead his polemic against the notion of "correspondence," leading to a construal of pragmatism which consists *"simply* in the dissolution of the traditional problematic about truth" (Rorty 1997, 334).

My interpretation gives due weight both to James's constructive remarks about truth and his will-to-believe doctrine, an interpretive project which is consistent with his polemic against correspondence, but not reducible to it. The interpretation's first axiom is drawn from Ayer's reading of James, noted in Chapter 5, according to which different types of propositions have different functions in our total system of beliefs. Truth is a species of good because, within a field of belief such as psychology (say), a belief has a certain *function,* which a true belief performs well, with reference to which function, consequently, it is good. True beliefs are those that work, generally speaking, but they work in different ways, relative to different contexts and the subsystem of beliefs that believers use in order to navigate those contexts. Assessment of belief will vary accordingly in algebra, physics, and religion; algebra aims at proof, physics at predictive power, religion at satisfaction of moral and emotional interests. The second axiom adds that within any context the appropriate evidential standards may not be met uniquely by one of the various live options for belief, in which case personal/subjective interests legitimately "incline the beam" toward this option or that. The second axiom, what I call "James's Tie-Breaker," was shown at work in the previous chapter with respect to the cause theory of attention and the effect theory, two incompatible options for belief in a context where the evidential standards of psychology aren't uniquely met by either of them. The second axiom concerns rational belief when evidential standards for truth are not uniquely met, and it may vary from person to person. The first axiom concerns truth, and it recognizes a notion of absolute truth that does not countenance variation from person to person.

In the next two sections I argue that evidential standards pertaining to the first axiom are fundamental, setting constraints on rational belief. Then I set out some of the logic of this constraint.

Constraining Subjectivity

Stephen Nathanson interprets James as endorsing the "shocking conclusion" that adoption of beliefs known to be false may be rational. ("All that is required for justification is a significant enough advantage" [Nathanson 1985, 88].) At this late stage in my argument I will assume that he is wrong and focus on providing a model that diagnoses why he is wrong. Here is the "Jamesian" frame that Nathanson supplies:

> I do not mean to retract my earlier "Jamesian" conclusion that the evidential irrationality of a belief might be overridden by its practical benefits. If embracing contradictions truly enhances the life of a Whitmanian romantic, then this might well provide an over-riding reason for holding inconsistent beliefs. Nonetheless, logical and evidential standards still apply in these cases. If there is evidence against a cherished belief, it provides reasons against that belief, even if it may be rational to reject the evidence in order to gain specific benefits. (Nathanson 1985, 119)

But why do "logical and evidential standards" still apply? Why should my rationality be in any way dependent on them? If my expected benefit or perceived advantage may outweigh the evidence as measured by these standards, why can't my expected benefit determine what counts as evidence? How, on Nathanson's view, does "the evidence" maintain itself as a constraint on belief formation? Failing an answer to this question, his view slides down a slippery slope to a vicious form of subjectivism that can't distinguish between rational agents and madmen.

Where do those logical and evidential standards come from? In James's reckoning they do not come from experience. They pertain to the "abstract order" rather than the "sensible order." The abstract order is not to be understood as a Platonic realm of eternal and immutable truths, but rather as a conceptual structure which is the historical upshot of evolution; it is the "back door" to the mind, while "the way of 'experience' proper is the front door, the door of the five senses" (PP, 1225).

The reference here is to a discussion of causes of mental modification of which we are not immediately conscious as such:

Some of them are molecular accidents before birth; some of them are collateral and remote combinations, unintended combinations, one might say, of more direct effects wrought in the unstable and intricate brain-tissue. Such a result is unquestionably the susceptibility to music, which some individuals possess at the present day. It has no zoological utility; it corresponds to no object in the natural environment; it is a pure *incident* of having a hearing organ, an incident depending on such instable and inessential conditions that one brother may have it and another not. Just so with the susceptibility to sea-sickness, which, so far from being engendered by long experience of its "object" (if a heaving deck can be called its object) is erelong annulled thereby. (PP, 1225)

Our higher aesthetic, moral, and intellectual life seems made up of affections of this "collateral and incidental sort, which have entered the mind by the back stairs, as it were, or rather have not entered the mind at all, but got surreptitiously born in the house. No one can successfully treat of psychogenesis, or the factors of mental evolution, without distinguishing between these two ways in which the mind is assailed" (PP, 1225). The pure or a priori sciences make up an entirely "of the house-born portion of our mental structure," forming a body of propositions "with whose genesis experience has nothing to do" (PP, 1237). Consistency is a house-born principle of the mind just as breathing is a house-born principle of the body: "After man's interest in breathing freely, the greatest of all his interests (because it never fluctuates or remits, as most of his physical interests do) is his interest in *consistency*, in feeling that what he now thinks goes with what he thinks on other occasions. We tirelessly compare truth with truth for this sole purpose. Is the present candidate for belief perhaps contradicted by principle number one? Is it compatible with fact number two? And so forth" (MT, 113). As James says elsewhere about scientific conceptions, "Their genesis is strictly akin to that of the flashes of poetry and sallies of wit to which the instable brain-paths equally give rise. But whereas the poetry and wit (like the science of the ancients) are their 'own excuse for being,' and have to run the gauntlet of no farther test, the 'scientific' conceptions must prove their worth by being 'verified'" (PP, 1232). This brings us a step closer to answering the question that Nathanson left unanswered, about how logical and evidential standards constrain subjectivity in James's account. Pure and empirical principles, affecting the mind's "back door" in their different ways and codified by the mathematical and scientific communities, are rationally coercive. The madman has failed to inherit the back-door inheritance of the human community with respect to "logical and evidential standards."

Absolute Truth and Half-Truth

James's will-to-believe doctrine argues the right, broadly speaking, to believe what will make one's life go best, and from the beginning it was charged with abandoning epistemic responsibility. He himself wrote, "I fornicate with that unclean thing [the will-to-believe], my adversaries may think, whereas your genuine truth-lovers must discourse in Huxleyan heroics, and feel as if truth ought to bring eventual messages of death to all our satisfactions" (James 1907, 404, quoted in Myers 1986, 44). There are a variety of interpretations of this doctrine. There are cautious readings, such as Timothy Sprigge's, which view it as of a piece with James's well-known sympathy for the mind-cure movement of his day, a popular philosophy of self-improvement which emphasized the power of positive thinking. In this reckoning James was simply drawing attention to unexpectedly wide-ranging and important contexts in which believing that such and such is true will initiate causal mechanisms producing good consequences. Sprigge credits James with rightly claiming that the power of the will in a quite ordinary sense is much greater than ordinarily thought, but he dismisses as error "the much bolder claim that cognitive enquiry quite properly as much creates its object as discovers it," on the grounds that the bolder claim implies that the existence or nonexistence of God, for instance, is "open to settlement by our way of thinking about the world," as though it were a matter for us to decide (Sprigge 1993, 43). The consequence of my interpretation for Sprigge's is simply that he is failing to distinguish the first and second axioms. The first axiom leaves open the possibility that the contexts that raise questions about God are susceptible to absolute truth, although rational belief may be subjective in just the way that Sprigge identifies.

Sprigge is not wrong to emphasize the optimistic, power-of-positive-thinking aspect of James's thinking about religion and other matters, and specifically his high opinion of the mind-cure movement, which James describes as "a living system of mental hygiene which may well claim to have thrown all previous literature of the *Diatetik der Seele* into the shade. This system is wholly and exclusively compacted of optimism: "'Pessimism leads to weakness. Optimism leads to power." "Thoughts are things," as one of the most vigorous mind-cure writers prints in bold type at the bottom of each of his pages; and if your thoughts are of health, youth, vigor, and success, before you know it these things will also be your outward portion" (VRE, 93). The difficulty with Sprigge's interpretation is not that it emphasizes James's optimism, but that it either restricts the will to believe to self-fulfilling prophecy or severs the optimism's connection with truth. Consider first the latter difficulty:

> These, then, are my last words to you: Be not afraid of life. Believe that life *is* worth living, and your belief will help create the fact. The "scientific proof" that you are right may not be clear before the day of judgment (or some stage of being which that expression may serve to symbolize) is reached. But the faithful fighters of this hour, or the beings that then and there will represent them, may then turn to the faint-hearted, who here decline to go on, with words like those with which Henry IV greeted the tardy Crillon after a great victory had been gained: "Hang yourself, brave Crillon! We fought at Arques, and you were not there." (WB, 56)

When James in this passage from "Is Life Worth Living?" urges his audience to believe that life is worth living, he does not mean only that their lives will go better if they do, though he does mean that, but also that by exercising their right to believe that the physical order is a part of a larger spiritual order their cognitive vision will expand. He compares that step to the transition from the vision of a dog to the vision of a human being: "Now turn from this to the life of man. In the dog's life we see the world invisible to him because we live in both worlds. In human life, although we only see our world, and his within it, yet encompassing both these worlds a still wider world may be there, as unseen by us as our world is by him; and to believe in this world *may* be the most essential function that our lives in this world have to perform" (WB, 53). James wants to establish epistemic warrant for acting on this "may be." Otherwise his address could have been much shorter, and he would not have had to launch the following argument:

> Now, I wish to make you feel, if I can in the short remainder of this hour, that we have the right to believe the physical order to be only a partial order; that we have a right to supplement it by an unseen spiritual order which we assume on trust, if only thereby life may seem to us better worth living again. But as such a trust will

seem to some of you sadly mystical and execrable unscientific, I must first say a word or two to weaken the veto which you may consider that science opposes to our act. (WB, 49)

Sprigge's interpretation limits James's optimism to a system of belief in which everything about the world is taken as given (apart from the causal mechanisms of mind cure), leaving no further creative role for human agency in arriving at rational belief about it, depriving the will-to-believe doctrine of its substance, which includes both the microagency of the human race in fashioning conceptual tools that serve its interests and act as its guides, and the microagency of individual agents who have opportunities, despite their minds' being tightly wedged between the sensible and abstract orders, to adjust their beliefs in life-enhancing ways when the evidence, or the lack of it, permits. I will expand on both of these modes of agency, with reference to Sprigge's example about God.

If the good consequences that flow from believing that p are restricted to the belief's helping bring about p, then Sprigge's account becomes the same as that of Richard Gale, who requires that a will-to-believe option include the condition that believing p play a causal role in making p true:

> It is very much in the spirit of James's Promethean pragmatism to have a causal requirement, since the significance and value of belief in general are the worldly deeds to which it leads. . . . Merely to be in a pleasurable belief or aesthetic state is not its own justification. There must be some behaviorally rooted reason for choosing to get oneself into such a state. Thus, it would violate the Promethean spirit of James's pragmatism to justify an epistemically nonwarranted belief solely in terms of its being a pleasurable state. Furthermore, by having a causal requirement James found yet another way, in addition to having the epistemic undecidability requirement, to protect his doctrine against the wishful-thinking objection. My ill-founded pleasurable delusions of grandeur were ones that my believing could not help to make true. (Gale 1999, 103)

The causal requirement is too strong. Believing that p can have symbolic, representational, or expressive aspects such that, when evidential minima are satisfied, these aspects justify the will to believe.

Not finding a notion of evidential minima in James, Gale has to require the causal condition in order to avoid wishful-thinking scenarios. But the coercions of the sensible and intelligible orders, of sense experience and the a priori, both work to supply evidential minima in James's system, as James wrote in *Pragmatism*. More generally, the function of a given belief in a given context fixes these minima. Consequently it is an oversimplification to characterize the difference between James and Bertrand Russell as amounting to the latter's recognizing that "our most basic duty is to believe in a way that is epistemically warranted, rather than in a way that maximizes desire-satisfaction" (Gale 1999, 151).

With evidential minima in place from sensory and a priori *background* to will-to-believe options, reasons for willing to believe can be found in addition to self-fulfilling prophecy cases that satisfy Gale's causal requirement.

Two Dimensions of Macroagency

Two dimensions of macroagency should be distinguished, retrospective and prospective. Prospective macroagency is an actual future human consensus, an absolute consensus:

> Truth absolute, [the pragmatist] says, means an ideal set of formulations towards which all opinions may in the long run of experience be expected to converge. In this definition of absolute truth he not only postulates that there is a tendency to such convergence of opinion, to such *absolute consensus*, but he postulates the other factors of his definition equally, borrowing them by anticipation from the true conclusions expected to be reached. He postulates the existence of opinions, he postulates the experience that will sift them, and the consistency which that experience will show. He justifies himself in these assumptions by saying that they are not postulates in the strict sense but simple inductions from the past extended to the future by analogy; and he insists that human opinion has already reached a pretty stable equilibrium regarding them, and that if its future development fails to alter them, the definition itself, with all its terms included, will be part of the very absolute truth which it defines. The hypothesis will, in short, have worked successfully all around the circle and proved self-corroborative, and the circle will be closed. (MT, 143–44)

So the first reply to Sprigge is that there can be an absolute truth about God, just in the case that, and just in the sense that, an ultimate consensus may come to pass.

But that future cash value of truth about God is not ours, at the various moments in history when we try to make sense of the world, and the cash value we must rely upon is that of the half-truths that guide us now: "This regulative notion of a potential better truth to be established later, possibly to be established some day absolutely, and having powers of retroactive legislation, turns its face, like all pragmatist notions, towards concreteness of fact, and towards the future. Like the half-truths, the absolute truth will have to be *made*, made as a relation incidental to the growth of a mass of verification-experience, to which the half-true ideas are all along contributing their quota" (P, 107). A historical community may find that belief in God does not conflict with the sensible order, nor with the abstract order of its principles for rational thinking and its theories about the world, and consequently a religion becomes entrenched for that community and becomes a bequest that the community's future generations inherit. Sprigge's question of truth, unless it is a question about ultimate consensus, is just the question that James wants to reject as idle, in favor of the question about the cash value of truth in context.

Sprigge presses: Can the existence or nonexistence of God really be open to settlement by our way of thinking about the world? Is this not too reminiscent of Tinker Bell's appeal in *Peter Pan* to children to believe in fairies in order to save them from extinction? If my earlier account of James's God is correct, a religious belief would be more appropriately compared to our appeal to the intentional stance because of its value in predicting what people are going to do. Whether fairies or the intentional stance is the better analogy will be borne out by ultimate consensus, if it comes to pass. In the meantime, that God exists may possess the cash value of truth, if only a half-truth, for a religious community. Remember James's second supposition in "The Dilemma of Determinism," quoted in the previous chapter: "if there be two conceptions, and the one seems to us, on the whole, more rational than the other, we are entitled to suppose that the more rational one is the truer of the two" (WB, 115). The tie between rational belief and truth is intimate, as it should be, but the first and second axioms laid out above preserve the two as distinct. The issue of the absolute truth about God is not closed by what passes for true in a given context, or by applications of James's Tie-Breaker under conditions of uncertainty.

So we have not arrived at Protagorean subjectivism, such that there is what is "true for me" and what is "true for you." Lawrence E. Johnson, however, argues this in *Focusing on Truth*, holding that the making-true relationship for James is entirely internal to the symbolic structures we create, such that "Whether a belief works seems likely to depend on what the believer asks of the belief, or what she or he is willing to put up with or count as 'working.' This suggests that whether a belief has the pragmatic value James identifies with the good of truth depends entirely on the believer's individual subjective constitution" (Johnson 1992, 66).

Johnson's reading is anchored in passages like one in *The Meaning of Truth* where James writes that the word *truth* "can only be used relatively to some particular trower," such that it may be true for me that Shakespeare wrote the plays attributed to him, whereas it may be true for a Baconian that Shakespeare never wrote the plays in question; given the workings of our opinions, and each of us being what we are (MT, 147). Moreover, there is the "faith ladder" that James invokes in *Some Problems Of Philosophy* and other post-1904 works:

1. There is nothing absurd in a certain view of the world being true, nothing self-contradictory;
2. It *might* have been true under certain conditions;
3. It *may* be true, even now;
4. It is *fit* to be true;
5. It *ought* to be true;
6. It *must* be true;
7. It *shall* be true, at any rate true for *me*. (SPP, 112)

Note, however, that the faith ladder separates truth from being true for me, and consequently it is fully compatible with the notion of absolute truth that my interpretation emphasizes in James.

But Johnson overlooks James's commitment to ultimate consensus as absolute truth, and the coercions of the sensible and abstract orders, and he ignores the peculiarities of James's example, referring to an issue about literary authorship which is shrouded in the past, such that both the Shakespearean and Baconian hypotheses are live options, neither being supported by such overwhelming evidence that the other is ruled out as a candidate for belief among informed members of the literary community. In this context, accepting it as described, differences in the workings of our opinions and differences in our personalities and dispositions ("each of us being what we are") give each of us the right to believe the hypothesis to which we are inclined, the cash value of truth splitting in our half-truths. But it does not follow that we are always free in this way to choose between incompatible hypotheses; belief is often coerced.

The coercions of the sensible and abstract orders are greater or lesser, depending on the interests at stake, the principles at play, and the evidence at hand. The principles of scientific method have been so successful in contexts where an interest in prediction is at stake that someone who defies them egregiously will be deemed an irrational believer in falsehoods, whatever the context in which the predictive question is raised. But scientific and religious purposes are different, and they can be fashioned to be more completely different, in order that they may consort in the same belief-system, as Rorty has recently emphasized:

> Still, to suggest that the tension between science and religion can be resolved merely by saying that the two serve different purposes may sound absurd. But it is no more absurd than the attempt of liberal (mostly Protestant) theologians to demythologize Christianity, and more generally to immunize religious belief from criticism based on accounts of the universe which trace the origin of human beings, and of their intellectual faculties, to the unplanned movements of elementary particles. . . .
>
> Tillich did nothing worse to God than pragmatist philosophy of science had already done to the elementary particles. Pragmatists think that those particles are not the very joints at which things as they are in themselves divide but are objects which we should not have come across unless we had devoted ourselves to one of the many interests of human nature—the interest in predicting and controlling our environment. (Rorty 1986, 91–92)

Thoughts like these lend some urgency to the question, How exactly do the coercions of the sensible and abstract orders set limits on freedom to believe as one will? More generally, How do the functions of beliefs in context constrain subjectivity? And pursuant to these questions about the first axiom, there are questions about the second: How exactly does subjectivity legitimately enter into rational belief? What epistemic conditions constrain and give rise to half-truth or what passes for true?

The Logic of Subjectivity in Belief

At this point it would be helpful to bring forth detail about how these standards operate, which will more clearly specify the role of subjectivity in rational belief. With this in view I outline Nozick's neural network model of reasons for and against, which ties in nicely with James's cerebralism as well as his will-to-believe doctrine. I interpret it as modeling an ideal of the human community's back-door inheritance, an ideal of rationality:

> A reason *r* for statement *S* sends a signal along a channel with a certain positive weight to the *S*-node. A reason *r'* against *S* sends a signal to *S* along a channel with a certain negative weight. An undercutter of *r* as a reason for *S* will send a signal along a channel with a certain weight to reduce the weight (perhaps to zero) on the channel between *r* and *S*. The result of this network is a credibility value for statement *S*. . . . There is room within this framework for many kinds of reasons with different weights. Thus we might hope to capture many methodological maxims from the philosophy of science literature, either within the network or as an emergent phenomenon of the total network. (Nozick 1993, 73)

Persons as learning systems of this type would generate credibility values: scores for each statement *h* that is being assessed. Nozick's first rule of acceptance would rule out Nathanson-style Whitmanesque beliefs, which, since they are known to be false *ex hypothesis*, have zero credibility value:

> *Rule 1:* Do not believe *h* if some alternative statement incompatible with *h* has a higher credibility value than *h* does. (Nozick 1993, 87)

With Rule 2, however, Nozick's model begins to explore the Jamesian will-to-believe doctrine, counseling a rule of acceptance having to do with the desirability of holding a belief, calculating practical objectives and utilities. This rule (and the reformulation in Rule 5) is what I called earlier "James's Tie-Breaker."

> *Rule 2:* Believe (an admissible) *h* only if the expected utility of believing *h* is not less than the expected utility of having no belief about *h*. (Nozick 1993, 88)

So rational belief is a combination of the theoretical and the practical, with the theoretical coming lexicographically first.

Myers was applying Rule 2, in effect, when he recommended (in "Pragmatism and Introspective Psychology") a Jamesian regulative principle for contemporary philosophizing, a principle that appeals to our aesthetic, emotional, and active needs to resolve the endemic inconclusiveness of philosophical arguments. "It is not only the debates about metaphysical issues of the sort that occupied James throughout his career but all the current ones—about abortion, the death penalty, just wars, professional responsibilities, as well as about physicalism, essentialism, realism, and so on—that have no bottom lines. Nothing remains but for the *personal* element to intrude, to weigh the arguments but also the special (possibly compromising) relations that may obtain between them and oneself, if a responsible decision or choice of belief is to eventuate" (Myers 1997, 23).

The lexicographical relationship between the theoretical and the practical, in the Nozickean reading of James, shows that it cannot be rational to embrace a principle according to which "We are always morally obligated to believe in a manner that maximizes desire-satisfaction over the other available options," a principle that Gale attributes to James on the logic of the premises "We are always morally obligated to act so as to maximize desire-satisfaction" and "Belief is a free action." The latter is the premise to question, bearing in mind James's assertion in *Pragmatism* that the mind is "tightly wedged" between the sensory and abstract orders, implying a necessity to believe that, for instance, *You are in agonizing pain* or *two plus two equals four*. Also James classifies belief as an emotion, in *The Principles*, and emotions are not entirely under voluntary control. Gale must be construing the will narrowly, so as to exclude such emotions, when he writes that James's "overall argument for belief being an action is based on his identification of belief with the will, and the will, at least in one of its senses, with effortful attention to an idea. Since effortful attention is something that we can do intentionally or voluntarily, it follows, by Leibniz's Law of the indiscernability of identicals, that belief is an intentional action, and thereby, provided it is free, subject to the casuistic rule" (Gale 1999, 50). As in the previous chapter, I recommend a principle of charity in interpretation at this point, over enforcement of Leibniz's Law on the basis of a questionable reading of James on the voluntariness of belief.

With Rule 3, Nozick's model captures the Jamesian idea that what counts as a sufficiently high score for credibility value should depend on what kind of statement is being considered. With reference to the preceding discussion of science and religion, Rule 3 would be less demanding for religious statements than for statements in particle physics.

Rule 3: Believe an (admissible) *h* only if its credibility value is high enough, given the kind of statement it is. (Nozick 1993, 88)

Nozick next fashions a sufficient condition for belief:

Rule 4: Believe a statement *h* if there is no alternative statement incompatible with *h* that has a higher credibility value than *h* does, and the credibility value of *h* is high enough, given the kind of statement that *h* is, and the expected utility of believing h is at least as great as the expected utility of having no belief about *h*. (Nozick 1993, 89)

Finally, Nozick offers Rule 5 as a possible replacement for Rule 2, in the spirit of his proposed "decision-value" revision of decision theory, which holds that we are to take into account not just expected utility but "symbolic utility" as well, in calculating both rational action and rational belief:

Rule 5: Believe (an admissible) *h* only if the decision-value of believing *h* is at least as great as the decision-value of having no belief about it. (Nozick 1993, 89)

If expected utility has to do with the consequences of taking an action or having a belief, symbolic utility has to do with the action or belief's meaning. So my bringing myself to believe in my freedom to lead my life for good or ill, to use a case close to James's heart, may not only have good consequences (high expected utility), as the mind-cure enthusiast would stress, but also the very believing of it may mean something positive and important about me and my relationship to the universe (high symbolic utility). One's beliefs "make a statement" about oneself, in addition to whatever further consequences they are likely to have.

Jamesians, I submit, should replace Rule 2 with Rule 5.

Neither Rule 2 nor Rule 5 is a violation of what Laurence Bonjour calls "epistemic responsibility," understood as the stricture that, in his words, "one accepts all and only those beliefs which one has good reason to think are true" (Bonjour 1985, 8). Nozick's neural-net model is designed to aim at the truth, but practical considerations enter into its processes in a significantly qualified way, namely, qualification by Rule 1. By contrast, Nathanson's "shocking conclusion" would be a straightforward violation of epistemic responsibility.

For illustrations of this model of the will to believe, one need look no farther than James's case for willing to believe that he is free. He did not believe so in defiance of the evidence but rather in view of the fact, as he perceived it to be, that the evidence for freedom-extinguishing determinism was inconclusive. So he did not violate Rule 1. As for Rule 2, there was no hypothesis incompatible with his belief in free will that obliged him to disbelieve that his will was free. The free-will hypothesis has sufficient credibility value. Moreover, the expected utility of believing that hypothesis is higher than that of having no belief at all on the matter. He reckoned that adopting belief in free will would lift him out of his depression and generally give him a more positive outlook on life. The free-will hypothesis also satisfies Rule 3, because it is a kind of hypothesis that one can rationally believe in the absence of conclusive evidence to the contrary, whereas higher evidential standards would be required for, say, the belief that it is safe to walk over a particular bridge. Finally, there are reasons to believe in free will apart from those that are covered by the expected utility of adopting the belief, namely, those that have to do with the symbolic utility of the very adoption of the belief, that is, utility having to do with the meaning or expressive quality of adopting it, as opposed to the expected consequences of doing so. Accepting the free-will hypothesis means that one views oneself and the world in a certain way, a view that has positive symbolic utility, in addition to whatever further good consequences, such as lifting a depression, the adoption may have. For instance, one views oneself as having originative value in shaping the course of events, rather than merely transmitting a cause-effect chain stretching back into the past. (I am not arguing that the reader should accept this view, necessarily, but I am illustrating the model by reference to a view that James held.)

Where two incompatible hypotheses are both live options for belief according to the first three rules, the application of Rule 5 in favor of one or the other hypothesis can be called an application of James's Tie-Breaker. It is applicable in moral dilemmas in which different premises about value lead to incompatible conclusions in comparably cogent arguments. It is also applicable in cases where there is no dispute about values but where the evidence is inconclusive for this course of action over that. Recognizing that symbolic considerations are a legitimate influence on belief formation is likely to lead to a more tolerant outlook, less certainty that others are irrational or ill-informed. They may be sufficiently informed while being influenced differently by symbolic utility. This is a plausible diagnosis of some disagreements about abortion, for instance, in which one side is influenced by the symbolic utility of beliefs that express respect for life, the other side expressing recognition of a woman's right to choose. Neither side need be in violation of Rules 1 through 5; each may have legitimately exercised James's Tie-Breaker. Isn't the scope for symbolic utility in rational belief formation a more plausible explanation of intractable differences in moral dilemmas than the explanation that the other side is irrational or ill-informed or unable to grasp the values that would lead to one's own side's conclusions? Instead of pessimistic diagnoses of our times, such as the notion that we live in an age of emotivism in which moral disagreement is inevitable because we lack the coherent moral theory that the ancient Greeks enjoyed, the Tie-Breaker diagnosis is that we live in a symbolically rich environment, so rich that possibilities for integrating symbolic utility into one's belief-system are plentiful. Our disagreements are not the result of our accepting different fragments of moral theory and using the fragments to proselytize for our inclinations, masking the basic emotivism that motivates us, but instead we may be guided differently by fully rational considerations, not simply urging our inclinations on others but rather incorporating symbolic utility into our beliefs in a manner that is legitimate, though not necessarily rationally coercive for others.

Realism and Correspondence

In important respects Johnson is mistaken, I argued two sections back, in holding that the making-true relationship for James is entirely internal to the symbolic structures we create. But there is one respect in which I think he is correct, and I will conclude by touching on it. James is an external realist, in the sense that he posits a world of pure experience external to our representations, in particular the conceptualizations that occur in our desires, beliefs, and other mental states. But there can be no "correspondences" between that external reality and our representations; there can be nothing which would make true statements of the form, "the sentence p is true if and only if p." Any candidate for p on the right side of this formula is going to have conceptual structure, if only the simple subject-predicate structure of "Snow is white" in the sentence "'Snow is white' is true if and only if snow is white," and consequently it won't be about the external reality of the world of pure experience, which is pre-conceptual, lacking the articulations that the human serpent creates.

This is at least part of what James is getting at when he writes, in *Pragmatism*, about experience in mutation: "Truths emerge from facts; but they dip forward into facts again and add to them; which facts again create or reveal new truth (the word is indifferent) and so on indefinitely. The 'facts' themselves meanwhile are not *true*. They simply *are*. Truth is the function of the beliefs that start and terminate among them" (P, 107). So although one would normally expect to see an external realist ontology and a correspondence theory of truth go hand in hand, they go separate ways in James's system. James acknowledges an ordinary sense in which true beliefs correspond to, copy, or agree with "their object," but this "invites pragmatistic discussion," as he says. Not only does truth as correspondence succumb to pragmatic deconstruction, but values of the right side of the correspondence formula p is true if and only if p are products of human creativity and conceptual innovation just as much as those of the left side are. The "copied" object is not external to our representations. In this sense, then, the making-true relationship for James is entirely internal to the symbolic structures we create. Yet he is an external realist, I have emphasized. The world of pure experience is external to our symbolic structures.

Conclusion

The pragmatic theory of truth should be factored into a theory of absolute truth, for which the context-relative function of a belief and the prospect of a future universal consensus are central, and a theory of half-truth, what passes for true, or rational belief, for which subjective considerations come into play while being constrained by the evidential standards appropriate to the function of belief in the given context. Although the pragmatic theory of truth in the present reading has the complexity of the two axioms, it does not hold that pragmatic justification aims at personal benefit while epistemic justification aims at truth (*pace* Richard Gale: "James, *when he is espousing his will-to-be-*

lieve doctrine, challenges Clifford's univocalist account of belief justification. At these times, he claims that there are *two* different ways to justify believing a proposition: the *epistemic* way, based on empirical evidence and proofs; and the *pragmatic* way based on the desirable consequences that accrue to the believer of the proposition. The former is directed toward establishing the truth of the proposition; the latter, to establishing the desirability of believing that the proposition is true, quite a different matter" [Gale 1999].)[1] Rather, consideration of personal benefits has a subsidiary role to play under the aegis of the second axiom, where it justifies belief in a manner that is consistent with pursuit of the truth. Furthermore, with reference to the first axiom, there are subsystems of belief, such as religion and metaphysics, whose function it is to satisfy moral and emotional needs, and these may legitimately provide benefits to individuals as part of their pragmatic, truth-making *work*. Consideration of personal benefits do not trump truth, pace Nathanson; they are a constitutive but subsidiary element in the pursuit of truth, and for the same reason they do not define the truth, despite Sprigge's qualms.

The prima-facie textual support for my interpretation is adequate but not overwhelming. What makes the case overwhelming is the requirement that textual evidence should not have implications that are massively inconsistent with *The Principles*; a principle of charity requires that one look for a harmonizing interpretation. This is especially so for popular lectures delivered within a few years of *The Principles*, but I would extend it through to James's last years: unless there is direct repudiation of *The Principles'* doctrine, find a harmonizing interpretation.

12

Ethics I:
Morality Made Flesh

Although James had relatively little to say about ethics, what he did say has acquired particular importance in the light of Richard Gale's recent book, *The Divided Self of William James*, in which his alleged desire-satisfaction utilitarianism contributes to the Master Syllogism that Gale uses to interpret James's philosophy generally. In this chapter I will argue against Gale's reading of James on ethical matters and in favor of a reading that construes a principle of utility as at most one among a plurality of principles that figure in a historical struggle for acceptance, as suggested in the following passage from "The Moral Philosopher and the Moral Life":

> The anarchists, nihilists, and free-lovers; the free-silverites, socialists, and single-tax men; the free-traders and civil-service reformers; the prohibitionists and anti-vivisectionists; the radical darwinians with their idea of the suppression of the weak — these and all the conservative sentiments of society arrayed against them, are simply deciding through actual experiment by what sort of conduct the maximum amount of good can be gained and kept in this world. These experiments are to be judged, not *à priori*, but by actually finding, after the fact of their making, how much more outcry or how much appeasement comes about. What closet-solutions can possibly anticipate the result of trials made on such a scale? Or what can any superficial theorist's judgment be worth, in a world where every one of hundreds of ideals has its special champion already provided in the shape of some genius expressly born to feel it, and to fight to death in its behalf? The pure philosopher can only follow the windings of the spectacle, confident that the line of least resistance will always be towards the richer and the more inclusive arrangement, and that by one tack after another some approach to the kingdom of heaven is incessantly made. (WB, 157)

In addition to the theme of historical pluralism, I will introduce the idea of an end-of-history universal moral consensus in order to secure a notion of absolute moral truth that will contrast with the half-truths that emerge in the history of moral progress. My constructivist interpretation of the moral element of James's system ties it closely to his theory of truth examined in Chapter 11: the (absolute) moral truth is what will be believed in an ultimate future consensus, just as absolute truth *simpliciter* is defined by reference to such a consensus.

James wanted to establish that the objectivity of morality did not require it to be understood as God's command, and he rejected the idea that morality was *abstractly* objective. But our "ethical republic here below" can generate the objectivity of absolute truth in morality just as it can in physics, just in case moral hypotheses actually come to be believed by humanity in an ultimate future consensus. This is James's "religion of humanity." James's commitment to a principle of utility should be understood as highly tentative and provisional upon a consensus that we do not at present have. Consequently, an interpretation such as Richard Gale's, which puts such a principle at the center of James's thinking and freezes it in a form that makes it prey to criticism, should be rejected in favor of one which explores sympathetically his historical form of consensualism, morality made flesh.

So I will honor Myers's interpretive theme that James "expressed the existentialist thesis that ethics rest finally upon choice and commitment" (Myers 1986, 389), while embedding it in a broader outline of a constructivist account of moral truth. Myers's theme is important in understanding the rationality of moral belief and morally inspired action and for understanding the mechanism of progress toward moral truth, something I will touch upon in discussion of James's essay "The Moral Equivalent of War." But it does not do justice to the idea of moral truth that is at work in James's thinking, and it is misleading if it suggests a world in which individual minds are the measures of all things. James explicitly rejects this world. "[T]his is the kind of world," he writes, "with which the philosopher, so long as he holds to the hope of a philosophy, will not put up" (WB, 147). Ultimately, the existentialist reading of James glosses over the subtlety of James's view and fuels a questionable "postmodern" reading that either invokes James to justify a "That's-what-we-do-around-here" moral relativism or criticizes him for failing to valorize a chaos of incommensurable political groups or falsely categorizes him as a Robinson Crusoe individualist in his moral thinking.

Gale takes this latter tack in his interpretive theme that James had a "Robinson Crusoe approach" to ethics: "James makes the surprising claim that there would be concrete values and obligations, understood in the concrete sense, if there were a single, isolated desirer, which sets him apart from his fellow pragmatists Mead and Dewey, who gave a socialized account of everything that pertained to the normative. This is one among many instances of James's Robinson Crusoe approach to philosophical topics" (Gale 1999, 29). Gale is evidently referring to two paragraphs near the beginning of "The Moral Philosopher and the Moral Life" in which James discusses the possibility of a moral solitude in which only a solitary thinker exists. But the point of the discussion is to underscore the mind-dependent nature of ethics.

> In its mere material capacity, a thing can no more be good or bad than it can be pleasant or painful. Good for what? Good for the production of another physical fact, do you say? But what in a purely physical universe demands the production of that other fact? Physical facts simply *are* or are *not*; and neither when present or absent, can they be supposed to make demands. If they do, they can only do so by having desires; and then they have ceased to be purely physical facts, and have become facts of conscious sensibility. Goodness, badness, and obligation must be *realized* somewhere in order really to exist; and the first step in ethical philosophy is to see that no merely inorganic "nature of things" can realize them. (WB, 145)

Though this is the first step, it is hardly James's last; it hardly defines his approach. Moreover, Gale should not be surprised that James turns out to be a Robinson Crusoe theorist in his interpretation, since he reads James as a desire-satisfaction utilitarian, and a utilitarian, finding that desire may or may not be maximized in a one-person world as well as any other, will find obligations in that world as in any other. On the other hand, since James begins the most pertinent essay, "The Moral Philosopher and the Moral Life," with the caution that "the main purpose of this paper is to show that there is no such thing possible as an ethical philosophy dogmatically made up in advance," isn't that sufficient warning that James should not be classified as a desire-satisfaction utilitarian? Secondly, James's ethical theory, such as it is in its vanishingly slight content and lightly sketched form, is highly socialized, in that the *content* of the right, as opposed to its casuistic criterion, is a function of a future consensus, as I will explain. This distinction between content and criterion also helps to solve Gale's puzzle about James being a utilitarian and endorsing deontological moral principles: people accepting certain imperatives categorically may be most likely to promote the best consequences; deontological content may best satisfy a consequentialist criterion. "I know of no way to reconcile James's deontological intuitions," Gale writes, with his casuistic rule that we are always to act so as to maximize desire-satisfaction (Gale 1999, 48). But here is the way: construe the casuistic rule as pertaining to the criterion for judging what is right and the deontological intuitions as pertaining to the moral content that best satisfies the criterion. James was after all a student of John Stuart Mill in his consequentialism, and Mill quite explicitly distinguished between the principle of utility, as the ultimate criterion of right, and various intermediate-level principles of a deontological sort, which people should use in their everyday moral thinking. However, this chapter will ultimately challenge Gale's interpretation of James's casuistic rule, assessing it not as desire-satisfaction utilitarianism but rather as an *ideal-maximizing consensualism*. The general moral of the preceding paragraph remains; distinguish casuistic principles from moral psychology.

James's commitment to moral truth is present even when he is making the point that we are not in a position to theorize informedly in any detail about what the moral truth might be, as he says in "The Moral Philosopher and the Moral Life":

> The main purpose of this paper is to show that there is no such thing possible as an ethical philosophy dogmatically made up in advance. We all help to determine the content of ethical philosophy so far as we contribute to the race's moral life. In other words, there can be no final truth in ethics any more than in physics, until the last man has had his experience and said his say. In the one case as in the other, however, the hypotheses which we now make while waiting, and the acts to which they prompt us, are among the indispensable conditions which determine what that 'say' shall be. (WB, 141)

Just as with truth in the empirical sciences, it is necessary to draw a sharp distinction between the ideal content of moral truth—namely, whatever beliefs will form the general consensus—and our situation as historically located here, where we can't use the future consensus as a guide for what we ought to do, since we don't know what the consensus will be. Of course there may be no future consensus. In that sense the fulfillment of morality in an objective ideal is at risk. There might be a humanity-destroying holocaust, or it might turn out that, despite our best efforts to find an inclusive morality or perhaps because of unfortunately provincial choices, cultures remain morally alien to each other.

In the first case, the holocaust would prevent objective moral truth from *coming to pass*. As I noted in the previous chapter, James has a notion of absolute truth that is tied to *actual* future consensus, and that remains so in the moral sphere: "If one ideal judgment be objectively better than another, that betterness must be made flesh by being lodged concretely in someone's actual perceptions" (WB, 147). So it would not be enough to articulate moral truth in the form of a counterfactual conditional sentence, such as "All moral agents in an ideal future consensus *would* agree that such and such," where "such and such" is what is morally true; such possibilities, even if they be as well supported as counterfactuals can be, are not sufficiently robust to ground objective morality. What's needed is the actuality of consensus, with all the contingency that entails.

In the second case, provincial choices would erect barriers between cultures that would prevent moral truth from emerging. Even if one might think that it would emerge if the barriers were removed, the actual historical achievement of their removal and a consequent consensus need to come about, as I have emphasized, and a politics that emphasizes difference has the potential to block this prospect (Cooper 1996).

Consequentialism and Deontology

Even assuming that objective moral truth will be made flesh, we don't *know* whether its content is "consequentialist" or "deontological." Here then, in the form of James's patent epistemic humility about morality, is another reason, in addition to those summoned in Chapter 10, to refrain from imposing Gale's Master Syllogism on James. Its major and minor premises both presuppose a certain utilitarian moral content; while he was sympathetic to it, his particular form of consensualism kept it at a distance from the center of his moral thinking.

The ideal of consensus at least induces the demand about inclusiveness:

that we ought to think of moral progress as fundamentally a matter of searching for common moral ground, upon which we stand and affirm that is good. This in turn yields a very general sense in which James can be classified as a consequentialist. We ought to act now to promote such progress and the good it aims at. "There is but one unconditional commandment," James wrote, "which is that we should seek incessantly, with fear and trembling, so to vote and to act as to bring about the very largest total universe of good which we can see" (WB, 158). For example, it would be a big mistake to destroy the human race. But there is nothing about consequentialism at this level which rules out deontology as the content of moral truth. For instance, it is compatible with the prospect of a consensus about the fundamentality of human rights, deontological side-constraints on conduct.

In our historical predicament, relying on moral half-truths in a context of many competing claims to truth, we cope by acknowledging that "every *de facto* claim creates in so far forth an obligation" (WB, 148). Then, "Since everything which is demanded is by that fact a good, must not the guiding principle for ethical philosophy (since all demands conjointly cannot be satisfied in this poor world) be simply to satisfy at all times *as many demands as we can?* That act must be the best act, accordingly, which makes for the *best whole*, in the sense of awakening the least sum of dissatisfactions" (WB, 155). Note that the claims in question are *moral* claims, reasons that appeal to moral ideals. So James is not justifying the immoral person who knows what he does is wrong but does it anyway, simply because he wants to. Only in a moral solitude does a want have moral weight ipso facto.

Notoriously, the immoralist's wants have weight on a utilitarian calculus for determining what is right, which leads to highly counterintuitive consequences in certain scenarios. For suppose that the immoralist is a *utility monster* whose desire to do evil is so intense that it outweighs the desires of those he kills; then it is right that he kills them. My point here, in my reading of an essay that admittedly admits of multiple readings, is that the utility monster is not James's problem, because he is not concerned with "the claims of desires," so to speak, but rather "the claims of ideals." This comes out in the continuation of the passage just quoted, about *the best whole:*

> In the casuistic scale, therefore, those ideals must be written highest which *prevail at the least cost,* or by whose realization the least possible number of other ideals

are destroyed. Since victory and defeat there must be, the victory to be philosophically prayed for is that of the more inclusive side — of the side which even in the hour of triumph will to some degree do justice to the ideals in which the vanquished party's interests lay. The course of history is nothing but the story of men's struggles from generation to generation to find the more and more inclusive order. *Invent some manner* of realizing your own ideals which will also satisfy the alien demands — that and that only is the path of peace! Following this path, society has shaken itself into one sort of relative equilibrium after another by a series of social discoveries quite analogous to those of science. Polyandry and polygamy and slavery, private warfare and liberty to kill, judicial torture and arbitrary royal power have slowly succumbed to actually aroused complaints; and though someone's ideals are unquestionably the worse off for each improvement, yet a vastly greater total number of them find shelter in our civilized societies than in the older savage ways. So far then, and up to date, the casuistic scale is made for the philosopher already far better than he can ever make it for himself. (WB, 155)

So a sadist's desire to inflict harm was long ago *defeated*, and it does not have the moral weight that it might have in a moral solitude, in James's reckoning, or that it would have at any historical juncture on a desire-satisfaction utilitarian's reckoning. But as I have emphasized, James's moral theory is not such a utilitarianism, and his idea that the most universal moral principle would satisfy demand is really a case for *moral pluralism*:

The best, on the whole, of these marks and measures of goodness seems to be the capacity to bring happiness. But in order not to break down fatally, this test must be taken to cover innumerable acts and impulses that never *aim* at happiness; so that, after all, in seeking for a universal principle we inevitably are carried onward to the *most* universal principle — that *the essence of good is simply to satisfy demand*. The demand may be for anything under the sun. There is really no more ground for supposing that all our demands can be accounted for by one universal underlying kind of motive than there is ground for supposing that all physical phenomena are cases of a single law. The elementary forces in ethics are probably as plural as those of physics are. The various ideals have no common character apart from the fact that they are ideals. No single abstract principle can be used so as to yield to the philosopher anything like a scientifically accurate and genuinely useful casuistic scale. (WB, 153)

To be satisfied, then, are demands that represent ideals that haven't been defeated in the course of history. This rules out the sadist's ideal, apart from an imaginable world in which he "harms" without really harming, a possibility that James entertains in the following passage.

> If the ethical philosopher were only asking after the best *imaginable* system of goods he would indeed have an easy task; for all demands as such are *prima facie* respectable, and the best simply imaginary world would be one in which *every* demand was gratified as soon as made. Such a world would, however, have to have a physical constitution entirely different from that of the one which we inhabit. It would need not only a space, but a time, "of n-dimensions," to include all the acts and experiences incompatible with one another here below, which would then go on in conjunction—such as spending our money, yet growing rich; taking our holiday, yet getting ahead with our work; shooting and fishing, yet doing no hurt to the beasts; gaining no end of experience, yet keeping our youthful freshness of heart; and the like. (WB, 153)

In the interpretation I am recommending, according to which the sadist's desire's prima-facie respectability has been defeated in the real world by moral ideals that condemn it, and has consequently lost its respectability, James's moral theory doesn't imply that such immoral desires must be counted by a utilitarian calculus in determining what is right, with the possibility that, if the mathematics of desire favors the sadist, it becomes right to harm others.

I am now in a position to solve an "aporia" posed by Gale: "We make things good by desiring them, yet that it is good that desires get satisfied seems to be something that is not made true by us but instead discovered. I am at a loss to extricate James from this aporia" (Gale 1999, 31). Here is my proposal for extrication: We do *not* make things good by desiring them, except in the limiting case where no conflicting ideals are threatened by desire, such as the one-person moral solitude and the imaginary world just described. There is a stark difference in readings here. In Gale's, James emerges from the essay as a desire-satisfaction utilitarian:

> Given that the good is what satisfies a desire, and so on, and that we have an obligation to promote goodness, it follows that we have an obligation to see to it that any desire gets satisfied, unless doing so would result in the denial of a greater quantity of other desires. The obligation is a prima facie one that can be canceled

> only if the satisfaction of this one desire requires that a greater quantity of other
> desires go unsatisfied. This is what James means by his remark that "all demands
> as such are *prima facie* respectable." (Gale 1999, 27)

That is *not* what James means by this remark, in the reading I am recommending. I view it as a consideration in favor of my reading over Gale's that it does
not require something like the following diagnosis of why, according to Gale,
even a sadist's desires are good in James's view. "I believe that there was another motivation for James's revisionary account of good in terms of desire-
satisfaction based on his inveterate hipsterism, which was discussed in the Introduction. He was an experience junky intent on having as many tingles and
thrills as possible. This is the object of his quest to have it all. Because we have
these tingles and thrills when our desires are satisfied, his absolute normative
principle should be to satisfy desire — the more the better" (Gale 1999, 32). Gale
notices that interpreting James as a desire-satisfaction utilitarian is hard to reconcile with James's own conception of moral duty as a free agent, which is
expressed in "The Moral Philosopher and the Moral Life" by the concluding
paragraphs about the moral superiority of the strenuous mood, which "makes
us quite indifferent to present ill, if only the greater ideal be attained." When
that mood is upon us, especially as occasioned and enhanced by belief in God,

> The more imperative ideals now begin to speak with an altogether new objectivity
> and significance, and to utter the penetrating, shattering, tragically challenging
> note of appeal. They ring out like the call of Victor Hugo's alpine eagle, "qui parle
> au précipice et que le gouffre entend," and the strenuous mood awakens at the
> sound. It saith among the trumpets, ha, ha! it smelleth the battle afar off, the thun-
> der of the captains and the shouting. Its blood is up; and cruelty to the lesser
> claims, so far from being a deterrent element, does but add to the stern joy with
> which it leaps to answer to the greater. All through history, in the periodical con-
> flicts of puritanism with the don't-care temper, we see the antagonism of the
> strenuous and genial moods, and the contrast between the ethics of infinite and
> mysterious obligation from on high, and those of prudence and the satisfaction of
> merely finite need. (WB, 161)

The reading of James as a moral pluralist classifies the ideal of maximizing
desire-satisfaction as allied to what he calls here the ethics of prudence and the
satisfaction of merely finite need; it is one among many casuistic principles,

and not even the one that James enjoins us to strive to implement, the ethics of infinite and mysterious obligation from on high. Gale recognizes the problem, but blames it on James rather than his own interpretation:

> James did not desire just that certain desirable states of affairs be realized but that they be realized as a result of his own free agency. Herein James recognized an intrinsic, deontological value to being a free agent who causes in the right way the realization of desirable ends. There is a serious question whether James can be committed consistently to both his casuistic rule and his deontological values. This is exactly the same problem faced by the utilitarian who says both that we always must choose that alternative which maximizes utility and that we always must act from considerations of virtue. This attributes to us inconsistent motivations, as the latter recognizes an intrinsic, deontological value to acting from considerations of virtue that the former does not. (Gale 1999, 35)

In the pluralistic interpretation consistency is readily established, since the principle that desire-satisfaction should be maximized is not an ultimate moral principle, but one among potentially many principles that must be harmonized in a civilized society.

Gale asks whether James's principle about maximizing desire-satisfaction calls for satisfying the desires of the greatest number of people, the greatest number of desires, or the greatest quantity of desires in which the amount or intensity of a desire is factored in. That he should discuss this question at considerable length is understandable, since he not only views it as the fundamental principle of James's ethical theory but also as figuring in the architectonic of his philosophizing as a whole, in the form of the "Master Syllogism" discussed in Chapter 10. He opts for the third answer, relying on the following passage.

> Take any demand, however slight, which any creature, however weak, may make. Ought it not, for its own sole sake, to be satisfied? If not, prove why not. The only possible kind of proof you could adduce would be the exhibition of another creature who should make a demand that ran the other way. The only possible reason there can be why any phenomenon ought to exist is that such a phenomenon actually is desired. Any desire is imperative to the extent of its amount; it *makes* itself valid by the fact that it exists at all. Some desires, truly enough, are small desires; they are put forward by insignificant persons, and we customarily make

light of the obligations which they bring. But the fact that such personal demands as these impose small obligations does not keep the largest obligations from being personal demands. (WB, 149)

The position of this passage in the argument of "The Moral Philosopher and the Moral Life" is important. It occurs near the beginning of the essay, in the context of securing the point that the first step in ethical philosophy is to see that no merely inorganic "nature of things" can realize ethical qualities. The passage simply is not intended to bear the immense burden that Gale's interpretation places on it, as defining the fundamental principle of James's ethical theory and the major premise of the Master Syllogism. It is only adding emphasis to the "first step," underscoring that morality presupposes sentience. Moreover, the passage doesn't even support the third option that Gale favors (maximize satisfaction of intensity-weighted desires), since James goes on to indicate that the relevant small-big continuum surrounding his notion of amount has to do with the significance of the people who have the desires in question. So in spite of the fact that a significant person like Jesus and an insignificant person have equally intense desires that we should love one another, nonetheless Jesus' desire is big and the other's is small; the former has more "amount." I do not find this passage particularly clear or helpful, but this seems all the more reason to avoid an interpretive strategy that depends so heavily on it as does Gale's. It simply contributes to taking the first step, the heart of the ethical theory coming later, when James speaks of how a plurality of ideals can come together in a consensus, acceptance in the "everlasting ruby vaults" of our own human hearts, about progressively more inclusive arrangements.

It is entirely gratuitous to impute confusion of staggering proportions to James, as in the following passage, based on Gale's interpretation of the greatest-in-amount rule:

Suppose that not God but Descartes's evil demon exists. Would James still hold that the demands of the de facto biggest kid on the block are to carry the day? Obviously James, being one of the nicest human beings of all time, would not continue to adhere to his greatest-in-amount version of the casuistic rule, but then he would be smuggling in deontological considerations to the effect that the reason why we should obey God but not the evil demon is because God is morally good and the demon is not. (Gale 1999, 36)

There is no need for "smuggling." The casuistic rule in question, whatever the version, is at most one among a plurality of principles that a society might accept, including deontological principles that *defeat* the prima-facie respectability of the demon's desires.

Gale sees smuggling at every turn: "Andrew Reck has suggested in correspondence that one might interpret James as holding that the sort of desires which the strenuous mood presses us to satisfy are of a qualitatively higher sort—the desires that we would have if we were to become our ideal selves. If this is the right interpretation, and it might well be, then James is guilty of inconsistently smuggling in deontological considerations" (Gale 1999, 41). Reck's suggestion is a good one. As for the alleged inconsistent smuggling, it is best dealt with by dropping the interpretation that creates the appearance of it. Nonutilitarian moral considerations have a role in James's ethical theory that they would not have in the interpretation that James was advocating desire-satisfaction utilitarianism as a fundamental moral principle.

James is not a desire-satisfaction utilitarian. More positively, he is generally speaking a consequentialist; acting so as to bring about *the best whole* is the criterion of rightness, a criterion which tends to justify a plurality of ideals—as opposed to the single ideal embodied in a principle of desire-satisfaction utilitarianism. This criterion is applicable both at the level of absolute truth and of half-truth. At the former, it is the background to the consensus, in that everyone is aiming at the best whole, and that motivation guides them to whatever content objective morality will happen to have. At the latter, it favors what might be called *overlapping-consensus pluralism*, the view, broadly speaking, that justice and other fundamental values are relative to societies in which there is convergence among a variety of divergent ideals, a realization of them that is as complete as historical conditions allow. Half-truth pluralism, an interim ethic for the long march through history toward the future consensus, is evident in the following passage: "An experiment of the most searching kind has proved that the laws and usages of the land are what yield the maximum of satisfaction to the thinkers taken all together. The presumption in cases of conflict must always be in favor of the conventionally recognized good. The philosopher must be a conservative, and in the construction of his casuistic scale must put the things most in accordance with the customs of the community on top" (WB, 156).

I read "the maximum of satisfaction to the thinkers" as ruling out the possibility that James is talking about desire-satisfaction utilitarianism, which of course does not limit itself to the desires of thinkers. Instead he is referring to the realization of the ideals that those thinkers fight for; what's best is the most inclusive realization of the ideals they represent. This reading also helps to clarify what is not clear in the passage quoted earlier, about "insignificant persons" and their "small desires." Gale brings a dark interpretation to it: "This has an elitist ring to it implying that nice guys do finish last. People deserve respect and consideration, for example to have their desires taken seriously, only when they have the courage to demand that they be accorded this status. Only 'significant' persons count, and to achieve significant personhood a person must pass the courage test by demanding that others accord her this status" (Gale 1999, 45–46). This doesn't sound right at all, and it is easily avoided by interpreting the passage in question as merely emphasizing that morality presupposes sentience (the "first step") and releasing it from the burden of defining the fundamental principle of ethics, in favor of the pluralistic account of the casuistic principles. The significant persons are the thinkers who lead a community's moral progress. Insignificant people are among those who do not lead. (Let us imagine a continuum here.) It is not that the latter do not deserve respect and consideration; on the contrary, a liberal community's thinkers would be united in holding that every citizen is entitled to equal concern and respect, even those who have "little" desires of morally retrogressive sort, like wanting to introduce capital punishment for shoplifting.

Internalism

James's responsiveness to moral claims yields internalism about the connection between moral truth and motivation. Moral truths, in particular the moral half-truths of our present hypotheses, are always made flesh in our being disposed to be moved by this or that moral claim:

> But the only force of appeal to *us* . . . is found in the "everlasting ruby vaults" of our own human hearts, as they happen to beat responsive and not irresponsive to the claim. So far as they do feel it when made by a living consciousness, it is life answering to life. A claim thus livingly acknowledged is acknowledged with a solidity and fullness which no thought of an "ideal" backing can render more complete; while if, on the other hand, the heart's response is withheld, the stubborn

phenomenon is there of an impotence in the claims which the universe embodies, which no talk about an eternal nature of things can glaze over or dispel. An ineffective *à priori* order is as impotent a thing as an ineffective God; and in the eye of philosophy, it is as hard a thing to explain. (WB, 149)

When James say that "the religion of humanity" affords a basis for ethics as well as theism does, he is understating the case. Without roots in human motivation, a theistic moral code would have no moral weight.

Moral Intuition

The "'gory nurse" of history has slowly taught us to seek a more and more inclusive moral order: "A 'gory nurse' has trained societies to be what they are" (ERM, 164). The course of history is nothing but the story of men's struggles from generation to generation to find the more and more inclusive order, and creativity in this regard has made for social discoveries "quite analogous to those of science" (WB, 155–56). Consequently we enjoy a social equilibrium that has proved itself in "an experiment of the most searching kind," namely, the dynamics of actual history. So a basic intermediate principle is a presumption in favor of the conventionally recognized good, as noted above.

This is James's moral intuitionism, belonging to the "half-truth" aspect of his moral theory. It is complemented by a mechanism for moral progress, noted at the beginning of this chapter, through the experiments of moral reformers that challenge the reigning intuitions. Note the admission of contingency here. No one, in particular no philosopher, is in a position to chart the course from here to objective moral truth. This passage and others I have drawn attention to here seem to count against Barry Allen's diagnosis of James's "blind spot": "It is James's blind spot to think there is some natural, simply given difference between adaptive and maladaptive mental habits, or that it is possible in principle ('anticipating the results of the general truth-processes of mankind') to judge this objectively" (Allen 1993, 68). The results that James is talking about, in the passage from *The Meaning Of Truth* quoted parenthetically by Allen, are the ultimate consensus about truth. James is clear that these results don't constitute a decision procedure for deciding whether these ideas or those ideas make for moral progress. The most that can be done, and this falls far short of wielding a measure of a "natural, simply given difference," is to conserve the social equilibrium while allowing moral geniuses to challenge our intuitions with their own ideals.

James guesses that the ultimate consensus will recognize a plurality of fundamental ideals ("The elementary forces in ethics are probably as plural as those of physics are"). Similarly, he guesses that the constituent ideals of these elementary ethical forces will be "butchered" by the requirements of coexisting with each other, rather than constituting a harmoniously unified whole. But these are schematic guesses that don't really imply anything about our power now to make objective judgments about how the future ought to unfold: "The actually possible in this world is vastly narrower than all that is demanded; and there is always a *pinch* between the ideal and the actual which can only be got through by leaving part of the ideal behind. There is hardly a good which we can imagine except as competing for the possession of the same bit of space and time with some other imagined good" (WB, 153). This too is a projection of moral history rather than an appeal to the objective standard that Allen derides when he concludes, "James should admit that his pragmatism cannot supply an interesting, practical difference between passing for true and really being so" (Allen 1993, 68). The requirement that objective moral truth should be made flesh, by actually being believed, makes the distinction between half-truths that pass for true, on one hand, and absolute truths on the other hand, a pragmatically interesting distinction. Could it be that Allen is attributing to James a nonpragmatic conception of an abstract moral order? This would explain why he thinks James can't supply a pragmatically interesting distinction between passing for true and being true. But James definitely rejected this conception as a superstition. Inquiring into the ground of obligation, he observes that

> In our first essays at answering this question, there is an inevitable tendency to slip into an assumption which ordinary men follow when they are disputing with one another about questions of good and bad. They imagine an abstract moral order in which the objective truth resides; and each tries to prove that this pre-existing order is more accurately reflected in his own ideas than in those of his adversary. It is because one disputant is backed by this overarching abstract order that we think the other should submit.
>
> I know well how hard it is for those who are accustomed to what I have called the superstitious view, to realize that every *de facto* claim creates in so far forth an

obligation. We inveterately think that something which we call the "validity" of the claim is what gives to it its obligatory character, and that this validity is something outside the claim's mere existence as a matter of fact. (WB, 148)

James rejects this conception and provides an alternative that is "pragmatically interesting," so there is reason to suspect that Allen's diagnosis of James's blind spot is either a failure to see the pragmatism in James's position or else a question-begging refusal to view it as pragmatically interesting.

Relatively Objective Moral Judgments

Insight into the content of the ultimate consensus is doubtful, but James makes a case for moral insight into the present and past. Presumption in favor of local moral knowledge does not rule out relatively objective moral judgments, in particular judgments that are critical of other moral cultures. One culture can be closer to the truth than another, even though no one is able to use the ultimate moral consensus as a yardstick. Something like Popperian "verisimilitude" is at work. The logic of scientific discovery, according to his philosophy of science, is such that, although no one can prove a theory to be true, a theory's withstanding more attempts at falsification than the others permits a sense to be defined in which it is *more true* than they. Is it possible that one culture's moral beliefs are more true than another's?

James thinks that some cultures have solved the problems thrown up by history better than others, especially by finding social equilibria of greater inclusiveness. So a cannibalistic culture rates lower on the scale of moral perfection than one that relates to strangers less inhospitably, as he remarks in this passage from a debate with one Grant Allen on whether James was guilty of hero worship for emphasizing the importance of great individuals in molding history. James is arguing that there can be large, objectively significant differences in moral culture, and that small objective differences within a culture properly loom large for the natives, in this case James and Allen:

> Layer after layer of human perfection separates me from the central Africans who pursued Stanley with cries of "meat, meat!" This vast difference ought, on Mr. Allen's principles, to rivet my attention far more than the petty one which obtains between two such birds of a feather as Mr. Allen and myself. Yet while I never feel

proud that the sight of a passer-by awakens in me no cannibalistic waterings of the mouth, I am free to confess that I shall feel very proud if I do not publicly appear inferior to Mr. Allen in the conduct of this momentous debate. To me as a teacher the intellectual gap between my ablest and my dullest student counts for infinitely more than that between the latter and the amphioxus: indeed, I never thought of the latter chasm till this moment. Will Mr. Allen seriously say that this is all human folly, and tweedledum and tweedledee? (WB, 192)

Passages like this one, from his essay "The Importance of Individuals," are an important reminder to those who would draw moral-relativist conclusions from James's pragmatism. This is not at all to imply that one should keep his pragmatism separate from his moral reflection. On the contrary, they fit together in a complex and coherent way, I am arguing here.

James's Tie-Maker

By his definition in "The Moral Philosopher and the Moral Life," James was not always a pure philosopher, writing essays like "The Moral Equivalent of War" in which he championed his own ideals, in this case the ideal of a pacifism with manly virtues sufficient to match the appeal of militaristic ones. "Pacifists ought to enter more deeply into the aesthetical and ethical point of view of their opponents," he stated, finding that "Militarism is the great preserver of our ideals of hardihood" but that these ideals could be served by other means, in particular by "a conscription of the whole youthful population to form for a certain number of years a part of the army enlisted against *Nature*," to ameliorate their society's condition by building bridges, digging mines, etc. He articulates here, in effect, a strategy for moral reform that might be called "James's Tie-Maker": When your ideal is deficient with respect to *x* compared to your opponent's, find a way to incorporate *x* or something sufficiently *x*-like in your ideal, so that, tied now with respect to *x*, the deficiencies of your opponent's view and the superiority of your own with respect to *y* can break the tie, moving the community toward your ideal. (*Y* in the "Moral Equivalent" case would be bloodshed and violent death on a large scale, the well-established militaristic evil that, *other things being equal*, makes pacifism look very good.)

The mechanisms of scientific and moral progress are analogous. In *The Principles* James insisted that science advances not by simple accumulation of experience but rather by the "back-door" of spontaneous brainstorms within the scientific community. Similarly, every now and then, "someone is born with the right to be original, and his revolutionary thought or action may bear prosperous fruit. He may replace old 'laws of nature' by better ones; he may, by breaking old moral rules in a certain place, bring in a total condition of things more ideal than would have followed had the rules been kept" (WB, 157). Note that this analogy between science and morality does not invite Allen's critique about pretending to have the objective truth by which to measure progress. Neither the scientific nor the moral communities have such a thing, and in James's account it would be superstitious, as we saw, to suppose that they did.

To conclude, the theme of the Two-Levels View can be extended to ethics, where the metaphysical level becomes a future consensus of all moral agents in some set of fundamental moral principles, and the empirical level is the history of progress toward greater convergence and unification of different moral ideals. James is a consequentialist in holding that the most general principle of moral progress counsels attaining "the best whole" that circumstances allow, but this is compatible with acknowledging that the best whole will include moral agents with nonconsequentialist moral psychologies; their thinking may take the form of moral intuitions or adherence to deontological rules. Moreover, the principles that determine the content of morality in this best whole are likely to represent a plurality of moral ideals, each of which gets trimmed somewhat in order to establish a consensus that makes a stable society possible.

13

Ethics II:
Jamesian Moral Constructivism

James's philosophical system is a live option for belief, I have argued. A *full Jamesian* would accept the proposition that the physical world and streams of consciousness are constructs out of pure experience, as detailed in Chapters 1 through 8. A *three-quarters Jamesian* would reject pure-experiential construction, probably in favor of a view according to which the physical world is fundamental, while accepting James's constructivism about truth, often called his "voluntarism," as sketched in Chapters 9, 10, and 11. Finally, a *half Jamesian* would accept only the moral constructivism outlined in Chapter 12, involving the idea of greater and greater consensus, with an actual future consensus of all moral agents as an ideal limit. In this concluding chapter I offer a half-Jamesian essay in moral constructivism, to add emphasis to the idea introduced in Chapter 1, that James's system is not only a live option for belief but also for doing philosophy.

We live in one world, fundamentally a world of pure experience in a full-Jamesian account, but in the spirit of half-Jamesianism we will assume in what follows that the physical world is fundamental.[1] We assume this much in order to explore the parity, or lack of it, between social and moral facts, especially when moral facts are understood as a naturalistic moral realist would understand them, as truths about the natural world (not about a transcendent order, not about a nonnatural order), and truths moreover that are *objective* and, by virtue of that, binding on all moral agents. We will examine the difference between two forms of (naturalistic moral) realism, one that secures objectivity in microstructure, and one that does so in reasons. Both forms appeal to parity with social facts. Microstructure realism (MSR) asserts that both moral and social facts are related to physical facts by property identity or supervenience.

Reason realism (RR), specifically in the form we lay out, proposes that both moral and social facts are collective intentional constructs, although we will take note of another form of RR that locates moral reasons and moral facticity by reference not to construction but rather to a hypothetical situation of full rationality. MSR's objectivity derives from the objectivity of physical facts, whereas RR's objectivity follows from the universally binding character of moral reasons.

The claimed parity with social facts is a challenge for both views, because it threatens to imply moral relativism. If moral facts emerge through collective intentionality, as our interpretation of RR has it, then a sober look at the world would detect a plurality of different and incompatible moral constructs, corresponding to a plurality of societies with different moral beliefs and institutions that anthropologists have dwelt upon convincingly. This is what parity with social facts would suggest, since nonmoral social facts have just this social-scientifically confirmed variety, from culture to culture, state to state, tribe to tribe, and so forth. But then it is equally mysterious how moral facts, on a par with social facts, could be identical with microstructure. If moral facts are like social facts in their mutually incompatible variety, how could they qualify for identity with physical microstructure? To think that the same microstructural configurations are present in all societies is simply false, and to suppose that they vary from society to society, while true, is to exchange realism for relativism, in the absence of a satisfactory explanation for why the parity of moral and social facts ends *here*. Parity of moral facts with social facts, together with the variety of the latter, leads to the relativist conclusion that there are different moral facts, corresponding to different microstructural states, rather than a single law-like correlation between moral and physical facts.

The responses of MSR and RR to the threat of relativism will have similarities and differences. MSR will hold that, although the actual world is not a microstructural exemplification of rightness, there is a possible world which is; moral facts in that world will exhibit the variety of social facts, because ultimately moral facts are not social facts, but rather objective physical facts. And RR, in the form we propose, will hold that, although different social institutions give people different reasons for acting in the actual world, there is a possible world in which there is a universal moral institution that is objectively binding by virtue of its universality and other features of its construction; objective moral facts are ultimately social facts, but social facts as constructed in the ideal possible world. But this ideal possible world must be an actual future world, in which we have created a universal moral institution. This is the first of two features that distinguish our version of RR from that of Smith (1994), which requires only the counterfactual possibility of universal acceptance under conditions of full rationality. The second feature is that our conception of full rationality is relativized to the degree of rationality that rational agents can actually muster in construction of moral institutions, whereas Smith's conception makes no such allowances for any limitations in the rationality of actual, historically situated moral agents.

Both MSR and RR can say that moral facts "supervene" on physical facts, but there is a crucial difference in the alleged supervenience. MSR, we will argue, can't offer a satisfactory explanation of the tie of supervenience between moral and physical facts. It has to be taken as a brute fact that they are, so to speak, slapped together as they are. (We assume that "God slapped them together, and that's an end to it" is not a satisfactory explanation, if only because the best defense of MSR, which we discuss below, favors naturalistic explanations that exclude traditional references to God.) But RR does have a satisfactory explanation, by reference to a process of construction that begins with physical facts and proceeds through social facts to objectively moral ones, at least in the ideal world.

This summary of our argument is somewhat overstated. We do not show that every form of MSR has a problem explaining supervenience, but we do show that arguably its currently most detailed and plausible defense, Brink, has that problem. And we do not quite show that RR has a satisfactory explanation of supervenience. Rather, we sketch one such explanation, Searle (1995), as exemplary of a *form* of explanation with the potential to elucidate the supervenience of the moral upon the physical. We do not need to show that his account is the best among those that have this form, but only that its illumination is sufficient to bolster confidence that some explanation of its constructivist form will solve the problem.

We begin by revisiting two criticisms by Mackie of the "queerness" of the realist's objective moral facts. The first criticism runs as follows: Paradigmatically, facts are things one may have a pro-, con-, or indifferent attitude towards, depending on what one's interests happen to be; so moral facts, if such there were, would be queer facts, for they would be intrinsically motivating. Brink replies that an adequate moral theory should recognize the possibility of "the amoralist," who is not motivated by recognition of moral facts, contrary to the assumption that morality, because it is essentially motivating, rules out him and his motivational structure a priori. Moral realism should be externalist about motivation, he maintains, tracing the motivating power of morality not to a queer internally-motivating property of moral facts but rather to an overall congruence between morality and self-interest.

Other realists, like Smith, accept that moral facts need not be motivating but hold instead that they have the property of inducing belief in fully rational agents and consequently give a moral agent a reason to act, without reference to the agent's motivation, or anyone else's. We propose an alternative that combines three hypotheses:

1. The amoralist is a genuine possibility.
2. Moral facts are intrinsically motivating.
3. We-beliefs figure in comprehending moralism and the limits of moral motivation.

Consider a form of hard case much discussed in the literature: someone, perhaps an addict or a pervert, who is constitutionally incapable of wanting to do that which he believes to be right. In our view such a person may or may not belong to a *we*, a social group that is capable of collective intentionality, specifically in creation of the group-relative moral fact that it is wrong to do such and such. Lacking such membership opens up one way to be an amoralist, who can "quotationally" observe that *they* believe it is "wrong" to do such and such, but not that *we believe it is wrong*.

Another form of amoralism, of the form "We believe it's wrong, but I don't," is possible for the group member, but it is parasitic on preponderantly shared moral beliefs with the community. "I disbelieve everything we believe to be wrong" is amoralism of the first type, disguised in communal language. Amoralism of the second type exposes the subject to moral self-criticism even without his motivation to do what's right, and not because, as Smith would say, he would believe doing so is right if he were fully rational, but rather because he belongs to an actual community which believes it's right. The intrinsically motivating character of what's right, whatever the individual's interests happen to be, derives from the incoherence of the group's having the moral beliefs it has without being motivated to act upon them. Coherence is compatible with a few individuals being amoral with respect to a few moral beliefs, but not with all members of the group being motivationally indifferent to all of them.

As a participant in a *we*, a rational agent may accept that the group is better placed to judge the desirability of his conduct than he, the community better fulfilling our potentiality for rationality and self-improvement than he has managed to do. Although a full treatment of this issue lies off our path, contrast with the view of Smith indicates how we would develop our own. His subject in "the evaluated world," the actual world in which he has an inextinguishable desire that he deplores, is criticizing himself from the perspective of "the evaluating world," a possible world in which he is fully rational. The desirability of acting in certain ways in the evaluated world is constituted by "facts about the desires we have *about* the desires we have *about* the evaluated world in the evaluating world" (Smith 1994, 151).

In our view Smith's evaluating world is too perfect, in part because it is hypothetical and also because it doesn't subject "the categorical demands of reason," as Smith styles them, to real-world, temporally located human subjects whose potential responsiveness to those demands is less than perfect, whether because of "blind spots" in the human condition of the sort that Nagel (1986) has explored, or limited potential determined by particularities of place, time, and culture. Rationality too falls within the compass of evolutionary theory; it is an animal trait and an evolutionary adaptation, with the measure of contingency and chance that implies (Nozick 1993). So although we agree with Smith, as against Williams, that a rational agent may have reasons for acting that go beyond the agent's "subjective motivational set" (Smith 1994, 102), we locate such reasons in the agent's membership in an actual community—at the limit, an actual future community which realizes the current community's potential for rationality. The limiting case is problematic, since the actuality of the future community is only presumed by the agent who judges himself and his community by the standard of future communal reasons. Like the revolutionary's appeal to God in Locke's *Second Treatise*,[2] the agent may have it wrong. Just as there may be no God or a God who judges the revolutionary to be unjustified, so too there may be no future consensus, or it may not judge as the agent thinks it will. We think this shows that moral life can be problematic, not that the communal reasons of the current *we* are beyond criticism. (This is a marker of the differences between our view and what might be called naive communitarianism.) What we call communal reasons are responses to the ties that bind one to the *we*, not to the categorical demands of reason; but the *we* can be, in the limiting case, a future universal moral community that stands to one's present community as, so to speak, its *best actual continuer*. We hope to bring the nature of the individual's tie to community into sharper focus in what follows; indeed, the capacity of constructivist RR to articulate this nature is its strength, by comparison with MSR's blunt posit of a lawlike relationship between microstructure and moral facts.

Mackie's second criticism impugns moral realism by associating it with Platonic or Moorean antinaturalism, that is, with commitment to transcendent or nonnatural facts, respectively. Realists counter the more biting form of this criticism with a *parity argument*: that moral facts are no more strange than social facts of the sort that social scientists refer to without controversy, so moral facts should be no more controversial than social facts; moral facts are just as "natural" as social facts, both of them nomically supervening upon natural facts, where supervenience is "a nomological or law-like relation" (Brink 1989, 60). Brink holds that realism about moral facts is compatible with naturalism because these facts can be *constituted* by natural facts. This is a somewhat special notion of constitution or makeup. He does not mean that large things are made up of smaller things and ultimately, if naturalism is correct, of atoms described in particle physics. Rather, moral *properties* are made up of constituent properties, and ultimately, if naturalism is correct, of the properties of atoms.

Against the objection that ethical naturalism would require identity rather than constitution, and that identity in turn would require synonymy of the predicates that pick out the properties in question, Brink concedes that these stringent requirements would undercut his ethical naturalism, but they equally would undercut the social sciences, since their proprietary predicates—their "ideologies" in Quine's sense—are different in meaning from the ideologies of the natural sciences. In short, if the property *being morally wrong* is queer, then so too is, say, the political scientist's property *being a federal law*; neither of the corresponding predicates is synonymous with any naturalistic predicate. But surely skepticism about the naturalistic credentials of being a federal law is unreasonable, so the nonidentity of moral properties with naturalistic ones shouldn't be a problem, as long as the relationship of constitution is in place. *This is the parity argument at work.* The microstructural moral realist should not worry that moral terms express nonnatural facts on a synonymy criterion of property identity, because this will be equally true about every discipline. The parity of moral realism with the natural and social sciences remains intact (Brink 1989, 164–65).

Moral facts, Brink wants to say, *supervene* upon the natural order, being constituted by the properties that figure in a natural-scientific description. Just as boiling water is constituted by molecules in motion, so too a murder is made up of matter's moving—a series of naturalistically describable events involving at least two bodies in which one life is caused to cease. The fact about water boiling supervenes upon its constitution, and the fact that a murder takes place, a morally wrongful killing, likewise supervenes upon its constitution. Supervenience, in Brink's account, is a *nomological* or lawlike relation, such that one property *f* supervenes on another property *g* just in case it is a law that if something is *g*, it is *f* (Brink 1989, 160).

A very short way with Brink's realism would premise Davidson's argument for the anomalousness of the mental (Davidson 1970). This is the view that there cannot be psychophysical correlation laws because of the disparate commitments of the mental and physical vocabularies, the physical vocabulary being "homonomic" in the sense that it is capable of being made indefinitely more precise in its measurements, the mental vocabulary being "heteronomic" in this sense because it is governed by considerations of rationality. In other words, in the homonomic domain of the natural sciences, the ruler rules; in the heteronomic domain of "folk psychology," rationality rules. This excludes psychophysical laws and makes problematic a notion of the supervenience of the moral on the physical which spells out this relationship in nomic terms.

While this short way strikes us as sound, as far as it goes, it does not get to the source of the problem with microstructure realism. It does not fully answer the question, What exactly about the social domain makes for heteronomy and anomalism? We are going to recommend the answer that the social domain in general, and the moral domain in particular, are marked by construction: *construction* of the social from the nonsocial, by way of collective agreement about rules that constitute or generate social facts. This constructivity explains how the social and moral *connect* to the (nonsocial) natural world. The parity that microstructure realism can achieve between moral and social facts is bound to be superficial because MSR overlooks constructivity. It succumbs to a naturalistic counterpart to Mackie's second "queerness" objection, because, by overlooking constructivity, it cannot illuminate the way in which social and moral facts connect to the natural world.

We will assume that objective physical facts, mind-independent and independent of the evidence we have for them, are fundamental, and that both subjective mental facts and communal (group-relative, collectively intentional) social facts are causally emergent from them. We use the word "emerge" here advisedly, contrasting it with supervenience in Brink's nomic sense. Omega emerges from alpha in the present sense if alpha causes omega to come into existence.

Communal facts come into existence with the exercise of collective intentionality, as when we, Dick and Jane, form the collective intention to have a conversation, that is, the intention that *we* should converse. Dick and Jane's conversing as an expression of collective intentionality is different, in Searle's hypothesis, from Dick's having the intention that he should talk to Jane and Jane's having the intention that she should talk with Dick—that is, intentions of the form "I do something with the other." This hypothesis of difference, or of the irreducibility of collective intentionality to individual intentionality, has the strengths of hypotheses such as that of the irreducibility of physical-object language to sense-data language. That is, attempts to carry out the reductions are incorrigibly incomplete and implausible. In the conversing example, the attempt would presumably take the form of requiring the presence of a certain individual, I-as-subject mental states, so that Dick's talking to Jane as though she were a recording machine, and conversely, wouldn't qualify as their expressing the collective intention to converse. But specifying these conditions for our conversing is not easy, and we will assume in what follows that it is impossible. *Our conversing* is sui generis. Its definitive mental states require we-as-subject. This is communal ontology, in which access to the intentional state is asymmetrical, and hence not objective, but not individual, and hence not simply subjective. Tom and Susan don't have Dick and Jane's mode of access to their conversing; Dick and Jane have first-person-plural access: "We are conversing." Tom and Susan have third-person access: "They are conversing." (Dick and Jane might be cultural anthropologists adopting a third-person stance toward their conversing, viewing themselves as a "they," but this complication can be ignored, though it's noteworthy that their objective stance would have to comprehend their subjectivity and community, on pain of behaviorism or a related form of overlooking the subject matter.)

Much more needs to be said about defining ontological categories in terms of their distinctive accessibility conditions. These conditions aren't a list of particular ways one might come to know something, but rather general conditions of the knowability of something, and in this sense they define a category of fact rather than a particular way in which someone might come to know a fact. Consider the third-person, objective ontology of the fact that water boils at 100 degrees centigrade. It has this ontology because it is directly knowable by anyone, in principle, even though, as it may happen, one may rely on another, such as the author of a book, to learn this. With first-person, subjective ontology, however, it is different. Consider being in pain. The subject can directly know this, but others can know it only indirectly, through behavior especially, and even then it is only *through* the subject that others can know this, in the sense that, in the absence of the pain's subjective ontology, others cannot know that the subject is in pain, but at most that he is behaving as though he were. Similarly, the first-person-plural, communal ontology of the fact that we are conversing is knowable by others only *through* us, the people who have a direct relationship to the group's collective intentionality. The accessibility conditions for communal facts are looser than for subjective ones, as shown by the possibility that an absent-minded person might become totally unaware of conversing with another, becoming engrossed in a restaurant's menu perhaps, and have to be reminded of it, whereas "total unawareness" of subjectivity is nothing but absence of subjectivity. (People aren't usually so absent-minded, but the idea of looseness of accessibility conditions is important for dealing with an individual's relationship to complex social institutions such as the law. So as we are using the direct/indirect distinction in these remarks, someone could participate in collective intentionality, and therefore have a direct relationship to it in contrast with an outsider's, while being totally unaware of that relationship, either because of passing awareness deficits caused by sleep, absent-mindedness, drugs, and so forth, or because the collective intentionality in question is an implication of some distinct collective intentionality which the subject *is* aware of, in the way that believing we are bound by the laws of the land implies that we believe we are bound by *this* law, of which we are totally unaware. (The implication is conversational rather than logical if our earlier point about amoralism of the second type is sound, and if an analogy between law and morality holds here: an individual can find a particular law so objectionable that his being bound by the law of the land is canceled in this particular case—"We believe that such-and-such is valid law, but I don't.")

Collective intentionality is the fulcrum by which we construct social reality, creating social institutions by accepting constitutive rules of the logical form *We accept that* X *counts as* Y *(in circumstance* C*)*, a form that we will detail immediately below. This is a point about logical form rather than psychological reality. The agreement need only be implicit, and typically it will be so for participants who enter into an ongoing social institution. For instance, they will develop a sense for the constitutive rules of tennis or English grammar, such that they will be *disposed* to criticize themselves as having made mistakes by violating those rules, without having any occurrent mental "I-am-following-a-rule" episode and without any past history of entering into a collective "We-hereby-accept-this-rule" ceremony.

Communal facts in general and social institutions in particular are expressions of collective intentionality, and as such they emerge from subjectivity in generally the same way that subjectivity emerges from objective physical facts about the brain.[3] If a subjective fact is a system feature of the brain, a communal fact is a system feature of a group of beings exercising collective intentionality, particularly in the creation and maintenance of social institutions. But whereas causal mechanisms in the brain are adequate to explain the emergence of subjectivity, constitutive rules are required to explain social institutions. This introduces the realm of communal construction and communal ontology, which we detail by distinguishing various kinds of *status functions* that collective acceptance can generate. (We are following Searle [1995] here, but the qualification introduced at the outset is in place: we invoke his account to illustrate communal construction and ontology, not to assert that it is the only such account or even the most plausible one.) Status and causal functions are theoretical duals, the latter theorizing things that function as they do because of their causal powers. A screwdriver functions to drive screws because it is built to have such effects when used correctly. But a thing or person functions with a status primarily or exclusively because of acceptance, such as English speakers' accepting certain inscriptions and sounds as words (a symbolic status function), an owner's having property rights and correlated duties (a deontic status function), a dog's being the best in the show (an honorific status function), and a doctoral student's being required to pass a candidacy examination (procedural status function). Acceptance of constitutive rules defining these statuses is capable of indefinite depth or iteration, status functions being stacked upon earlier-accepted status functions (we form a club, then create officers, then let them make rules for us, etc.), indefinite breadth of interlocking systems of rules (a system of rules defining marriage engages rules of property, and both connect to the political system, and so forth in a vast web). Deontic and honorific status functions are particularly important to the communal ontology of morality, yielding its rights and duties, and its virtues and vices.

Considerations about communal ontology cast a shadow over realist theory about objective, mind-independent moral facts. Social reality is mind-dependent, an expression of collective intentionality, and the moral facts that we know, or think we know, are a function of how we express our collective intentionality in building up moral institutions through status functions, moral institutions being systems of constitutive rules about what we accept as morally right and wrong. But objective moral facts in Brink's sense, if such there are, must stake a claim outside of social reality and therefore must do without the parity argument that compares them to the facts that the social sciences study. The scope of this point extends beyond MSR to versions of RR, such as Smith's, that purport to derive moral reasons and moral facts from full rationality under hypothetical ideal conditions. Our objection to these versions of RR is that they are not constructive in the sense we have sketched.

The length of the shadow does not extend to constructive RR. Despite its constructivity, our account can still assign a *kind* of mind-independence to communal moral facts. They are more public than subjective facts, by virtue of their first-person-plural ontology, and they can approach third-person publicity as a limit, at least in principle, since all rational beings might belong to the makeup of a ubiquitous social fact. We might all believe that we are members of a Kantian kingdom of ends, say. (Conceivably the social fact of our believing this could obtain without all rational agents in the universe knowing of each other's existence, just as a social fact can emerge from large groups in which no one knows everyone else.) So publicity can amount to a kind of objectivity. Further, social facts can have constituents other than individual minds, such as artifacts and procedures that compensate for the lack of connection between the social fact and individual minds. For instance, a society's laws can set out what we are proscribed from doing, even if most of us happen to be ignorant of the fact. We are aware of ourselves as citizens, and consequently as parties to a system of status functions, including laws that bind us despite ignorance, lapses of memory, etc. So institutional infrastructure can amount to a kind of mind-independence.

This is another instance of a theme we have been emphasizing: Constructivity illuminates the connection between objective physical facts and higher-level facts without abandoning naturalism or the aspiration toward moral objectivity. All facts are ultimately physical, but emergent ones have subjective or communal ontologies that distinguish them from the objective (third-person) ontology of brute physical facts. In the light of this logical structure, the nomic relationship between microstructure and higher-level facts alleged to exist according to MSR has a strange quality. Of course Brink holds, on the strength of the parity argument, that the metaphysical commitments of his version of ethical naturalism are no stranger than materialist versions of any other higher-order properties (Brink 1989, 179). But this isn't true. Brink's commitments *are* stranger than the constructivist's, because the higher-order properties generated by the constructivist model are consistent with materialism while not depending on (nomic) supervenience. This supervenience is strange, it has been argued, because the third-person objectivity and mind-independence that Brink's version of ethical naturalism seems to call for is hard to reconcile with communal moral facts. There would have to be a reconciliation if Brink's parity argument were to show that moral facts in his sense have the same logical status as social facts. In its absence, his moral facts remain mysterious. Brink claims that the only problem with MSR's nomic relationship is identifying the relata, and that this should be no more surprising than our inability to state the set and organization of physical properties that realize an economic property like inflation (Brink 1989, 179). This won't do, though, because the analogy is false. Inflation is *inconceivable* apart from social institutions that we create, from small businesses to money. It is a creature of social infrastructure. This is true of injustice as well, as an object of communal ontology. But what Brink has in mind is a notion of injustice that is not tethered to institutions. And so the analogy to inflation, which is so tethered, fails.

The point we are making here is closely related to a familiar one in the philosophy of social science. Peter Winch argued that technical concepts that are not taken from the object of investigation, such as those that would figure in MSR's nomic relationships, must presuppose the participant's unreflective understanding of the object:

> For example, liquidity preference is a technical concept of economics: it is not generally used by business people in the conduct of their affairs but by the econo-

mist who wishes to *explain* the nature and consequences of certain kinds of business behavior. But it is logically tied to concepts which do enter into business activity, for its use by the economist presupposes his understanding of what it is to conduct a business, which in turn involves an understanding of such business concepts as money, profit, cost, risk, etc. It is only the relation between his account and these concepts which makes it an account of economic activity as opposed, say, to a piece of theology. (Winch 1958, 89)

Taylor (1995) has made similar points in such influential essays as "Interpretation and the Sciences of Man." Indeed, the general idea has become a staple of introductory texts in the philosophy of social science (Little 1991). Certain high-level social phenomena that can be captured in statistical generalizations or perhaps even in exceptionless laws are logically parasitic upon lower-level rule-constituted social phenomena. In this sense inflation and economic laws about it are parasitic on the social institution of *money*, which involves our accepting rules that constitute coins and pieces of paper as legal tender. Inflation is simply inconceivable apart from this intentional imposition of status functions.

If social facts are created by the imposition of status functions through collective intentionality, as we are hypothesizing here, then the objects of study in social science will have a communal ontology, constructively emergent from the subjective ontology of a community's members' psychological states, especially those that fall under the rubric of collective intentionality; and in that fundamental way they will be different both from the objects that the natural sciences study, which have an objective ontology, and also from the simply subjective ontology of psychologists and social scientists who study mental states, such as pains and opinions, that aren't expressive of collective intentionality. We are signaling agreement here with Taylor's critique of individualistic social science as being incapable of explaining what it means to have an objective social reality, an objectivity that Taylor labels "intersubjective" and we have called "communal." As long as political culture is understood simply as the "psychological dimension" of a given political system, without reference to collective intentionality, constitutive rules, and communal ontology, or their theoretical equivalents or continuers, the student of culture will be blind to social and moral facts.

Brink's frame for the discussion of moral theory classifies the main options as "realism about science and antirealism about ethics," "realism about science and ethics," and "harder to classify: either global subjectivism or antirealism, [or] . . . a sophisticated realism" (Brink 1989, 61). He favors the second option, straight realism all around. But he does not acknowledge a fourth option: straight realism about (natural) science, "sophisticated realism" about ethics. This would be compatible with the social constructivism outlined here, which is grounded in "realism about science" because of its commitment to objective, mind-independent physical facts. The present model requires that impositions of status functions on less basic functions should bottom out in impositions of status functions on the physical world. (The argument has two stages: Bottoming-out onto the nonsocial is needed to avoid an infinite regress or circularity, and the physical world is the most plausible candidate for the nonsocial bottom.) Furthermore, the model assigns a degree of objectivity and mind-independence to an ontological category of communal moral facts, and leaves it an open question whether these are, or might become, global or universal. It is capable of being a vehicle for sophisticated realism about ethics.

Our collective intentionality expresses itself, for instance, in the belief that it is wrong to cause unnecessary suffering. The communal moral fact that this is wrong may be universal in scope, comprising everyone capable of thinking rationally and informedly about the matter. On this reckoning, our constructive activity in integrating this fact into our social world would be a *ladder* by use of which we gain access to a universally communal moral ontology, a universal moral *we*. Even if this doesn't obtain at the moment, it might obtain in the future, and sophisticated realism about ethics could maintain itself with a conception of moral progress as movement toward that future. This would not be "straight realism" in Brink's sense, because it doesn't fit within a third-person ontology. It would express itself with a metaphor like a ladder rather than, say, an *auger* for boring into the soil of objective physical fact. It would still be naturalistic, however, in that communal ontology is causally emergent from, and ultimately constituted by, the objective physical particles described by physics.

The case for the nomic supervenience of the moral on the physical is murky at best, and it certainly isn't supported by Brink's parity argument. Nor is an antimaterialist account required in order to provide a nonreductive alternative, as indicated by the social constructivism set out here, which replaces nomic supervenience by causal emergence, collective intentionality, and status functions, and remains consistent with a naturalistic world view. The communal ontology of moral facts implies a degree of objectivity and independence of mind, relative to the subjective ontology of the mental. A sophisticated realism about ethics can be formulated in terms of it, about which we will have one further thing to say in a moment. Sophisticated realism may not be enough for a moral realist like Brink, but it may have to do until a less murky notion of straight realism about ethics comes along.

What remains is the relative objectivity of shared community. It is possible that there are, or are potentially, human moral universals in this sense, even moral universals among all intentional agents. Let us begin to explore, in closing, the implications of collective intentionality for this speculation. We assume that the mind is a biological phenomenon: it is a product of our brains' microstructure, and a system feature of our brains. In particular, then, collective intentionality is a biological phenomenon, and it is a brute fact about beings with biologies like ours that we have the capacity for it. Now assume further that there are ideal conditions for the exercise of this capacity, such that, when these conditions are satisfied, each of us engages every other in the construction of social reality. (Similarly, smog-filled air is not ideal for the exercise of our capacity to breathe.) The implication is that there is something less than ideal about conditions in which our constructive activity has more limited scope, for instance, limited to members of *this* culture, an implication one might begin to justify by noting that, in the present account, culture is an expression of biology, and since we all have comparable biology with respect to the capacity for collective intentionality, we should expect it to be exercised with *universal scope* under ideal conditions for culture building. Of course it might turn out that our capacity for expanding the scope of our collective intentionality is limited in the way that the same capacity in wolves is limited to *packs*. But there is ample evidence of potential for expansion in human history, none among wolves. Is there reason to think we have arrived at a limit?

It follows from such speculation, and is hardly surprising on the face of it, that the human race has been living in less-than-ideal times all these years, with respect to the ideal conditions for the exercise of collective intentionality. But this is changing, as we respond to global environmental and military threats by creating global institutions, like the United Nations, in which collective intentionality is exercised with universal scope; as we universalize and enhance our communications infrastructure with new technologies such as the Internet;

and so on. We can set ourselves toward helping bring about better conditions for the exercise of our collective intentionality by becoming better informed, subjecting our shared understandings to examination, exploring other cultures and engaging them in dialogue, looking for underlying common purposes beneath a variety of social constructions, and so forth.

The ideal conditions posited in this speculation encourage a comparison between universal moral facts and Lockean secondary qualities such as color, sound, and smell—dispositions of the primary qualities of objectively physical matter to produce qualia in us. If the comparison were tight, moral realism would be triumphantly vindicated, since its moral facts could be fully *constituted* by the microstructure that produces beliefs and desires in the normal moral agent—for instance, the motion of matter that subserves an injustice, and there would be nothing further to the story. But there is an important further story to be told, we have been arguing. The construction of moral reality is not simply a slapping-together of objective matter and subjective qualia, but a more complex process of imposition of status functions through collective intentionality. The constitution of moral facts includes institutional facts as well as, ultimately, the objectively physical facts that moral realism focussed upon in its attempt to naturalize morality. But there is nothing nonnatural about institutional facts. They are an expression of our biology, specifically of our biological capacity for collective intentionality. However, they have a communal ontology that moral realism overlooked, and consequently this speculative vindication of moral realism is not quite complete. The convergence with moral realism is closest on those versions of realism that surrender Brink's ontological claim for a subjectivist interpretation of moral facts that defines objectivity solely in terms of such a possible consensus. Thus, Smith construes objectivity in terms of the prospect of convergence of moral views under idealized conditions of reflection (Smith 1993, 400, 409), and he urges that "only time will tell" whether it will come to pass. With much of this we agree, but what exactly will time tell? In our view it will tell whether a universal *we* will construct objective (communal) moral facts. The objectivity of such facts is an artifact of the historically situated construct, not evidence that we harmonize with an ahistorical ideal consensus of perfectly rational beings. In Smith's view such a construction, the actual convergence, would only be a *sign* that moral facts exist, for the true test, in his account, is what fully rational agents would choose in a hypothetically ideal world. He acknowledges that we have "little choice" but to engage in normative ethical debate to see whether convergence unfolds (Smith 1994, 202), whereas our view is that we have *no* choice.

Our ideal world is what James once called "morality made flesh" in a contingent future construction, and it is different from Smith's ideal in the way that James's historical notion of a future consensus is different from Peirce's counterfactual notion of what a future community *would* agree upon.[4]

We are not now denying the moral and cultural diversity we emphasized earlier. In particular, we am not now denying the hypothesis in Rawls that a plurality of world views is "the natural outcome of the activities of human reason under enduring free institutions" (Rawls 1993, xxiv). Rather, our view underscores the phrase "under enduring free institutions," for those institutions were created by collective intentionality with relatively broad scope, within the overlapping consensus among a plurality of comprehensive doctrines that had previously been in violent conflict. The *we* that created those institutions was broader than the *we* of the adherents of this or that world view; it was all of *us*, qua participants in the consensus. Cultural evolution, we have speculated, will be similarly conditioned by convergence toward an overlapping consensus of increasingly broad scope, serving as a countervail to reasonable pluralism, as history enters closer-to-ideal conditions for the exercise of collective intentionality. We have offered no argument here for the prospect of such a consensus. Rather, we have simply posited it by way of explaining the possibility of a way in which moral realism might be partially vindicated. Wrong in its ontology, it might be right about the future conditions that it would accept as confirming it. But the future consensus would be not a mere confirmation of the existence of objective moral facts but rather the very construction of them, morality made flesh.

Moral realism as we have criticized it aims to secure objective moral facts, on a par with the facts that the natural sciences describe. We have not rescued this aspiration, but we have approximated it with a case for communal moral facts, where the community is universal in scope. We have criticized Brink's parity argument, showing how it founders because the nomic relationship it asserts between moral facts and their natural-scientific constitution has a queer slapped-together quality, in comparison to a relationship spelled out by the social construction of moral institutions. Moral realism can back away from the nomic relationship free of mind-dependent entities such as collective intentionality and constitutive rules, and content itself with causal connections reaching from natural-scientific constitution up to moral facts, connections thoroughly mediated by intentionality and rules. We have shown in barest outline how this might be done. The resulting moral facts are natural in a straightforward sense: they are physical. But they don't have the third-person ontology of natural-scientific facts, and so they lack a quality that belonged to the Brinkian moral-realist aspiration. We don't see how *that* quality can be rescued.

Notes

Chapter 1

1. I include James's "voluntarism" within his pragmatism. Otherwise, one would refer to his legacy not as a pair of innovations but as a triad.
2. Parfit (1984, 478) endorses the theory for many cases, while holding that it breaks down in some science fiction thought-experiments.
3. From a letter to his sister, Alice, dated November 14, 1866: "Your first question is, 'where have I been?' To C. S. Peirce's lecture, which I could not understand a word of, but rather enjoyed the sensation of listening to for an hour" (Hardwick 1961, 24).
4. "The thesis of this book," Gale writes, "is that James's underlying quest was to find a philosophy that would enable us, as the beer commercials enjoin, to have it all, to grab for all the gusto we can" (Gale 1999, 4).
5. See Simon (1998) for an excellent recent biography that highlights his shortcomings from a broadly feminist perspective.

Chapter 2

1. James acknowledges this early inclination toward epiphenomenalism in a footnote in *The Principles* (130–31).
2. See his review of Wundt's *Grundzuge der physiologischen Psychologie*, in *Essays, Comments, and Reviews*, 296.
3. James also mentions a fifth characteristic: thought "always appears to deal with objects independent of itself." This is dropped in the *Briefer Course*.

Chapter 3

1. See also his article in *Transactions of the Charles S. Peirce Society* (Bailey 1998a).

Chapter 5

1. See Kenneth Gergen's *The Saturated Self* for a lively recounting of the stresses and strains of what he calls our postmodern condition. (Gergen 1991).

Chapter 6

1. So it might be said that our short-term memory would be quicker if it weren't for conflicting evolutionary pressures for the brain to perform other functions. (Steinberg's work suggests such a measure of the bargain Mother Nature has struck with respect to memory.)

Chapter 7

1. Russell speaks of "the true metaphysic, in which mind and matter alike are seen to be constructed out of a neutral stuff, whose causal laws have no such duality as that of psychology, but form the basis upon which both physics and psychology are built" (Russell 1921, 287).

Chapter 8

1. I take the formalism from Michael Smith's exposition, which is particularly lucid (Smith 1994).

2. Contemporary physicalists can fall prey to the same problematic reliance on ostension, as Frank Jackson demonstrates when he proposes that "physicalists can give an ostensive definition of what they mean by physical properties and relations by pointing to some exemplars of non-sentient objects—tables, chairs, mountains, and the like—and then say that by physical properties and relations, they mean the kinds of properties and relations needed to give a complete account of things like them" (Jackson 1998, 7). But the doctrine of pure experience implies that the ostensive gesture could be pointing *either* to a physical table *or* to the voluminous spatial quale that figures in one's perceptual construction of the physical table. Jackson goes on to add a qualification, writing that "There will be a problem for this way of elucidating the notion of physical properties and relations if panpsychism is true (as Ian Ravenscroft reminded me). For then there are no exemplars of the non-sentient. Everything has a mental life. But I think that we can safely set this possibility to one side" (Jackson 1998, 7). I think Jackson has in mind by "panpsychism" the view that every physical thing has a sentient quality. James's doctrine of pure experience is not panpsychism. For one thing, the mental is not predicative of the physical, in James's account, but rather both are predicative of pure experience. Further, ostending pure experience isn't *eo ipso* ostending the mental; James isn't defending idealism. Although I argued in Chapter 2 that pure experience has some features of the mental, the operative word here is *some*. Pure experience lacks those characteristics of the mental, such as privacy, which would prevent it from constructing a public world of physical objects. In any event, panpsychism and James's theory represent two ways in which the physicalist's ostension might fail to refer uniquely to the physical. And one of my aims in this chap-

ter is to provide a reconstruction of James's theory that physicalists won't be able to "safely set to one side," because the functionalism about the mind that many of them accept will lead, when carried to its logical conclusion, to global functionalism.

Chapter 9

1. James is not without contemporary allies on this score. See Searle (1987), for one, for a sharp critique of Quine's view.

Chapter 10

1. Gale actually replaces 2´ with 2*, but I find it helpful to give them separate names, 2´ and 2*.

2. "What we need in the case of sense experience is not little colored shapes (muffled sounds, etc.) in the head, but a stage in the processing of sensory information about these properties in which such information is made available to cognitive centers for conceptual utilization—for the fixation of belief" (Dretske 1991, 182).

Chapter 11

1. Quite cheerful as usual about attributing inconsistencies to James, Gale confines this dual-track account of belief-justification to James's discussion of the will-to-believe doctrine, maintaining that elsewhere he is committed to a univocal account: "I added the qualification 'when he is espousing his will-to-believe doctrine' because . . . James, like Clifford, has a univocalist account of belief justification, only it is the reverse of Clifford's, based on maximizing desire-satisfaction, with epistemic considerations entering in only in a rule-instrumental manner as useful guiding principles" (Gale 1999, 95). I criticized this interpretation in Chapter 10.

Chapter 13

1. This chapter is largely taken from Cooper and Frimpong-Mansoh (2000); I will use the first-person plural in what follows to acknowledge the coauthorship.

2. "But, farther, this question, Who shall be judge? cannot mean that there is no judge at all. For where there is no judicature on earth to decide controversies amongst men, God in heaven is judge. He alone, 'tis true, is judge of the right. But every man is judge for himself, as in all other cases so in this, whether another hath put himself into a state of war with him, and whether he should appeal to the supreme Judge, as *Jeptha* did" (Locke 1966, 142).

3. For one philosophical account of the emergence of subjective physical facts from objective ones, see Searle (1992).

4.   Putnam makes the observation about James and Peirce that we are mapping onto ourselves and Smith:

> [A]lthough Peirce does speak of "the opinion which is fated to be ultimately agreed to by all who investigate," he later glosses this as the opinion which *we would converge* to if inquiry were indefinitely continued, and I asked if James would accept a similar modification. The answer is that he would not. For in Peirce's view, the *counter-factual* "If investigation *had been* indefinitely prolonged, such-and-such a statement *would have been* verified" might be true even though no actually experienced fact supports that counter-factual. A statement may "agree" with reality although the "conjunctive relation" which constitutes that agreement exists only as a counter-factual possibility and not as a 'conjunctive experience"; truth does not have to "happen" for an idea to be true, it only has to be the case that "it would have happened if." James's metaphysics has no place for such a claim. (But James does not object to counterfactuals as such. Many counterfactuals actually get verified. But those counterfactuals have had truth "happen" to them; they are not made true by a mysterious kind of potentiality ("Thirdness") but by the "cash-value" of incorporating them in our system of beliefs. (Putnam 1997, 178)

Bibliography

Allen, B. 1993. *Truth in Philosophy.* Cambridge: Harvard University Press.

Ayer, A. 1968. *The Origins of Pragmatism.* San Francisco: Freeman, Cooper.

Bailey, A. 1998a. "The Strange Attractions of Sciousness: William James on Consciousness." *Transactions of the Charles S. Peirce Society* 34 (2): 414–34.

Bailey, A. 1998b. "William James, Chaos Theory, and Conscious Experience." In *Systems Theories and A Priori Aspects of Perception,* ed. J. Jordan. Oxford: Elsevier Science B.V.

Bird, G. 1986. *William James.* London: Routledge and Kegan Paul.

Bonjour, L. 1985. *The Structure of Empirical Knowledge.* Cambridge: Harvard University Press.

Brink, D. O. 1989. *Moral Realism and the Foundations of Ethics.* Cambridge: Cambridge University Press.

Chalmers, D. 1996. *The Conscious Mind: In Search of a Fundamental Theory.* New York: Oxford University Press.

Cook, J. 1994. *Wittgenstein's Metaphysics.* Cambridge: Cambridge University Press.

Cooper, W. 1996. "Culture Vultures and the Re-enchantment of Citizenship." In *Do We Need Minority Rights?: Conceptual Issues,* ed. J. Räikkä. The Hague: Kluwer Press.

Cooper, W., and A. Frimpong-Mansoh. 2000. "Moral Realism, Social Construction, and Communal Ontology." *South African Journal of Philosophy* 19 (2): 119–32.

Davidson, D. 1970. "Mental Events." In *Experience and Theory,* ed. L. Foster and J. Swanson. Amherst: University of Massachusetts Press.

Dennett, D. 1987. *The Intentional Stance.* Cambridge: MIT Press.

Dennett, D. 1991. "Real Patterns." *Journal of Philosophy* 88 (1): 27–51.

Dretske, F. 1991. "Dretske's Replies." In *Dretske and His Critics,* ed. B. McLaughlin. Cambridge, Mass.: Blackwell.

Flanagan, O. 1984. *Naturalizing the Mind: The Philosophical Psychology of William James.* Cambridge: MIT Press.

Flanagan, O. 1997. "Consciousness as a Pragmatist Views It." In *The Cambridge Companion to William James,* ed. R. Putnam. Cambridge: Cambridge University Press.

Flugel, J. 1964. *A Hundred Years of Psychology*. New York: Basic Books.

Ford, M. P. 1982. *William James's Philosophy*. Amherst: University of Massachusetts Press.

Gale, R. 1999. *The Divided Self of William James*. Cambridge: Cambridge University Press.

Gavin, W. J. 1992. *William James and the Reinstatement of the Vague*. Philadelphia: Temple University Press.

Gergen, K. J. 1991. *The Saturated Self: Dilemmas of Identity in Contemporary Life*. New York: Basic Books.

Goldman, A. I. 1970. *A Theory of Human Action*. Englewood Cliffs: Prentice-Hall.

Gordon, R. M. 1987. *The Structure of Emotions*. Cambridge: Cambridge University Press.

Hardwick, E. 1961. *The Selected Letters of William James*. New York: Farrar, Straus, and Cudahy.

Hilgard, E. R. 1987. *Psychology in America: A Historical Survey*. San Diego: Harcourt Brace Jovanovich.

Jackson, F. 1998. *From Metaphysics to Ethics: A Defence of Conceptual Analysis*. New York: Clarendon.

James, H. 1920. *The Letters of William James*. Vol. 2. Boston: Atlantic Monthly Press.

James, W. 1907. "A Word More about Truth." *Journal of Philosophy* (18 July 1907).

James, W. 1975. *The Meaning of Truth*. Cambridge: Harvard University Press.

James, W. 1976. *Essays in Radical Empiricism*. Cambridge: Harvard University Press.

James, W. 1978. *Essays in Philosophy*. Cambridge: Harvard University Press.

James, W. 1979a. *Pragmatism*. Cambridge: Harvard University Press.

James, W. 1979b. *Some Problems of Philosophy*. Cambridge: Harvard University Press.

James, W. 1979c. *The Will to Believe*. Cambridge: Harvard University Press.

James, W. 1981. *The Principles of Psychology*. Cambridge: Harvard University Press.

James, W. 1982. *Essays in Religion and Morality*. Cambridge: Harvard University Press.

James, W. 1983. *Essays in Psychology*. Cambridge: Harvard University Press.

James, W. 1984. *Psychology: Briefer Course*. Cambridge: Harvard University Press.

James, W. 1985. *The Varieties of Religious Experience*. Cambridge: Harvard University Press.

James, W. 1987. *Essays, Comments, and Reviews*. Cambridge: Harvard University Press.

James, W. 1988. *Manuscript Essays and Notes*. Cambridge: Harvard University Press.

Johnson, L. E. 1992. *Focusing on Truth*. London: Routledge.

Leahey, T. H. 1980. *A History of Psychology*. Englewood Cliffs: Prentice-Hall.

Little, D. 1991. *The Varieties of Social Explanation*. Boulder: Westview Press.

Locke, J. 1966. "An Essay Concerning the True Original, Extent, and End of Civil Government." In *Social Contract*, ed. J. Gough. Oxford: Blackwell.

Mackie, J. 1977. *Inventing Right and Wrong*. Harmondsworth: Penguin.

McGinn, C. 1991. *The Problem of Consciousness*. Oxford: Blackwell.

McGinn, C. 1999. *The Magic Flame*. New York: Basic Books.

Myers, G. 1986. *William James: His Life and Thought*. New Haven: Yale University Press.

Myers, G. 1997. "Pragmatism and Introspective Psychology." In *The Cambridge Companion to William James*, ed. R. Putnam. Cambridge: Cambridge University Press.

Nagel, T. 1979. *Mortal Questions*. Cambridge: Cambridge University Press.

Nagel, T. 1986. *The View from Nowhere*. New York: Oxford University Press.

Nathanson, S. 1985. *The Ideal of Rationality*. Atlantic Highlands, N.J.: Humanities.

Nozick, R. 1981. *Philosophical Investigations*. Cambridge: Harvard University Press.

Nozick, R. 1989. *The Examined Life*. New York: Simon and Schuster.

Nozick, R. 1993. *The Nature of Rationality*. Princeton: Princeton University Press.

Parfit, D. 1984. *Reasons and Persons*. New York: Oxford University Press.

Peirce, C. 1982. *Writings of Charles S. Peirce: A Chronological Edition*, Vol.1, 1857–1866. Bloomington: Indiana University Press.

Perry, R. 1935. *The Thought and Character of William James*. Cambridge: Harvard University Press.

Popper, K., and J. C. Eccles. 1977. *The Self and Its Brain*. Berlin: Springer.

Putnam, H. 1997. James's Theory of Truth." In *The Cambridge Companion to William James*, ed. R. Putnam. Cambridge: Cambridge University Press.

Rawls, J. 1993. *Political Liberalism*. New York: Columbia University Press.

Rorty, R. 1986. "Pragmatism, Davidson, and Truth." In *Truth and Interpretation*, ed. E. Lepore. Oxford: Blackwell.

Rorty, R. 1997. "Faith, Responsibility, and Romance." In *The Cambridge Companion to William James*, ed. R. Putnam. Cambridge: Cambridge University Press.

Russell, B. 1921. *The Analysis of Mind*. London: George Allen and Unwin.

Searle, J. 1987. "Indeterminacy, Empiricism, and the First Person." *Journal of Philosophy* 84: 123–46.

Searle, J. 1992. *The Rediscovery of the Mind*. Cambridge: MIT Press.

Searle, J. 1995. *The Construction of Social Reality*. New York: Free Press.

Seigfried, C. 1978. *Chaos and Context: A Study in William James*. Athens: Ohio University Press.

Simon, L. 1998. *Genuine Reality: A Life of William James*. New York: Harcourt Brace and Company.

Smith, M. 1993. *Realism: A Companion to Ethics*. Oxford: Blackwell.

Smith, M. 1994. *The Moral Problem*, Oxford: Blackwell.

Sprigge, T. 1993. *James and Bradley: American Truth and British Reality*. Chicago: Open Court.

Taylor, C. 1995. "Interpretation and the Sciences of Man." In *Readings in the Philosophy of Social Science*, ed. M. Martin and L. McIntyre. Cambridge: MIT Press.

Taylor, E., and R. Wozniak. 1996. *Pure Experience: The Response to William James*. Bristol: Thoemmes.

Wild, J. 1969. *The Radical Empiricism of William James*. Garden City, N.Y.: Doubleday.

Williams, B. 1981. *Moral Luck*. Cambridge: Cambridge University Press.

Wilshire, B. 1968. *William James and Phenomenology*. Bloomington: Indiana University Press.

Wilshire, B. 1969. "Protophenomenology in the Psychology of William James." *Transactions of the Charles S. Peirce Society* 5: 25–43.

Winch, P. 1958. *The Idea of a Social Science and Its Relation to Philosophy*. London: Routledge and Kegan Paul.

Wittgenstein, L. 1963. *Tractatus Logico-Philosophicus*. Trans. D. Pears and B. McGuinness. Frankfurt: Suhrkamp Verlag.

Index